MARY SHELLEY AND EUROPE
ESSAYS IN HONOUR OF JEAN DE PALACIO

LEGENDA

LEGENDA is the Modern Humanities Research Association's book imprint for new research in the Humanities. Founded in 1995 by Malcolm Bowie and others within the University of Oxford, Legenda has always been a collaborative publishing enterprise, directly governed by scholars. The Modern Humanities Research Association (MHRA) joined this collaboration in 1998, became half-owner in 2004, in partnership with Maney Publishing and then Routledge, and has since 2016 been sole owner. Titles range from medieval texts to contemporary cinema and form a widely comparative view of the modern humanities, including works on Arabic, Catalan, English, French, German, Greek, Italian, Portuguese, Russian, Spanish, and Yiddish literature. Editorial boards and committees of more than 60 leading academic specialists work in collaboration with bodies such as the Society for French Studies, the British Comparative Literature Association and the Association of Hispanists of Great Britain & Ireland.

The MHRA encourages and promotes advanced study and research in the field of the modern humanities, especially modern European languages and literature, including English, and also cinema. It aims to break down the barriers between scholars working in different disciplines and to maintain the unity of humanistic scholarship. The Association fulfils this purpose through the publication of journals, bibliographies, monographs, critical editions, and the MHRA Style Guide, and by making grants in support of research. Membership is open to all who work in the Humanities, whether independent or in a University post, and the participation of younger colleagues entering the field is especially welcomed.

ALSO PUBLISHED BY THE ASSOCIATION

Critical Texts
Tudor and Stuart Translations • *New Translations* • *European Translations*
MHRA Library of Medieval Welsh Literature

MHRA Bibliographies
Publications of the Modern Humanities Research Association

The Annual Bibliography of English Language & Literature
Austrian Studies
Modern Language Review
Portuguese Studies
The Slavonic and East European Review
Working Papers in the Humanities
The Yearbook of English Studies

www.mhra.org.uk
www.legendabooks.com

STUDIES IN COMPARATIVE LITERATURE

Editorial Committee
Chairs: Dr Emily Finer (University of St Andrews)
and Professor Wen-chin Ouyang (SOAS, London)

Dr Ross Forman (University of Warwick)
Professor Angus Nicholls (Queen Mary, University of London)
Dr Henriette Partzsch (University of Glasgow)
Dr Ranka Primorac (University of Southampton)

Studies in Comparative Literature are produced in close collaboration with the British Comparative Literature Association, and range widely across comparative and theoretical topics in literary and translation studies, accommodating research at the interface between different artistic media and between the humanities and the sciences.

ALSO PUBLISHED IN THIS SERIES

20. *Aestheticism and the Philosophy of Death: Walter Pater and Post-Hegelianism*, by Giles Whiteley
21. *Blake, Lavater and Physiognomy*, by Sibylle Erle
22. *Rethinking the Concept of the Grotesque: Crashaw, Baudelaire, Magritte*, by Shun-Liang Chao
23. *The Art of Comparison: How Novels and Critics Compare*, by Catherine Brown
24. *Borges and Joyce: An Infinite Conversation*, by Patricia Novillo-Corvalán
25. *Prometheus in the Nineteenth Century: From Myth to Symbol*, by Caroline Corbeau-Parsons
26. *Architecture, Travellers and Writers: Constructing Histories of Perception*, by Anne Hultzsch
27. *Comparative Literature in Britain: National Identities, Transnational Dynamics 1800-2000*, by Joep Leerssen
28. *The Realist Author and Sympathetic Imagination*, by Sotirios Paraschas
29. *Iris Murdoch and Elias Canetti: Intellectual Allies*, by Elaine Morley
30. *Likenesses: Translation, Illustration, Interpretation*, by Matthew Reynolds
31. *Exile and Nomadism in French and Hispanic Women's Writing*, by Kate Averis
32. *Samuel Butler against the Professionals: Rethinking Lamarckism 1860–1900*, by David Gillott
33. *Byron, Shelley, and Goethe's Faust: An Epic Connection*, by Ben Hewitt
34. *Leopardi and Shelley: Discovery, Translation and Reception*, by Daniela Cerimonia
35. *Oscar Wilde and the Simulacrum: The Truth of Masks*, by Giles Whiteley
36. *The Modern Culture of Reginald Farrer: Landscape, Literature and Buddhism*, by Michael Charlesworth
37. *Translating Myth*, edited by Ben Pestell, Pietra Palazzolo and Leon Burnett
38. *Encounters with Albion: Britain and the British in Texts by Jewish Refugees from Nazism*, by Anthony Grenville
39. *The Rhetoric of Exile: Duress and the Imagining of Force*, by Vladimir Zorić
40. *From Puppet to Cyborg: Pinocchio's Posthuman Journey*, by Georgia Panteli
41. *Utopian Identities: A Cognitive Approach to Literary Competitions*, by Clementina Osti
43. *Sublime Conclusions: Last Man Narratives from Apocalypse to Death of God*, by Robert K. Weninger
44. *Arthur Symons: Poet, Critic, Vagabond*, edited by Elisa Bizzotto and Stefano Evangelista
45. *Scenographies of Perception: Sensuousness in Hegel, Novalis, Rilke, and Proust*, by Christian Jany
46. *Reflections in the Library: Selected Literary Essays 1926–1944*, by Antal Szerb
47. *Depicting the Divine: Mikhail Bulgakov and Thomas Mann*, by Olga G. Voronina
48. *Samuel Butler and the Science of the Mind: Evolution, Heredity and Unconscious Memory*, by Cristiano Turbil
49. *Death Sentences: Literature and State Killing*, edited by Birte Christ and Ève Morisi
50. *Words Like Fire: Prophecy and Apocalypse in Apollinaire, Marinetti and Pound*, by James P. Leveque

Mary Shelley and Europe

Essays in Honour of Jean de Palacio

Edited by Antonella Braida

Studies in Comparative Literature 55
Modern Humanities Research Association
2020

Published by Legenda
an imprint of the Modern Humanities Research Association
Salisbury House, Station Road, Cambridge CB1 2LA

ISBN 978-1-78188-548-2 (HB)
ISBN 978-1-78188-552-9 (PB)

First published 2020

All rights reserved. No part of this publication may be reproduced or disseminated or transmitted in any form or by any means, electronic, mechanical, photocopying, recording or otherwise, or stored in any retrieval system, or otherwise used in any manner whatsoever without written permission of the copyright owner, except in accordance with the provisions of the Copyright, Designs and Patents Act 1988, or under the terms of a licence permitting restricted copying issued in the UK by the Copyright Licensing Agency Ltd, Saffron House, 6–10 Kirby Street, London EC1N 8TS, *England, or in the USA by the Copyright Clearance Center, 222 Rosewood Drive, Danvers MA 01923. Application for the written permission of the copyright owner to reproduce any part of this publication must be made by email to legenda@mhra.org.uk.*

Disclaimer: Statements of fact and opinion contained in this book are those of the author and not of the editors or the Modern Humanities Research Association. The publisher makes no representation, express or implied, in respect of the accuracy of the material in this book and cannot accept any legal responsibility or liability for any errors or omissions that may be made.

Trademark notice: Product or corporate names may be trademarks or registered trademarks, and are used only for identification and explanation without intent to infringe.

© *Modern Humanities Research Association 2020*

Copy-Editor: Dr Isabel Schlinzig

CONTENTS

	Acknowledgements	ix
	Notes on Contributors	x
	List of Illustrations	xiv
	Abbreviations	xv
	Introduction: The European Mary Shelley: From Jean de Palacio to the Twenty-First Century ANTONELLA BRAIDA	1
	PART I: APPROACHING THE MARY SHELLEY CANON AND SCHOLARSHIP	
1	Re-Collecting Mary Shelley and Percy Bysshe Shelley JEAN DE PALACIO	21
2	But How Do We Know that It Is by Mary Shelley? NORA CROOK	33
3	Mary Shelley as Editor, Translator, and European: A Tribute to the Scholarship of Jean de Palacio MICHAEL ROSSINGTON	48
4	Mourning in Mary Shelley's 'The Choice', and the Work of Editing VALENTINA VARINELLI	57
	PART II: MARY SHELLEY ACROSS LANGUAGES AND CULTURES	
5	'Sa "lutte solitaire"': Mary Shelley's Liberal Authority and the Philosophic Radicals LISA VARGO	71
6	'Write my story and translate': Mary Shelley's *rambles* in the Italian Language, Literature, and Country MARIA PARRINO	81
7	Mary Shelley's Italian Scenes ANNA MERCER	90
	PART III: THE RECEPTION OF MARY SHELLEY: INTERDISCIPLINARY APPROACHES (TRANSLATION, THEATRE, AND ICONOLOGY)	
8	The British Reception of *Frankenstein* (1818) and the Culture of Early Nineteenth-Century Science MARJEAN D. PURINTON	105

9 Jules Saladin's 1821 Translation of *Frankenstein* 118
   ANNE ROUHETTE

10 Becoming Human: *Frankenstein* at the National Theatre 128
   CATHERINE PUGH

11 Iconographic Portraits of Mary Shelley: A Postmodern Perspective 143
   JEAN-MARIE LECOMTE

   Bibliography 167

   Index 185

ACKNOWLEDGEMENTS

This volume is the result of a series of discussions, meetings, and conferences that took place from 2016 to the time of its publication. I thank Jean de Palacio and Marie-France de Palacio for their hospitality and their collaboration at the start of this project. The present publication was made possible by the research centre IDEA (Interdisciplinarity in English Studies), its past and current directors, John Bak and Isabelle Gaudy-Campbell, and the research cluster TELL (Temps, Espaces, Lettres, Langues), that generously supported my research and the conferences I organized in Nancy.

From the very beginning I could benefit from the expert advice of Professor Michael Rossington, and I am very grateful for his support and generous help and advice. I owe thanks to Nora Crook and Keith Crook for putting me in contact with Professor Jean de Palacio, and for their generosity in sharing their knowledge about Mary Shelley and her circle. I thank the illustrators for generously agreeing to publish their portraits of Mary Shelley, and Jean-Marie Lecomte for liaising with them: Esao Andrews, Sarah Dolby, Salvador Heras, Derek Marks, Abigail Larson, Alison Silva, Tim Seeley, Alan Vest, and Fernando Vicente. The editor thanks Nick Dear for his interviews and his availability and Catherine Pugh who conducted them. I thank the Bodleian Library for permission to publish Reginald Easton's portrait and the National Portrait Gallery for Richard Rothwell's portrait. Graham Nelson, managing editor of Legenda, as well as Wen-chin Ouyang and Emily Finer have provided their guidance during the slow progress of this project, and I would not have succeeded in completing it without their help. I wish to thank Marie Isabel Matthews-Schlinzig for revising the volume for publication. I am very grateful to the readers who have offered their time and expertise to improve the coherence of the volume.

Robin Mackenzie, Philippe Laplace, Emily Hoy, and Michael Rossington helped me with the challenging task of translating quotations from the French. Moreover, Philippe Laplace provided significant editorial help and advice throughout the project.

I thank my colleagues, especially Céline Sabiron and Jeremy Tranmer, Bérengère Stassin and Michael Latham, for their precious research and teaching exchanges, and last but not least, Anna and Philippe for sharing my interest in Mary Shelley.

A.B., June 2020

NOTES ON CONTRIBUTORS

Antonella Braida completed her DPhil at St Catherine's College, Oxford. She has taught in Britain (Oxford, Durham) and France (Besançon, Belfort, Nancy). She is lecturer in English at the Université de Lorraine, Nancy, France, and member of the research centre IDEA (Interdisciplinarity in English Studies). She has published articles and essays on the reception of Dante, Anglo-Italian relations, and British women writers. She has published two volumes on the reception of Dante: *Dante and the Romantics* (Houndmills, Basingstoke: Palgrave, 2004), *Dante on View*, co-edited with Luisa Calé (Aldershot, Hampshire & Burlington, VT: Ashgate, 2007). On British Romanticism she has published *Inconstances romantiques: Visions et revisions dans la littérature britannique du long XIXe siècle*, co-edited with Sophie Laniel-Musitelli and Céline Sabiron (Nancy: PUN, 2019), and on the relationship between word and image, *Image and Word: Reflections of Art and Literature from the Middle Ages to the Present*, co-edited with Giuliana Pieri (Oxford: Legenda, 2003). In 2016, she organized the one-day conference 'Beyond Frankenstein's Shadow' and a workshop in honour of Professor Jean de Palacio.

Nora Crook is Professor Emerita at Anglia Ruskin University, Cambridge, UK. She is General Editor of the Pickering and Chatto editions of Mary Shelley's novels and miscellaneous writings (1996, 2002), and editor of *Frankenstein* and *Valperga*. She has published articles on various aspects of Mary Shelley, some of which concern attribution, in *RaVon*, *Keats-Shelley Journal*, *Keats-Shelley Review*, *Créature au féminin*, ed. by Marianne Camus (Dijon: EUD, 2006), and in Japanese and Italian collections. In 2006, she received the award of Distinguished Scholar from the Keats-Shelley Association of America. In 2013, she found thirteen previously unknown letters written to Horace Smith and his family by Mary Shelley. As part of her role as General Editor of *Complete Poetry of Percy Bysshe Shelley* (Baltimore, Maryland: Johns Hopkins, 2000–), she is at present seeing through the press poems first edited posthumously from Percy Bysshe Shelley's notebooks by Mary Shelley.

Jean de Palacio is Professor Emeritus at the Université de la Sorbonne, Paris, France. He has published two monographs on Mary Shelley and her circle: *Mary Shelley dans son œuvre* (Paris: Kincksieck, 1970) and *William Godwin et son monde intérieur* (Lille: Presses Universitaires de Lille, 1980). Both volumes are still untranslated in English. He has also published numerous monographs, editions, and edited volumes on French and European *fin de siècle* literature (1870–1914): *Pierrot fin-de-siècle, ou, Les Métamorphoses d'un masque* (Paris: Librairie Séguier, 1990); *Les Perversions du merveilleux: 'Ma Mère l'Oye' au tournant du siècle* (Paris: Nouvelles Éditions Séguier, 1993); *Figures et formes de la Décadence* (Paris: Séguier, 1994); *Les*

Métamorphoses de Psyché: Essai sur la décadence d'un mythe (Paris: Séguier, 2000); *Figures et formes de la décadence [deuxième série]* (Paris: Séguier, 2000); *Le Silence du texte* (Leuven: Peeters, 2003); *Configurations décadentes* (Leuven: Peeters, 2007). His monograph, *La Décadence: Le Mot et la chose* (Paris: Les Belles Lettres/Essais, 2011) was awarded the 2012 Émile Faguet prize by the Académie Française. In 2014, he co-edited with Marie-France de Palacio *Le Crépuscule des royautés: Essai sur la décadence du droit divin* (Paris: Honoré Champion, 2014). He has also published four novels: *Le Portrait* (Barr: Calleva, 2009); *Ascagne* (Barr: Calleva, 2012); *L'Apparition* (Paris: Théolib, 2012); *Les Ciseaux d'Atropos* (Toronto: Kobo, e-scriptoria, 2015); *Veturia* (La Plaine Saint Denis: Edilibre, 2017); *Journal de Bérénice* (Paris: Éditions Complicités, 2018).

Jean-Marie Lecomte is a researcher in literature and audio-visual studies at the Université de Lorraine, France. His teaching and research areas include nineteenth-century studies, Victorian poetry, early cinema, and the advent of film sound. He wrote his PhD thesis on the poetry of Gerard Manley Hopkins. He has published extensively on nineteenth-century literature and film adaptation, mostly investigating the ways in which literature interacts with film speech and film sound. He also specializes in videography.

Anna Mercer is a Lecturer in English Literature at Cardiff University. She studied at the University of Liverpool (BA) and at the University of Cambridge (MPhil), and completed her AHRC-funded doctorate in English Literature at the Centre for Eighteenth Century Studies, University of York, UK, in 2017. Anna's research focuses on the collaborative literary relationship that existed between Percy Bysshe Shelley and Mary Wollstonecraft Shelley from their initial meeting in 1814 through to Percy Shelley's death in 1822, as well as considering Mary Shelley's later work. Her thesis — which was published as a monograph entitled *The Collaborative Literary Relationship of Percy Bysshe Shelley and Mary Wollstonecraft Shelley* (London: Routledge, 2019) — aims to identify the textual connections between the works of the two authors, considering the Shelleys' relationship in terms of literary and stylistic ideas. Anna is also interested in literary relationships in the Romantic period more generally and has published an essay in *The Coleridge Bulletin* on the poetical dialogue of Samuel Taylor Coleridge and Sara Coleridge. She won the Keats-Shelley Essay Prize in 2015 (runner-up) for her piece 'Beyond *Frankenstein*'. Anna works at Keats House Museum, Hampstead, and for the Keats-Shelley Association of America. She is the Communications Officer for the British Association for Romantic Studies.

Maria Parrino obtained her first PhD in English Studies from the University of Genova, Italy, in 1989 with a dissertation on Italian-American women's autobiographies. She then pursued her studies and obtained a second PhD at the University of Bristol in 2014 with a thesis on nineteenth-century English Gothic Literature. She is currently a full-time teacher of English Language and Literature at a Secondary School in Vicenza, Italy. She has taught at the faculty of Political Science at the University of Padova. She has published textbooks on short stories and Gothic literature. She has written essays and articles which include 'Crossing the Borders: Hospitality in Bram Stoker's *Dracula* and Florence Marryat's *The Blood of the Vampire*' (in *Hospitality, Rape and Consent in Vampire Popular Culture: Letting the Wrong One in*, ed. by David Baker and others (Cham: Palgrave Macmillan, 2017), pp. 19–35), and 'Gothic and Earlier Painting: Nightmares and Premature Burials in Fuseli and Wiertz' (in *Gothic and the Arts*, ed. by David Punter (Edinburgh: Edinburgh University Press, 2019), pp. 107–21). In February 2018 she co-organized the International Bicentenary Conference on Mary Shelley's *Frankenstein* which was held at the University of Venice, Italy.

Catherine Pugh completed her PhD at the University of Essex, UK, and is now a writer and independent scholar. Working with horror and science fiction in all their forms, she is particularly fascinated by ideas of monstrosity and mental illness versus literary madness. Her research interests concern disability, mental illness/madness, metamorphic monsters, and horror landscapes. She has contributed essays to *At Home in the Whedonverse: Essays on Domestic Place, Space and Life*, ed. by Juliette C. Kitchens (Jefferson, NC: McFarland & Co., 2017) and *The Politics of Race, Gender and Sexuality in 'The Walking Dead': Essays on the Television Series and Comics*, ed. by Elizabeth Erwin and Dawn Keetley (Jefferson, NC: McFarland & Co., 2018).

Marjean D. Purinton is Professor of English at Texas Tech University, USA, where she also teaches in the Women's Studies Program as Affiliated Faculty. She is the author of numerous essays and articles on British Romantic drama and women writers as well as *Romantic Ideology Unmasked: The Mentally Constructed Tyrannies in Dramas of William Wordsworth, Lord Byron, Percy Shelley, and Lord Byron* (Newark: University of Delaware Press, 1994). She is completing a book project entitled 'Staging Grotesques and Ghosts: British Romantic Techno-Gothic Drama'. In 2008, Dr Purinton received a Professing Excellence Award in recognition of excellence in teaching and service to students; she also received the President's Excellence for Teaching Award in 2003. Dr Purinton served as president of the International Conference on Romanticism from 2002 to 2004. At Texas Tech University, she served eight years as Associate Dean for the Honors College, four years as Associate Chair for the English Department, and three years as Director of Literature, Linguistics, and Creative Writing.

Michael Rossington is Professor of Romantic Literature at Newcastle University, UK. His research expertise is focused on textual editing and eighteenth- and nineteenth-century literature, especially the writing of, and research relating to, the Romantic period (*c.* 1780–*c.* 1830), including: the work of Percy Bysshe Shelley and Mary Wollstonecraft Shelley; poetry; textual criticism, manuscript studies, and bibliography; republicanism; life-writing; and comparative approaches to European writing. He edited poetry and drama for volumes II, III, and IV of the Longman Annotated English Poets edition of *The Poems of Shelley* (2000, 2011, 2013). He is currently editing poems and plays for, and coordinating, the fifth and final volume of *The Poems of Shelley*, which is to be published by Routledge. His Oxford World's Classics edition of Mary Shelley's *Valperga* was published in 2000.

Anne Rouhette is a Senior Lecturer in the English Department of the Université Blaise Pascal, Clermont-Ferrand, France. She works on the English novel at the turn of the nineteenth century and on translation studies. She has published books and articles on Jane Austen, Frances Burney, and Matthew Arnold's lectures on translating Homer, but her main focus of interest is Mary Shelley's works, on which she has written several articles. She has also translated into French Shelley's *The Fortunes of Perkin Warbeck* (Paris: Classiques Garnier, 2014) and *History of a Six Weeks' Tour* (Aix-en-Provence: Presses Universitaires de Provence, 2015).

Lisa Vargo is Professor of English at the University of Saskatchewan, Saskatoon, Canada. Her research interests are in Romantic women's writing and textual editing. She has produced editions of Thomas Love Peacock's *Nightmare Abbey* and Mary Shelley's *Lodore* with Broadview Press (Peterborough, Ontario, Canada, 1997) and *Lives of the Portuguese and Spanish Writers* for *Mary Shelley's Literary Lives and Other Writings* under the general editorship of Nora Crook (London: Pickering & Chatto, 2002). Recent essays and book chapters include as their subjects Mathilde Blind, Mary Shelley's sources for *Frankenstein*, Anna Barbauld's poem 'Inscription for an Ice-House', representations of the moose in late eighteenth-century literature, Mary Shelley's short story 'The Swiss Peasant', Charlotte Smith's writings for children, and Romantic Gothic suicide. She is a recipient of the 2017 Keats-Shelley Association Distinguished Scholar Award.

Valentina Varinelli is an AHRC-funded PhD student at Newcastle University, UK. Her research project consists in a literary and linguistic analysis and a new edition of Percy Bysshe Shelley's verse and prose writings in Italian. Her research interests include the works of Mary Shelley; Romantic theories and practice of translation; Anglo-Italian literary relations; travel writing in Italy; and textual editing. Valentina is assistant editor and co-translator of the latest two-volume Italian anthology of Percy Bysshe Shelley's works (Milan: Mondadori, 2018) and is responsible for the translation and editorial commentary of a number of prose pieces, including the Shelleys' *History of a Six Weeks' Tour*.

LIST OF ILLUSTRATIONS

❖

FIG. 11.1. Reginald Easton, *Mary Shelley*, between 1851 and 1893, watercolour, Bodleian Library, University of Oxford, Shelley relics (d).

FIG. 11.2. Richard Rothwell, *Mary Shelley*, exhibited 1840, oil on canvas, 73.7 × 61 cm, National Portrait Gallery, London, NPG 1235, © National Portrait Gallery.

FIG. 11.3. Fernando Vicente, *Mary Shelley*, 2009, book illustration/print, © Fernando Vicente.

FIG. 11.4. Salvador Heras Muños, *Mary Shelley as her own Dr Frankenstein's Monster Character*, 2007, analogue/digital mixed media, © Salvador Heras Muños.

FIG. 11.5. Tim Seeley, *Mary Shelley Lovecraft*, 2009, comics/print, © Tim Seeley.

FIG. 11.6. Abigail Larson, *Mary Shelley and her Creation*, 2010, pencil & ink drawing/print, © Abigail Larson.

FIG. 11.7. Sarah Dolby, *Portrait of Mary Shelley*, 2008, painting/print, © Sarah Dolby.

FIG. 11.8. Esao Andrews, *Young Mary Shelley*, 2010, oil on wood/print, © Esao Andrews.

FIG. 11.9. Alan Vest, *Portrait of Mary Shelley*, 2016, watercolour drawing/print, © Alan Vest.

FIG. 11.10. Alison Silva, *He Comes to Life*, 2017, painting/print, © Alison Silva.

FIGS. 11.11–14. Derek Marks and Charles Cuykendall Carter, *An Illustrated Biography of Mary Shelley*, [n.d.], comics/print, © Derek Marks and Charles Cuykendall Carter.

ABBREVIATIONS

MWS Journals   *The Journals of Mary Shelley: 1814–1844*, ed. by Paula R. Feldman and Diana Scott-Kilvert, 2 vols (Oxford: Clarendon Press, 1987; repr. (with light corrections and in one volume) Baltimore: Johns Hopkins University Press, 1995). Both editions are used for citation in this volume, pagination being the same.

MWS Letters   *The Letters of Mary Wollstonecraft Shelley*, ed. by Betty Bennett, 3 vols (Baltimore: The Johns Hopkins University Press, 1980–88).

PBS Letters   *The Letters of Percy Bysshe Shelley*, ed. by Frederick L. Jones, 2 vols (Oxford: Clarendon Press, 1964).

INTRODUCTION

The European Mary Shelley: From Jean de Palacio to the Twenty-First Century

Antonella Braida

This volume has been conceived as a Festschrift in honour of Jean de Palacio in order to acknowledge his unique contribution to Mary Shelley studies and to continue his legacy in the twenty-first century. His volume *Mary Shelley dans son œuvre: Contributions aux études shelleyennes* (1969) has inspired the contributors' approaches which are aimed at assessing the European background of Mary Shelley's works and exploring their impact, reception, and transformation in European drama, art, literature, and media.

Mary Shelley belongs to a generation of writers who lived through major changes in Britain and Europe. Born in 1797, she crossed the Channel for the first time (as Mary Godwin) in 1814 for a six-week journey that already revealed to her and her fellow travellers — Percy Shelley and Claire Clairmont — the dire consequences of the Napoleonic wars in north eastern France. She started composing her first novel, *Frankenstein*, during her second, much-remembered stay in Switzerland in 1816. Her longest residence outside Britain lasted from March 1818 to July 1823. During these five years she lived in various Italian towns, became a fluent speaker of the language, and acquired a good knowledge of Italian literature. She was able to accomplish two more extended journeys around Europe — in 1840 and 1843 — that resulted in her two-volume publication *Rambles in Germany and Italy*.

It is significant that Mary Shelley's creative career started outside Britain. British women writers had been able to write successfully about Europe without leaving the country.[1] However, it is because of her travels that Mary Shelley developed in her works a particular interest in European culture that is reflected in profound ways in her writings. Three among her six novels — *Frankenstein*, *Valperga*, *The Last Man*, — involve a European setting, with one fully set in medieval Italy. Some of her short stories are set in Greece and Italy and her biographies for Dionysius Lardner's *Cabinet Cyclopædia* concern Italy, France, Spain, and Portugal. As the essays included in this volume will show, for Mary Shelley European culture was a complex construct including places, languages, literatures, and artistic production, namely music, art, and sculpture.[2] In one of her late journeys to Italy she reflected on the importance of becoming acquainted with the language and literature of the country in which she resided as a central aspect of the process of acculturation:

> I read a great deal to beguile the time, chiefly in Italian; for it is pleasant to imbue one's mind with the language and literature of the country in which one is living: and poetry — Italian poetry — is in harmony with these scenes.[3]

While here the process is one of reaching a balance and 'harmony' between oneself and the surrounding world, Mary Shelley posited the possibility of constructing an Anglo-Italian identity in a series of articles that she published in the 1820s and 1830s. At that time she was living in Britain and was striving to establish her role as paid writer and self-styled promoter of Percy Shelley's memory. In the review article 'The English in Italy' (1826) she clearly identifies herself with a 'new race or sect among our countrymen, who have late been dubbed Anglo-Italians' and capable, in Byron's wake, of producing a school of Anglo-Italian literature.[4] Around the same time she also signed two articles as 'Anglo-Italicus'.[5] Maria Schoina has provided an important contribution to understanding Mary Shelley's hyphenated identity. Her analysis illustrates that she was thus creating her space in a community of writers who expressed in various degrees their attraction to a composite identity, one in which a woman's space could be freed from the constraints of propriety. According to Schoina:

> Mary Shelley carefully utilizes Italy and Italianness in the construction of a new personality, a new cultural model with which she identifies, the Anglo-Italian, which she wishes to prescribe as a standard of taste, learning and aesthetic competency. In addition, she exploits the dynamics of this discursive configuration in order to construct a distinct literary and political identity as a woman writer of her age.[6]

Should critics take into account this specificity by creating an Anglo-Italian category within European Romanticism? Rather than introducing new distinctions to an already fragmented European literary space, this volume intends to overcome the artificial barriers established by national critical traditions and to analyse Mary Shelley's works as belonging to European as well as to British literary traditions. This approach has been introduced by critics who come to British Romanticism as well-qualified 'outsiders'. Not unlike the contribution to postcolonial studies brought about by Edward Said first, and later Homi Bhabha,[7] a new turn in British Romanticism is being introduced by scholars belonging to different cultural traditions, namely Greece (Schoina), Italy (Lilla Maria Crisafulli, Diego Saglia), Germany (Christoph Bode), and British scholars sharing a European interest that is turning the national into an international European framework.[8] Their findings are collected by new ambitious critical studies that introduce a European dimension into British Romanticism, while focusing on particular micro 'events' in literary history.[9] Among these approaches, Steve Clarke and Tristanne Connolly's project has been 'to consider what British Romanticism looks like when its own international connections and circulations are taken into account'.[10] They pursue with confidence the analysis carried out by Christoph Bode who has expressed the need to introduce a historical perspective to the concept of European Romanticism:

> For it is, of course, perfectly permissible to speak of a singular European Romanticism provided one keeps in mind that we are speaking of a *construct* (a concept that we have developed because we have reason to believe it is useful as a tool) that focuses our discussion and helps to detect both similarities and discrepancies that may have escaped our notice before.[11]

Surprisingly few European 'constructs' have caused as many difficulties to literary historians as 'Romanticism'. One can speak of 'the Renaissance', 'the Enlightenment', and 'fin de siècle' with a more confident European perspective. It is perhaps telling that Europe is still a contentious concept today. Just as it can be said that the bases for modern Europe were laid in the period between the French Revolution and the Napoleonic wars, so it can be argued that the two constructs in fact overlap: Romanticism is European in so far as it witnessed the development of modern Europe in the form of many national constructs. Thus, one can speak with Bode about 'the European cultural scene' and 'a truly international literature' created by cosmopolitan figures such as Madame de Staël, August Wilhelm Schlegel, or Samuel Taylor Coleridge. Their work can be seen 'as a vast range of possible responses within a new framework'.[12] Similarly, Paul Hamilton invokes the need for a comprehensive view of the movement:

> We should perhaps recognize that it is in its European or comparative character that the post-neoclassical period behaves in what became known as a Romantic manner. A resistance to generic boundaries of all kind, and a cultural investment in the transgression of inherited boundaries permitted a choice of the traditions with which one defined oneself.[13]

This collection of essays on Mary Shelley's works intends to respond to her own 'transgression of boundaries', between genre, gender, as well as geographical boundaries.

Mary Shelley and Europe: Biography, Translation, and 'Cosmopolitanism'

Mary Shelley's interest in European languages and cultures can be seen in her novels and short stories, as well as in her non-fictional works, most notably in the biographies for Lardner's *Cabinet Cyclopædia*.[14] The *Literary Lives* can be considered as a kind of testimony reflecting her own curiosity in European culture. As Charles E. Robinson pointed out,

> these more than 60 biographies of writers as diverse as Ficino, Calderón, and Pascal were written later in Mary Shelley's life, but they also draw our attention to her earlier works when she frequently employed mottoes and quotations from continental texts.[15]

Moreover, the *Literary Lives* illustrate the importance of translation in her work. As de Palacio was the first to suggest and is confirmed by the editors of the Pickering & Chatto edition, the *Literary Lives* comprise long translations from primary or secondary sources in Italian, French, and Spanish.[16] As de Palacio pointed out, her choice to go back to sources in the original even when translations were available testifies her unfaltering interest in European languages:

Très attentive au génie propre des langues qu'elle possédait, on la voit déclarer, avec Foscolo, 'how fallacious and trivial all translations are', déplorer l'impuissance du traducteur à faire passer dans une langue d'emprunt les beautés de l'original, ou s'efforcer, au contraire, de les rendre sensibles au lecteur étranger. D'où chez elle quelques réactions caractéristiques, dont la première consiste à proposer, chaque fois que la chose est possible, le texte original à côté de la traduction.[17]

[Mary Shelley was always very attentive to the 'genius' of the languages she mastered, and thus she lamented, following Foscolo, 'how fallacious and trivial all translations are', and deplored the translator's impotence when trying to transfer the beauties of the original into a new language, or she strived to make foreign readers aware of them. Hence some of her personal translating choices, among which the first was to print, whenever possible, the translation alongside the original text.][18]

Parts I and II of the present volume focus on Mary Shelley's engagement with Europe in a variety of ways and with the help of different critical approaches. As they will show, it is significant that her initiation into creative writing happened when travelling through Europe.

It is possible to identify a consistent interest in the consequences of despotism in European countries from her first travel narrative, *History of a Six Weeks' Tour*, to her last published work, *Rambles in Germany and Italy*. In the review article she published in 1826, Mary revisits her earlier experience: recalling the desolation she witnessed in northern France, she uses for herself and her companions the epithet of 'migrants', as if to stress the fact that their voluntary exile was marked by the same 'miseries' suffered by other Europeans forced away by wars or poverty.[19] Paul Stock has identified Mary Shelley's and Percy Shelley's frequent reference to an idea of what 'European' civilization meant in their writings of 1817–18.[20] *Frankenstein*, in particular, is seen to embody the French revolutionary ideals as '[i]t associates "European" with potentially dangerous radical thought and the concept of "progress"'.[21] As Lisa Vargo's contribution to this volume points out, the articles Mary Shelley wrote for the *Westminster Review* demonstrate her continued allegiance to revolutionary ideals, in terms that Vargo defines as 'a form of liberal authority', namely a consistent separation between private and public spheres. Within this framework, Mary Shelley's articles reveal her support for the revolutions in Italy and Greece of the 1820s. Until her last years, she thus continued to focus on Britain's role as the inspiration and source for the establishment of 'free institutions' in Europe. In *Rambles*, she comments on the restored governments' repression of revolts with the claim that 'the peace of Europe will be disturbed' and supports the need for a 'peaceful mediation and a strong universal sense of justice'.[22]

Anna Mercer, Valentina Varinelli, and Maria Parrino's essays reveal how complex and multifaceted Mary Shelley's Italian experience was. Parrino's essay follows in the line of Schoina's analysis and shows that the Italian language offered Mary the access to a bicultural identity that she strived to endorse through cultural practices available to Italian women: namely reading contemporary authors, joining salons and 'conversazioni', attending the opera, and translating. For Parrino, language learning and translating from the Italian contributed to the 'Gothic trope for *otherness* and multiple identities' that characterizes some of Mary's works.[23] Moreover, her inclusion of phrases in Italian in her letters or even in her published works suggests her intention of participating in the creation of a selective network of 'Anglo-Italian' readers and correspondents. The first and foremost among these was Percy Shelley, as Anna Mercer's essay points out. Mercer's analysis of Mary Shelley's use of Italian settings intends to move beyond the critical dichotomy concerning Percy's contribution to her work, or, inversely, Mary's critical revision of his poetry. By analysing their unique cohabitation and collaboration as writers, editors, and poets, Mercer considers 'the interrelationship between the Shelleys' texts and their Italian scenes'. Mercer shows the ambiguity of Mary Shelley's representation of Italy: both in her letters and in the fictional works that draw inspiration from them, she depicts Venice and Rome as places of alienation, but insists on their thriving multicultural communities and the remains of their glorious past. While taking part in the contemporary cultural scene in Italy, Mary Shelley shared Percy's wish to create a small, secluded community of kindred spirits. As Mercer demonstrates, they shared an interest in episodes and characters from Italian history and literature — Beatrice Cenci, Dante's *Divina Commedia* and his *Vita Nuova* — and cross-referenced each other's work. At Percy Shelley's death, the Italian landscape acquired a more nostalgic connotation: Valentina Varinelli singles out the poem 'The Choice' as the composition that best illustrates the ambiguity of this transformation. Well versed in the contemporary poetic tradition of mourning, Mary Shelley's poetry, in Mark Sandy's words, 'acts as a defence against, and encounter with, the final silence of death that challenges poetry's eloquent capacity for meaning.'[24] Varinelli illustrates how for Mary the act of mourning became one and the same with the act of reappropriation and reinterpretation of Percy's poems written in Italy. Varinelli's contribution, like Crook's and Mercer's, belongs to the recent turn in Mary Shelley studies aimed at understanding her work as less influenced by, and more notably exerting an influence on, Percy Shelley's work, thus reinstating her authorial awareness both as a writer and as an editor.

American and European Scholarship: Betty T. Bennett and Jean de Palacio

It is generally agreed that a new impulse in Mary Shelley scholarship arrived in the 1980s and 1990s with Betty T. Bennett's editorial and critical work, from the publication of the *Letters* (1980–88) and the *Mary Shelley Reader* (1990), to her *Mary Wollstonecraft Shelley: An Introduction* (1998).[25] Her publications coincided with the progressive deposit of the Abinger papers at the Bodleian Library on loan, between 1974 and 1993.[26] Jean de Palacio's monumental work, *Mary Shelley dans son œuvre* (1969) was the result of research undertaken before this event. It has remained the most important publication based on the manuscripts and collections housed at Lord Abinger's property in Bures. Yet its importance is far from being merely the source of a footnote in the history of Mary Shelley's manuscripts. As Nora Crook claims in this volume, de Palacio was 'her first true bibliographer'. A cursory reading of the volumes of *The Novels and Selected Works of Mary Shelley* illustrates the profound impact his research has had on editing and on literary criticism.

This volume opens with a chapter by Jean de Palacio. I hope that modern readers and students of Mary Shelley's works will find his account as inspirational as it was for the editor. A short biographical note is important in order to understand de Palacio's contribution.

Born in 1931 in Paris, de Palacio took the prestigious 'agrégation' (1953) set of exams aimed at combining a teaching and research career,[27] but then chose to continue his studies with a BA in Italian (1958). He later registered for a 'doctorat ès lettres' on Mary Shelley's works with Professor Jean-Jacques Mayoux at the 'Faculté des Lettres et Sciences Humaines' in Paris. The thesis that resulted from his degree was published in its complete form — reaching 717 pages — in 1969 by the publisher Klincksieck. The structure of the French doctorate called 'thèse d'état' must be taken into account in order to understand the length and scope of this volume. Left in place after the introduction of a three-year doctorate ('doctorat troisième cycle') in 1958,[28] this higher degree was often but not exclusively obtained after the first, shorter doctorate, and — up until the reform of 1984 — was a means of acceding to the position of University Professor, while holding non-permanent teaching positions.[29] The historian Antoine Prost refers to an indicative time span of ten years to complete the thesis and mentions the difficulty of reaching a sufficiently specialized readership for the lengthy tomes produced.[30] He also points out the training required as being both an advantage, in terms of teaching and research experience, and a disadvantage due to the non-permanent nature of the posts held by the researchers. Thus, while undertaking his research on Mary Shelley in the late 1950s, de Palacio held various non-permanent positions, before becoming University Lecturer and Professor at Lille III (1965–78).[31] He then obtained a chair at the Sorbonne University in Paris (1979–99), a post that he held until his retirement. The 'Preface' of his thesis includes a veiled, but clear reference to his disappointment at not having been offered the possibility of research leave.[32] De Palacio's research on Mary Shelley was carried out alongside a full-time teaching career and took eleven years to complete.

Critical studies on the situation of academics at French universities have pointed out a hierarchical structure among institutions and disciplines, with the existence of independent research centres (École Nationale des Chartes, Collège de France, École Pratique des Hautes Études, CNRS).[33] De Palacio's career reveals significant originality in its combination of three different disciplines: English, Italian, and Comparative Literature. This choice, and the nature of his research, place him in the French tradition of comparative studies that he eventually joined. The academic discipline of English Studies became well established in the nineteenth-century, with the creation of chairs in 'Foreign Literature', aimed, as Michel Espagne has pointed out, at 'establishing, from a French official perspective, specific cultural areas with their alleged specificities, thus establishing a science of "the foreign"'.[34] Comparative Literature developed after World War II as a discipline with a national association in existence since 1956;[35] only one journal, the *Revue de littérature comparée* (1921–) could boast of an early inception.[36] Moreover, French Comparative Literature soon adopted a preference for interdisciplinary approaches across the arts, progressively abandoning the framework of 'influence' in favour of a more cosmopolitan and pan-European one based on transfers, contacts, travels, and cross-cultural mediators.[37] However, after the 1966 Fouchet undergraduate reform, Comparative Literature Studies were fully integrated into French Studies, thus requiring the teaching of European and World literature in French translation.[38]

De Palacio's work could thus be seen as a fruitful continuation of the work undertaken by his predecessors in English Studies, and the comparatists at the Sorbonne, in particular by André Koszul and Charles Dédéyan.[39] André Koszul opened the way for a systematic study of Mary Shelley's works with his doctoral thesis on 'La jeunesse de Mary Shelley' (1910) and his edition of the mythological dramas 'Proserpine' and 'Midas'.[40] Moreover, de Palacio's approach could be defined as 'a literary cosmopolitanism' in the wake of Dédéyan's,[41] with a specific focus on European culture and literature in which the Italian medieval poet Dante occupies an important place.[42] Like his predecessors, de Palacio's eventual appointment to a chair in Comparative Literature in 1979 required him to teach research seminars on French Studies and Comparative Literature. By the end of the 1970s, his impressive publication record shows that, after a considerable contribution to the study of British Romanticism with articles written in French and English and two monographs, his interests progressively migrated to the European *fin de siècle*.[43] In the Festschrift volume *Anamorphoses décadentes* the authors outline his methodology:

> Appréhender une époque en fonction des critères qu'elle s'est elle-même données en mettant en résonance les motifs et les enjeux qui la constituent par le croisement des arts, l'étude de la presse, du contexte ou de l'édition.[44]
>
> [Endeavouring to understand a period on the basis of the criteria it had chosen for itself, to outline its themes and issues by identifying the interconnection between the arts, the study of periodical publications, the historical context, and publishing history.]

De Palacio's earlier studies on Mary Shelley display a similar attention for the literary context of her work, with research and publications on her links with Percy Shelley, William Godwin, and Lord Byron, thus mapping the network of writers with whom she associated.

It is significant that both Betty T. Bennett and de Palacio foregrounded Shelley's European sensitivity. According to Bennett:

> Her lengthy stay in Scotland as an adolescent, the Geneva Summer, and the five years she spent in Italy (1818–23) extended her sense of geography and history as well as literature onto a pan-European plane, giving her a perspective rare among writers of the day and rarer still among prominent female writers.[45]

De Palacio writes in similar terms about her 'italianisme', which he defines thus:

> Par *italianisme*, on entend d'une part l'intérêt porté par Mary Shelley à la littérature italienne et le degré de connaissance qu'elle avait de la langue; en second lieu, l'influence proprement dite que les écrivains italiens ont exercée sur son œuvre; enfin l'image de l'Italie telle qu'elle apparaît dans ses divers écrits.[46]

[By 'Italianism' I mean the following: first, Mary Shelley's interest in Italian literature and her knowledge of the Italian language; secondly, the direct influence of Italian writers on her work; and finally, the image of Italy as it appears in her various works.]

De Palacio's insight into Dante's influence anticipates recent developments in Mary Shelley studies. When identifying the omission from the 1831 edition of *Frankenstein*, of the reference to *Inferno*, XXIII, de Palacio offers an interesting speculation:

> La raison la plus probable est que Mary, souvent accusée dans ses romans précédents de faire étalage de son savoir, aura voulu y remédier ici en allégeant sa phrase. Mais peut-être y a-t-il une intention plus profonde. En l'associant aux damnés du chant XXIII, le texte de 1818 semblait dès le départ condamner Frankenstein pour la promesse faite au monstre. La rédaction de 1831, plus nuancée à cet égard, pourrait traduire l'hésitation du nouveau Prométhée sur le fondé de la requête faite par sa créature; elle substitue en quelque sorte la compassion à l'inflexible justice, toute dantesque, qui vouait le monstre à une éternelle solitude.[47]

> [The most probable reason is that Mary, who had already been accused of showing off her knowledge in her previous novels, must have decided to remedy this by simplifying her style. However, there might be a more profound intention. By introducing the association with the damned of canto XXIII, the 1818 text seemed to condemn Frankenstein from the start for the promise he had made to the monster. The 1831 version, more nuanced from this viewpoint, could be seen to translate the hesitation of the new Prometheus about the validity of his creature's demand; somehow, she has substituted compassion for the inflexible justice, typical of Dante, that condemned the monster to eternal solitude.]

This suggestion offers a plausible justification for the revision that is now acknowledged in contemporary scholarly editions of *Frankenstein*.[48] De Palacio's second important contribution to the current appreciation of Mary Shelley concerns her interest in the visual arts and music. His approach, derived from European comparative literature studies, highlights the inter-arts discourse in Shelley's works. *Mary Shelley dans son œuvre* encompasses essay writing, fictional writing, and autobiography, and identifies her interest in Italian medieval and Renaissance art, and her own personal readings in art history through contemporary and earlier works: Luigi Lanzi, Alexis-François Rio, and Vasari. Jeanne Moskal in her edition of *Rambles in Germany and Italy* accepts de Palacio's suggestions about the importance of Rio, while claiming that Mary Shelley 'transmutes [Rio's] exclusive attention to religious inspiration in paintings into her more inclusive response, expressing her enthusiasm for mythological and secular subjects and for sculpture'.[49] More recently, her interest in the Italian Primitives, and in particular of Domenico Ghirlandaio, has been analysed by J. B. Bullen and Rieko Suzuki, both of whom acknowledge de Palacio's findings.[50]

Likewise, de Palacio's long-lasting contribution concerns Mary Shelley's interest in music: in this particular field, his reading of *The Last Man* has revealed the importance of music as the deepest structural bond of the novel. His analysis touches upon the cohesiveness and complexity of the 'musical structure' of the *The Last Man*, as he explained:

> Mary ne s'en tient pas dans son livre à la déclaration de principe qu'elle prête à l'écrivain Lionel Verney: la musique y sert effectivement la technique romanesque. En règle générale, elle fait usage de la musique dans le roman lorsque les procédés habituels de la narration, analyse, description ou dialogue, se révèlent insuffisants pour exprimer dans toute leur intensité les états d'âme des personnages; elle s'associe au bonheur et au malheur dans leurs degrés extrêmes. Elle préside ainsi aux tournants de l'action, à la veille de dramatiques changements ou de catastrophes pressenties; elle apparaît aux apogées, aux points culminants, aux moments de crise ou de liesse. Les rappels musicaux sont en quelque sorte le signe du déroulement romanesque, auquel ils fournissent sa scansion et son rythme.[51]

> [In her novel, Mary does not limit herself to the declaration of principle she attributed to the writer Lionel Verney: music is in fact part of the narrative technique. In general, she uses music in the novel whenever the usual methods of narration, analysis, description, or dialogue are not capable of expressing the emotional intensity of the characters' feelings; music is associated with extremes of happiness or unhappiness. Music thus presides over the turning points of the action, the anticipation of dramatic changes, or of impending catastrophes; it appears at climaxes and moments of crisis or jubilation. The musical references are in a sense the characteristic of the novelistic plot to which they offer scansion and rhythm.]

De Palacio's assessment had the merit of opening new ground before American and British criticism returned to the novel in the 1990s with the new inspiring readings by Paul A. Cantor, Morton D. Paley, Audrey Fisch, Barbara Johnson, Betty T. Bennett, Anne K. Mellor, and Pamela Clemit,[52] and more recently Zachary Tooman, Lauren Cameron, and Ranita Chatterjee and Lucy Morrison.[53] Despite the richness and variety of these new readings, Morrison still finds de Palacio's contribution relevant in claiming that the novel 'draws its readers beyond language' and that

> the sound emanates from the pages of Mary Shelley's book [...]. Mary Shelley's interdisciplinarity more specifically takes readers beyond her pages into music as one significant facet of her engagement with the popular cultural scene in which she was involved.[54]

De Palacio's contribution to textual editing and new attributions of Mary Shelley's articles and letters has been acknowledged by all subsequent editors.[55] Michael Rossington's article in this volume focuses on his contribution to the study of Mary Shelley's role as editor of Percy Shelley's works. Setting de Palacio's scholarship in the complex context of early editions of Percy Shelley's works, Rossington claims that de Palacio's editorial work rehabilitates Mary Shelley as an editor, both by restoring her editorial choices and by making her role as editor more visible. As editor of Percy Shelley's works, Rossington, like de Palacio, finds Mary Shelley's editorial choices sensible and perceptive, with few genuine errors of judgment. Moreover, by focusing on de Palacio's groundbreaking study of Shelley's translations, Rossington highlights his contribution to an understanding of the importance of Italy and continental Europe in her writings.

Nora Crook's essay in this volume is essential to underlining de Palacio's scholarship, but also points the way forward for Mary Shelley's scholarship. As general editor of the standard scholarly edition of Mary Shelley's works, Crook comments on the urgent need to revise the author's canon. W. H. Lyles's *Annotated Bibliography* (1975) is still often used as the main reference, despite the progression in scholarship over the last forty-five years. A certain number of dubious or even erroneous attributions still exist and require renewed editorial treatment and the updating of existing editions. In particular, Mary Shelley's reviewing for periodicals during the 1820s and 1830s still invites further investigation in order to achieve a canon with stronger foundations. Crook's article provides significant examples of good practice in attributing anonymous articles, a field in which de Palacio led the way for future textual criticism. Her contribution opens the programme for the creation of a network of Mary Shelley scholars at European and international levels. This project will involve the creation of an interactive Digital Humanities tool to which researchers will be able to freely contribute in order to advance our knowledge about articles newly attributed to Mary Shelley and the still evolving canon of her works.

Mary Shelley's Afterlife in Europe: Translation, Reception, and Rewriting(s)

Understanding Mary Shelley in the twenty-first century means coming to terms with the Frankenstein myth, its origins, and its potency. As Chris Baldick points out, contemporary readers and critics inevitably approach the novel *Frankenstein* as a text that has been transformed in a variety of media and forms: 'that series of adaptations, allusions, accretions, analogues, parodies, and plain misreading which follows upon Mary Shelley's novel is not a supplementary component of the myth; it *is* the myth.'[56] Section III of this volume thus continues de Palacio's comparative project by applying contemporary developments in cultural studies and particularly in intermediality. Among the many definitions intermediality has acquired, its meaning implies, according to Werner Wolf, 'a direct or indirect participation of more than one medium in the signification and/or structure of a given semiotic entity ("a work") and involvement that must be verifiable within this entity'. In its broader meaning the term implies a transgression of boundaries 'not only within individual works, texts or performances, but also as a consequence of relations and comparisons between different semiotic complexes'.[57] In terms of literary afterlife, as Maddalena Pennacchia Punzi has pointed out, literary intermediality occurs, as in *Frankenstein*'s case, 'when "a literary message" has been disseminated in many different media, undergoing a transformation, or *mediamorphosis* (Fidler)'.[58] Mary Shelley's novel belongs to a special category of literary works that have been able to respond to technological changes and attract *mediamorphosis* in new media. Various interpretations have been offered for this creativity; the novel has been considered a 'readerly text', namely a literary work that invites the reader to provide closure to the narrative.⁵⁹ Furthermore, it was written at a time of transition, in which the scientific culture that still dominates our world was timidly emerging. Whatever the interpretation, this afterlife is interesting not only in itself, but also as a means of revealing new approaches to the novel, as pointed out by Fred Botting and Chris Baldick.⁶⁰ When reading *Frankenstein* through its literary posterity, the contemporary critic/reader thus acknowledges his/her contribution to the myth-making process. I would like to adapt Matthew Reynolds's original concept of 'prismatic translation' and extend it to claim the existence of a 'prismatic reading':⁶¹ contemporary readings and rewritings of *Frankenstein* are superimposed on earlier ones, but rather than replacing them they coexist side by side, and interact, like the facets of a prism. With this approach in mind, theatrical performances of *Frankenstein* are indeed essential to the afterlife of the novel: in Mary Shelley's lifetime the first theatrical adaptation by Richard Brinsley Peake, *Presumption, or The Fate of Frankenstein* (1823), had already planted the seed of myth-creation.⁶² Marjean D. Purinton focuses on the initial British reception of the novel: in the first thirty years from its publication, illegitimate adaptations of the novel capitalized on large audiences attracted by the supernatural and by medical or pseudo-medical shows of deformity and disease. This early reception bears an uncanny similarity with the contemporary one, in which scientific discourse is eager to appropriate the metaphor of the reconstructed body for a variety of modern practices, from genetic engineering to artificial intelligence.⁶³ Anne Rouhette's article retraces the tenuous separation of translation, adaptation, and rewriting in the French nineteenth-century context. Rouhette's analysis is essential to understanding the European reception of *Frankenstein*, because Jules Saladin's 1821 translation offered readers in Europe access to the novel at a time in which French was the language of communication for European intellectuals and readers.⁶⁴ The lack of translations of *Frankenstein* in other European languages until the twentieth century is important for the understanding of its reception. This absence can be explained partly through the editorial history of the novel, as pointed out by William St Clair: the circulation of the volume was limited to the 500 copies of the first Lackington edition and to the Bentley Standard Novels edition, and 'for the first fourteen years of its life in print, *Frankenstein* existed in about a thousand copies'.⁶⁵ More importantly, its circulation did continue — but through its stage adaptations, as St Clair explains: 'during the nineteenth century, it was not the reading of the text of the book, but seeing adaptations of the story on the stage which kept Frankenstein alive in culture.'⁶⁶ Rouhette's analysis shows that this tendency prevailed in France, where Saladin's translation was soon turned into adaptations, among which was Jean-Toussaint Merle and Antony Béraud's play *Le Monstre et le magicien* (1826).⁶⁷ More importantly, Rouhette contextualizes the French translation and its adaptations within the contemporary evolution of the 'Romantisme frénétique', thus introducing a significant contribution to the European reception of the novel.⁶⁸

Twentieth-century performances have been influenced to different degrees by James Whale's *Frankenstein* films, with the creature impersonated by Boris Karloff. Yet, the fact that Whale's *Frankenstein* was based on a dramatic adaptation of the novel demonstrates that the interplay and transfer across media has always been extremely productive within the Frankenstein myth.

Current adaptations of the novel worldwide illustrate the dramatic potential of the Frankenstein myth. Yet, putting *Frankenstein* on stage still challenges directors into coming to terms with Mary Shelley's text as well as the myth it created. Catherine Pugh analyses the choices Nick Dear faced when staging a play based on the novel at the London National Theatre in 2011. Through a perspective that aims at taking into account the requirements of a contemporary performance as well as its impact on the audience's understanding of the novel, Dear's approach becomes relevant for the current reception of *Frankenstein*. Thus, the decision to have the lead actors Benedict Cumberbatch and Jonny Lee Miller alternate roles as Frankenstein and the creature invites the viewer to appreciate the doppelgänger theme in the novel, an approach that has often been omitted in theatrical adaptations in favour of 'a simplified Byronic hero-villain (Frankenstein)'.[69] Dear's production seeks to break away from tropes and traditions in putting the novel on stage and establishing a closer dialogue with the text.

The Frankenstein myth has generated in turn a Mary Shelley myth. De Palacio's *Mary Shelley dans son œuvre* aimed at fighting against a literary and biographical tradition that relegated her to a secondary role as Percy's wife. Contemporary scholarly approaches share a similar objective, as Nora Crook has pointed out, to access the 'inclusive Mary Shelley', namely the study of a writer who — while often overshadowed by the Frankenstein myth — produced a variety of texts that range from the novel to the short story, to the review and to travel writing — without neglecting her autobiographical and editorial work. With the contemporary interest in autobiography and in women's studies, Mary Shelley's authorial persona and her own singular life as a woman writer in Napoleonic and post-Napoleonic times has not failed to attract attention. She has increasingly been associated with her mother's work and ideology, in biography and scholarly publications.[70] Jean-Marie Lecomte demonstrates that the twentieth century witnessed a proliferation of images of Mary Shelley that developed alongside the Frankenstein myth. Starting from the few surviving portraits, Lecomte retraces the contemporary iconography of Mary Shelley in popular media and across new art forms — from comics and graphic design to advertisement and digital art. Lecomte's contribution introduces a taxonomy of these visual interpretations: Mary Shelley's likeness becomes the signifier of a variety of discourses, from feminism to literary theory to commercial advertising. This transformation of the image of the author into a visual icon was facilitated by the presence of visuality in Mary Shelley's and the Romantics' sensibility, as Johnathan Crary has pointed out: this sensibility is part of 'the continuous unfolding of a Renaissance-based form of vision, in which photography, and eventually cinema, are simply later instances of an ongoing deployment of perspectival space and perception'.[71] While the name *Frankenstein* has progressively become an intersemiotic object,[72] referring to a series of images reproduced in multiple media, originating from a novel adapted into plays and films, Mary Shelley has become the signifier of the female author, of the Gothic genre, and of her own fictional creations.

While this volume was in preparation, academic communities in Europe and across the world celebrated the bicentenary of the publication of *Frankenstein*. In 2018, the conferences that took place in Nancy, London, Venice, Clermont-Ferrand, Bologna, and Rome, as well as the global *Frankenreads* initiative testified to a new commitment by the academic community to continue the research undertaken by European scholars after Jean de Palacio's groundbreaking publication.[73] This volume has had the privilege of bridging the gap between scholars belonging to different countries and of laying the foundations for an ongoing collaboration among them regardless of the threats associated with Brexit. It aims to show that Mary Shelley scholarship is a collaborative enterprise characterized by the very cosmopolitanism she endorsed in her work.

Notes to the Introduction

1. See, for example, Felicia Hemans's poems about Italy, Spain, and Greece, and Ann Radcliffe's novels set in Italy as presented in Felicia Hemans, *Selected Poems, Prose and Letters*, ed. by Gary Kelly (Peterborough, Ontario: Broadview Press, 2002), and Pam Perkins, 'John Moore, Ann Radcliffe and the Gothic Vision of Italy', *Gothic Studies*, 8.1 (May 2006), 35–51 (p. 17).
2. As Maria Schoina has pointed out, Stuart Hall's approach to cultural identity and language is particularly relevant to Mary Shelley's insistence on the importance of language as a means of acculturation. See Stuart Hall, 'New Cultures for Old', in *A Place in the World? Places, Cultures and Globalization*, ed. by Doreen Massey and P. M. Jess (Oxford: Oxford University Press, in association with The Open University, 1995), pp. 175–214, and Stuart Hall, 'Cultural Identity and Diaspora', in *Identity and Difference*, ed. by K. Woodward (London: SAGE Publications, 1997), pp. 51–59. See Maria Schoina, *Romantic 'Anglo-Italians': Configurations of Identity in Byron, the Shelleys and the Pisan Circle* (Farnham: Ashgate, 2009; Abingdon: Routledge, 2016), p. 10.
3. Mary Shelley, *Rambles in Germany and Italy*, in *The Novels and Selected Works of Mary Shelley*, The Pickering Masters, ed. by Nora Crook and others, 8 vols (London: Pickering & Chatto, 1996), VIII: *Travel Writing*, ed. by Jeanne Moskal, p. 124. Hereafter cited as *Travel Writing*. All references to Shelley's works are to this edition unless indicated otherwise.
4. [Mary Shelley], 'The English in Italy', *The Westminster Review*, 6 (October 1826), 325–41, in *The Novels and Selected Works of Mary Shelley*, II: *Matilda, Dramas, Review and Essays*, ed. by Pamela Clemit, pp. 147–63 (p. 149). Hereafter *Matilda, Dramas, Review and Essays*.
5. She used the pseudonym in an article entitled 'Velluti', published in the *Examiner*, 12 June 1826, pp. 372–73; see Jean de Palacio, *Mary Shelley dans son œuvre: Contribution aux études shelleyennes* (Paris: Klincksieck, 1969), p. 582. A second article remained in draft form. See *MWS Letters*, I, 520–24.
6. Schoina, *Romantic 'Anglo-Italians'*, p. 10.
7. See also *Global Romanticism: Origins, Orientations, and Engagements, 1760–1820*, ed. by Evan Gottlieb (Lewisburg: Bucknell University Press, 2015).
8. Most scholars in British Romanticism have touched upon its European background. Among those more specifically focusing on the Romantics and Italy are: Laura Bandiera, Will Bowers, Charles Peter Brand, Luisa Calé, Carmen Casaliggi, Roderick Cavaliero, Lilla Maria Crisafulli, Nora Crook, Lia Guerra, Nicholas Havely, Maurizio Isabella, Joseph Luzzi, Ralph Pite, Alan Rawes, Michael Rossington, Diego Saglia, Jane Stabler, Peter Vassallo, Edoardo Zuccato, Alan M. Weinberg, among others, and the editor of this volume. However, attempts to separate the study of the Romantics and Europe from British Romanticism are bound to be unsatisfactory. Recent scholarship has tended to overcome binary distinctions and focus on approaches that take into account a global perspective.
9. Their studies can be compared to the historical turn towards microhistory. For some well-known examples of microhistorical approaches, see Carlo Ginzburg, *The Cheese and the Worms:*

The Cosmos of a Sixteenth-Century Miller (1976), trans. by John and Ann C. Tedeschi (Baltimore: The Johns Hopkins University Press, 2013 [1980]), and Giovanni Levi, 'On Microhistory', in Peter Burke, *New Perspectives on Historical Writing* (Cambridge: Polity Press, 1991), pp. 93–94.
10. *British Romanticism in European Perspective: Into the Eurozone*, ed. by Steve Clarke and Tristanne Connolly (London: Palgrave Macmillan, 2015), p. 1.
11. *Romanticism: An Oxford Guide*, ed. by Nicholas Roe (Oxford: Oxford University Press, 2008 [2005]), pp. 126–36 (p. 127).
12. Ibid., pp. 126–36.
13. *The Oxford Handbook of European Romanticism*, ed. by Paul Hamilton (Oxford: Oxford University Press, 2016), p. 2.
14. These biographies, edited by Tilar J. Mazzeo (Italian lives), Lisa Vargo (Spanish and Portuguese lives), and Clarissa Campbell Orr (French lives) are now collected in volumes I–III of *Mary Shelley's 'Literary Lives' and Other Writings*, ed. by Nora Crook and others, The Pickering Masters, 4 vols (London: Pickering & Chatto, 2002). The lives are supplemented by a fourth volume, *Life of William Godwin, Poems, Uncollected Prose, Translations, Post-Authored and Attributed Writings*, ed. by A. A. Markley and Pamela Clemit.
15. Charles E. Robinson, review of *Mary Shelley's 'Literary Lives' and Other Writings*, ed. by Nora Crook and others, 4 vols (London: Pickering & Chatto, 2002), in *Romanticism on the Net*, 43 (August 2006) <https://www.erudit.org/fr/revues/ron/2006-n43-ron1383/013595ar/> [accessed 19 February 2020].
16. De Palacio identified her translations from Spanish poetry. De Palacio, *Mary Shelley dans son œuvre*, p. 524.
17. Ibid.
18. Unless otherwise indicated, all translations are the editor's.
19. 'The English in Italy', in *Matilda, Dramas, Reviews and Essays*, p. 147.
20. Paul Stock, 'The Shelleys and the Idea of "Europe"', *European Romantic Review*, 19.4 (2008), 335–49.
21. Ibid., p. 337.
22. *Travel Writing*, p. 68.
23. On the importance of the Gothic for Mary Shelley, see Angela Wright, *Mary Shelley, Gothic Authors: Critical Revisions* (Cardiff: University of Wales Press, 2018).
24. Mark Sandy, *Romanticism, Memory, and Mourning* (Farnham: Ashgate, 2013), p. 1.
25. See *The Mary Shelley Reader*, ed. by Betty T. Bennett and Charles E. Robinson (New York: Oxford University Press, 1990); Betty T. Bennett, *Mary Wollstonecraft Shelley: An Introduction* (Baltimore: Johns Hopkins University Press, 1998); Graham Allen, *Mary Shelley*, Critical Issues (Houndmills, Basingstoke: Palgrave MacMillan, 2008).
26. They were acquired in 2004. See Michael Rossington, 'Mary Shelley's Short Stories Notebook in the Bodleian Library', *La Questione Romantica*, Mary Shelley special issue in memory of Betty T. Bennett, n.s., 1.1 (1 June 2009), 113–18 (p. 113).
27. These exams were introduced by Louis XV in 1766. The 'agrégation' continued in the XIX century as a means of recruiting high school teachers. According to André Chervel, in the twentieth century this exam maintained its prestige. See André Chervel, *Histoire de l'Agrégation* (Paris: Institut National de Recherche Pédagogique, Éditions Kimé, 1993).
28. See André Tuilier, *Histoire de l'Université de Paris et de la Sorbonne*, 2 vols (Paris: Nouvelle Librairie de France, 1994), II: *De Louis XIV à la crise de 1968*, 519–20.
29. The old French terminology was 'maître assistant' or 'assistant de faculté'.
30. Antoine Prost 'Faut-il rétablir la thèse d'état ?', in *Vingtième Siècle, Revue d'histoire*, 47.1 (1985), 191–93. Prost expresses his reservations against the HDR because he finds that the minimal requirements to have access to the degree are not clearly defined.
31. He was an 'Assistant' at Paris Sorbonne University (1959–64) and 'Maître-Assistant' at Rennes (1964–65).
32. Research leave could and can still be granted by becoming a member of the CNRS (Centre National de la Recherche Scientifique). De Palacio applied unsuccessfully in 1964. See de Palacio, *Mary Shelley dans son œuvre*, p. 11.

33. See Pierre Bourdieu, *Homo Academicus* (Paris: Éditions de Minuit, 1984); *Le Personnel de l'enseignement supérieur aux XIXe et XXe siècles*, ed. by Christophe Charle and Régine Ferré (Paris: Éditions du CNRS, 1985); Emanuelle Picard, 'L'Histoire de l'enseignement supérieur français: Pour une approche globale', in *Histoire de l'éducation*, 122 (1 April 2009), 11–33.
34. Michel Espagne, *Le Paradigme de l'étranger: Les Chaires de littérature étrangère au XIX siècle* (Paris: Cerf, 1993), p. 18.
35. The first chair in comparative literature was created in 1896 in Lyon.
36. During the 1940s, it was published in Britain by Priory Press (Cardiff) in order to avoid censorship. Yves Chevrel has compiled the history of the French Society of Comparative Literature (Société Française de Littérature Générale et Comparée) in an article published on the society's website. Yves Chevrel, 'La Société Française de Littérature Générale et Comparée (1956–2006)', (2007) <http://sflgc.org/sflgc/notre-histoire/> [accessed 22 February 2020].
37. See D. H. Pageaux's summary of the evolution of the discipline in which he confirms its interdisciplinarity and its associations with the human sciences, namely psychology, sociology, anthropology, and history, and the fact that it was not well represented at the CNRS. Cited in Chevrel.
38. The teaching of 'foreign' authors became compulsory in the first year of the two-year DUEL (Diplôme universitaire d'études littéraires) 'Lettres Modernes' that was introduced before the three-year bachelor's degree.
39. Dédéyan occupied the chair at the Sorbonne from 1949 to 1979.
40. André Koszul, *Proserpine and Midas: Two Unpublished Mythological Dramas* (London: Milford, 1922).
41. According to Jean-Yves Masson, 'on peut reprendre à propos du comparatisme de Charles Dédéyan l'expression que lui-même a employée à propos de Charles Du Bos: c'est bien d'un "cosmopolitisme littéraire" qu'il s'agit, sous-tendu par une interrogation presque exclusive sur la culture européenne.' ['In order to define Charles Dédéyan's comparative approach, his own definition concerning Charles Du Bos can be applied: it is in fact "literary cosmopolitanism" underpinned by a research almost exclusively devoted to European culture.'] Jean-Yves Masson, 'Le Cosmopolitisme littéraire de Charles Dédéyan', *Revue de littérature comparée*, 336 (2010), 485–92.
42. See Charles Dédéyan, *Dante en Angleterre*, 2 vols (Paris: Didier, 1961), and de Palacio's articles 'Shelley and Dante: An Essay in Textual Criticism', *Revue de littérature comparée*, 35.1 (January–March 1961), 105–12, and 'Shelley traducteur de Dante: Le Chant XXVIII du *Purgatoire*', *Revue de littérature comparée*, 36.4 (October–December 1962), 571–78.
43. His impressive contribution to the concept of 'decadence' has been awarded the 2012 Académie française 'Emile Faguet' prize for *La Décadence: Le Mot et la chose* (Paris: Les Belles Lettres/Essais, 2011).
44. *Anamorphoses décadentes: L'art de la défiguration (1880–1914), Etudes offertes à Jean de Palacio*, ed. by Isabelle Krzywkowski and Sylvie Thorel-Cailleteau (Paris: Presses Universitaires de Paris Sorbonne, 2002), p. 15.
45. *Mary Shelley in her Times*, ed. by Betty T. Bennett and Stuart Curran (Baltimore: The Johns Hopkins University Press, 2000), p. ix. Hereafter *Mary Shelley in her Times*.
46. De Palacio, *Mary Shelley dans son œuvre*, p. 23.
47. Ibid., p. 38.
48. See for instance *The Novels and Selected Works of Mary Shelley*, 1: *Frankenstein*, ed. by Nora Crook with an introduction by Betty Bennett, p. 40 n. and *Frankenstein*, ed. by J. Paul Hunter, (New York: Norton, 2012 [1996]), p. 105. The narrator compares his feelings at having accepted the creature's demand for a companion to the punishment of the hypocrites in Dante's *Inferno*, canto XXIII, condemned to walk with the burden of an iron cowl.
49. Jeanne Moskal, 'Introductory Note', in *Rambles in Germany and Italy*, in *Travel Writing*, pp. 49–57, (p. 51).
50. For Suzuki, Robert Browning's harsh treatment of Mary Shelley's *Rambles* must be put into context 'in the light of his own distance from Romanticism, and from P. B. Shelley in particular'. Rieko Suzuki, 'Browning on Romanticism: "Fra Lippo Lippi" and Leigh Hunt',

The Keats-Shelley Review, 27.1 (2013), 31–38 (p. 31). On the topic, see also Stephen Cheeke, 'Browning, Renaissance Painting, and the Problem of Raphael', *Victorian Poetry*, 49.4 (Winter 2011), 437–61; J. B. Bullen, 'Browning's "Pictor Ignotus" and Nineteenth-Century "Christian" Art', *Nineteenth-Century Contexts*, 26.3 (September 2004), 273–88 (p. 276). I must thank Nora Crook for alerting me to this aspect of Mary Shelley criticism.
51. De Palacio, *Mary Shelley dans son œuvre*, p. 328.
52. See *The Novels and Selected Works of Mary Shelley*, IV: *The Last Man*, ed. by Jane Blumberg with Nora Crook; Anne K. Mellor, 'Introduction', in *The Last Man*, ed. by Hugh J. Luke, Jr (Lincoln: University of Nebraska Press, 1993), pp. vii–xxvi; Morton D. Paley, '*The Last Man*: Apocalypse without Millennium', in *The Other Mary Shelley: Beyond Frankenstein*, ed. by Audrey A. Fisch, Anne K. Mellor, and Esther H. Schor (New York: Oxford University Press, 1993), pp. 107–23; Barbara Johnson, '*The Last Man*', in *The Other Mary Shelley*, ed. by Fisch, Mellor, and Schor, pp. 258–66; Audrey A. Fisch, 'Plaguing Politics: AIDS, Deconstruction, and *The Last Man*', in *The Other Mary Shelley*, ed. by Fisch, Mellor, and Schor, pp. 267–86; Betty T. Bennett, 'Radical Imaginings: Mary Shelley's *The Last Man*', *Wordsworth Circle*, 26.3 (Summer 1995), 147–52; Paul A. Cantor, 'The Apocalypse of Empire: Mary Shelley's *The Last Man*', in *Iconoclastic Departures: Mary Shelley after 'Frankenstein'*, ed. by Syndy M. Conger, Frederick S. Frank, and Gregory O'Dea (Madison, NJ: Associated University Presses, 1997), pp. 193–211. These contributions were preceded by Robert Lance Snyder, 'Apocalypse and Indeterminacy in Mary Shelley's *The Last Man*', *Studies in Romanticism*, 17.4 (Autumn 1978), 435–52, and William Lomax, 'Epic Reversal in Mary Shelley's *The Last Man*: Romantic Irony and the Roots of Science Fiction', in *Contours of the Fantastic: Selected Essays from the Eighth International Conference on the Fantastic in the Arts*, ed. by Michele K. Langford (Westport, CT: Greenwood Press, 1990), pp. 7–17.
53. This list cannot be exhaustive, as *The Last Man* has become the most popular novel with literary critics after *Frankenstein*. See Zachary Tooman, 'Her "Whole Soul Was Ear": Novel Sound, Experimental Music, and Artistic Community in Mary Shelley's *The Last Man*', *Style: A Quarterly Journal of Aesthetics, Poetics, Stylistics, and Literary Criticism*, 51.2 (2017), 167–86; Lauren Cameron, 'Mary Shelley's Malthusian Objections in *The Last Man*', *Nineteenth-Century Literature*, 67.2 (September 2012), 177–203; the special issue on Mary Shelley's *The Last Man*, ed. by Ranita Chatterjee, *European Romantic Review*, 25.1 (February 2014).
54. Lucy Morrison 'Listen While You Read: The Case of Mary Shelley's *The Last Man*', in *Mary Shelley, her Circle and her Contemporaries*, ed. by Adam Meckler and Lucy Morrison (Newcastle: Cambridge Scholars Publishing, 2010), pp. 151–68 (pp. 151–55).
55. For example, de Palacio's support for the attribution of Mary's contribution to the poem 'Orpheus' from line 35, with a joint authorship, is quoted by Pamela Clemit as a viable editorial interpretation when facing 'an insoluble riddle' (*Matilda, Dramas, Reviews and Essays*, p. 439). For de Palacio's discussion of the fragment, see *Mary Shelley dans son œuvre*, pp. 464–72.
56. Chris Baldick, *In Frankenstein's Shadow: Myth, Monstrosity, and Nineteenth-Century Writing*, Clarendon Paperbacks (Oxford: Oxford University Press, 1990 [1987]), p. 4.
57. Werner Wolf, 'Literature and Music: Theory', in *Handbook of Intermediality: Literature, Image, Sound, Music*, ed. by Gabriele Rippl (Berlin: De Gruyter, 2015), pp. 459–73 (p. 460). See also *Afterlives of Romantic Intermediality: The Intersection of Visual, Aural and Verbal Frontiers*, ed. by Leena Eilittä and Catherine Riccio-Berry (Lanham, Maryland: Lexington Books, 2016).
58. *Literary Intermediality: The Transit of Literature through the Media Circuit*, ed. by Maddalena Pennacchia Punzi (Bern: Peter Lang, 2007), p. 10. On intermediality and 'iconotexts' see also *Icons — Texts — Iconotexts: Essays on Ekphrasis and Intermediality*, ed. by Peter Wagner (Berlin: De Gruyter, 1996). See also the discussions by W. J. T Mitchell, *Iconology: Image, Text, Ideology* (Chicago: University of Chicago Press, 1986); Werner Wolf, *The Musicalization of Fiction: A Study in the Theory and History of Intermediality* (Amsterdam: Rodopi, 1999); *Selected Essays on Intermediality by Werner Wolf (1992–2014): Theory and Typology, Literature-Music Relations, Transmedial Narratology, Miscellaneous Transmedial Phenomena*, ed. by Walter Bernhardt (Leiden: Brill, 2018); Irina Rajewsky, *Intermedialität* (Tübingen: Francke, 2002).
59. For the definition, see Roland Barthes, *S/Z*, trans. by Richard Millen (Oxford: Blackwell, 2002 [1990]).

60. Fred Botting, *Making Monstrous: Frankenstein, Criticism, Theory* (Manchester: Manchester University Press, 1991).
61. Matthew Reynolds, *Translation: A Very Short Introduction* (Oxford: Oxford University Press, 2016).
62. For adaptations of *Frankenstein* for the stage and film, the following select bibliography cites some useful studies: Donald Glut, *The Frankenstein Archive: Essays on the Monster, the Myth, the Movies and More* (Jefferson, NC: McFarland, 2002), and his *The Frankenstein Catalog* (Jefferson, NC: McFarland,1984); Shane Denson, *Postnaturalism: Frankenstein, Film and the Anthropotechnical Interface* (Bielefeld: Transcript, 2014); Radu Florescu and Matei Casacu, *Frankenstein* (Paris: Tallandier, 2013); Caroline Joan S. Picart, *Remaking the Frankenstein Myth on Film: Between Laughter and Horror* (Albany: State University of New York Press, 2003); *Actes du colloque 'Frankenstein': Littérature/cinéma*, ed. by Jean-Marie Graitson, with a preface by Gilles Ménégaldo, Les Cahiers de paralittérature (Liège: Éditions du Céfal, 1997); *Frankenstein: Creation and Monstrosity*, ed. by Stephen Bann (London: Reaktion Books, 1994); Steven Earl Forry, *Hideous Progenies: Dramatizations of 'Frankenstein' from the Nineteenth Century to Present* (Philadelphia: University of Pennsylvania Press, 1990), and his '"The Foulest Toadstool": Reviving *Frankenstein* in the Twentieth Century', in *The Fantastic in World Literature and the Arts*, ed. by Donald E. Morse (New York: Greenwood, 1987), pp. 183–209; Albert LaValley, 'The Stage and Film Children of *Frankenstein*', and William Nestrick, 'Coming to Life: *Frankenstein* and the Nature of Film Narrative', in *The Endurance of Frankenstein*, ed. by George Levine and U. C. Knoepflmacher (Berkeley: University of California Press, 1974), pp. 243–89; pp. 290–316. See also 'Responses to and Adaptations of Frankenstein in Film and Elsewhere: A Selective Chronological Bibliography', taken from the NASSR-L discussion list, September 1999, compiled by Melissa J. Sites for *Romantic Circles Scholarly Resources* (1999) <https://www.rc.umd.edu/reference/misc/ficrep/frankenstein.html> [accessed 03 November 2019].
63. For an example of contemporary uses of *Frankenstein* in science see for instance, Jon Turney, *Frankenstein's Footsteps: Science, Genetics and Popular Culture* (Yale: Yale University Press, 1998), and Monette Vacquin, *Frankenstein aujourd'hui: Égarements de la science moderne* (Paris: Belin, 2016). For a recent article on AI, Adam Briggle, 'As Frankenstein Turns 2000, Can We Control our Modern "Monsters"?', *Scientific American* (29 December 2017), online edition, <https://www.scientificamerican.com/article/as-frankenstein-turns-200-can-we-control-our-modern-monsters/?wt.mc=SA_Twitter-Share> [accessed 03 November 2019].
64. See *Histoire de traductions en langue Française, XIX siècle (1815–1914)*, ed. by Yves Chevrel, Lieven d'Hulst, and Christine Lombez (Paris: Verdier, 2012). Marc Fumaroli retraces the earlier history of the French language in Europe in his *Quand l'Europe parlais français* (Paris: Éditions de Fallois, 2001). Christophe Scheidhauer, 'Les Langues de l'Europe: un régime paradoxalement durable', *Langage et société*, 125.3 (2008), 125–43.
65. William St Clair, *The Reading Nation in the Romantic Period* (Cambridge: Cambridge University Press, 2004), pp. 358–73 (p. 365).
66. Ibid. p. 367.
67. Antony Béraud and Jean-Toussaint Merle, *Le Monstre et le magicien: Mélodrame Féerique en trois actes* (Paris: Bezou Libraire, 1826).
68. See Gideon Toury, *Translation Studies and beyond* (Amsterdam: Benjamins, 1995).
69. Forry, *Hideous Progenies*, p. x
70. See for example the volume *Mary versus Mary: Saggi per il bicentenario di Mary Wollstonecraft e Mary Shelley*, ed. by Lilla Maria Crisafulli and Giovanna Silvani (Napoli: Liguori, 2001); Charlotte Gordon's biography, *Romantic Outlaws: The Extraordinary Lives of Mary Wollstonecraft and Mary Shelley* (London: Windmill Books, 2016 [2015]); or the anthology *Mary Wollstonecraft, 'Mary and Maria'; Mary Shelley, 'Mathilda'*, ed. by Janet Todd (London: Penguin, 1991).
71. J. Crary, *Techniques of the Observer: On Vision and Modernity in the Nineteenth Century* (Cambridge, MA: Massachusetts Institute of Technology, 1992), p. 4.
72. For a recent definition of intersemiotics, see Kubilay Aktulum, 'What is Intersemiotics? A Short Definition and some Examples', *International Journal of Social Science and Humanity*, 7.1 (January 2017), 33–36. Roman Jakobson used the term in his *Essais de linguistique générale* (Paris: Minuit, 1963).

73. The conferences are: 'Beyond Frankenstein's Shadow', Université de Lorraine, Nancy (29 April 2016); 'The Shelley Conference 2017', Institute of English Studies, University of London (15 September 2017); 'The Bicentenary Conference on Mary Shelley's *Frankenstein*', University of Venice Cà Foscari (21–22 February 2018), '"With shut eyes, but acute mental vision": Dream and Literary Creation in Women's Writings in the Eighteenth and Nineteenth Centuries', Université Clermont-Auvergne — CELIS, Clermont-Ferrand, (5–6 April 2018); 'Mary Shelley's *Frankenstein*, 1818–2018: Circuits and Circulation', University of Bologna (19–21 September 2018). *Frankensreads* was organized by the Keats-Shelley Association of America and took place worldwide in November 2018. Other conferences took place all over Europe and in the USA. Moreover, other initiatives involved the media, like for example the series of podcasts on Mary Shelley by the French radio channel France Culture: see, for instance: 'Frankenstein: Les 200 ans de premier monstre de la science', *La Méthode scientifique*, Radio France Culture, 02 March 2018, <https://www.franceculture.fr/emissions/la-methode-scientifique/la-methode-scientifique-du-vendredi-02-mars-2018> [accessed 4 November 2019].

PART I

Approaching the
Mary Shelley Canon and Scholarship

CHAPTER 1

Re-Collecting Mary Shelley and Percy Bysshe Shelley

Jean de Palacio

1.1 Re-Collecting Mary Shelley[1]

In 1957, some sixty years ago, it was paradoxical, not to say preposterous, to choose Mary Shelley as the subject of a PhD thesis. Nobody really cared for her in France at that time. Even her *Frankenstein*, which nobody read, although it had been aptly translated by Germain d'Hangest as early as 1922,[2] and the main character whom everybody mistook for the creature, was only known through James Whale's filmic adaptation in 1931, starring Boris Karloff as the monster.

Searching my memory, my first encounter with Mary Shelley dates back to 1952. As an MA student, I had to work on 'Love and Woman in Shelley's Poetry'. I then devoted much space and attention to Percy Bysshe Shelley's poem *Epipsychidion*. I had been struck by Mary's allegorical portrait therein as 'the cold chaste moon' (l. 281),[3] the woman who warms but does not illumine, in contradistinction to Teresa Emilia Viviani's 'eternal sun' (l. 280), which fills the soul out of its 'urn of / Golden fire' (ll. 375–76).[4] Another striking derogatory feature was that of 'the cold chaste bed' (l. 299).[5] All these lines Mary had obviously not forgotten in 1839, when she wrote in her diary: 'There are other verses I should well like to obliterate for ever',[6] and refrained from devoting a note on the poem for Edward Moxon's four-volume edition of Percy Shelley's *Poetical Works*.

Another indirect or 'transverse' reason for my interest in Mary arose from one of Percy Shelley's prefatory sentences to the poem: 'The stanza on the opposite page is almost a literal translation from Dante's famous canzone 'Voi, ch'intendendo, il terzo ciel movete, etc.'[7] I had then begun learning Italian, so as to be able to trace Dante's influence upon Percy Shelley's poetry. Newman Ivey White's major biography of Shelley was always close at hand, and I kept in mind his statement about 'the Dantean, Petrarchan, and Platonic conception of love' as the 'spiritual basis' of the poem.[8] In 1956, I undertook to study Shelley's translation of Dante's canzone. I had at my disposal only Richard Garnett's 1862 version as contained in his *Relics of Shelley*,[9] a version which all subsequent editors of Shelley had blindly reprinted. In a later article,[10] I explained how I toiled for months over the first stanza, the meaning of which I failed to grasp; and how I made up my mind at last to go to the Bodleian Library and consult the manuscript notebook there. I discovered Garnett had 'forgotten' a line (among other misconstructions), which Mary had successfully restored, although she failed to decipher the last two words.

The whole 'literary' family retained my attention. I intended at first to work on the father, William Godwin, but was apprised that the subject was withheld from present use for the benefit of another scholar; in fact, that study hung fire and was never completed. I therefore decided to take Mary as the subject of my work and wrote to a Professor at the Sorbonne for approval of my topic. I remember the exact words of his reply: 'Mary Shelley, moi, je pense qu'on en a tout de suite fait le tour. Mais vous me convaincrez du contraire'[11] ['Mary Shelley, in my opinion, is an author whose work will be covered in a short space of time. But you will convince me that the opposite is the case'].[12] An undisguised lack of enthusiasm! But I was at liberty to pursue my work unhindered.

Percy Shelley criticism in France was then at a low ebb. Mary was considered only as his wife. She deserved to be considered in her own right. But the path was uneasy. No novel of hers except *Frankenstein* had been reprinted at that time. The Bibliothèque Nationale de France held only one: *The Last Man*, in the 1826 Galignani version. It soon proved necessary to acquire the scarce first editions of *Valperga*, *The Last Man* (the 1826 Colburn version), *The Fortunes of Perkin Warbeck*, and *Falkner*. This became my pursuit, with the help of such well-informed booksellers as Maggs Bros., Bernard Quaritch, and Henry Sotheran, not to mention Norman Colbeck in Bournemouth. But I could not lay my hands on a copy of *Lodore*. Photocopying did not exist at that time. I resolved to copy out the nine hundred pages of the novel in the Rare Books Reading Room of the British Museum in the North Library, off the Tottenham Court Road. I could also acquire a copy of *Rambles in Germany and Italy*, a much-neglected book, notwithstanding Robert Browning's strictures,[13] and patiently collected copies of the *Keepsake*, one by one, containing all of Mary's tales. And I bought from Colbeck a pristine copy of the first illustrated edition of *Frankenstein*, number 9 in Bentley's 'Standard Novels' (1831), for 20 shillings,[14] an important book, containing the text of Mary's new preface and the famous plate by Theodore von Holst showing the monster awakening to life.[15] Another task consisted in establishing the catalogue of Mary's library and all the books she read, possibly including Lady Charlotte Bury's and Caroline Norton's novels, and, of course, her father's novels, *Caleb Williams*, *Fleetwood*, *Mandeville* (in which she may have had a hand), *Cloudesley*, and *Deloraine*. Here is a sample:

— Thomas Hope, *Anastasius; or, Memoirs of a Greek* (1820)
— Thomas Alexander Boswell, *Recollections of a Pedestrian* (1826) (In 1957, a copy of the book, bearing Mary's holograph signature, was owned by a London bookseller, Messrs. B. F. Stevens and Brown.)
— Horace Smith, *Brambletye House* (1826) (In 1985, a copy of the book, bearing Mary's holograph signature, with the Boscombe Manor bookplate of her son Percy Florence, was owned by Bernard Quaritch.)
— Catherine Gore, *The Hamiltons; or, The New Era* (1830)
— E. J. Trelawny, *Adventures of a Younger Son* (1830).
— William Johnson Neale, *Cavendish; or, The Patrician at Sea* (1831)
— William Godwin, Jr, *The Orphans of Unwalden* (1835)
— Harriet Martineau, *Deerbrook* (1839)

Manuscripts were quite another matter. They had to be consulted either at the British Museum or at the Bodleian. But those specifically relevant to Mary Shelley were in private hands — those of James Richard Scarlett, eighth Baron Abinger. In 1960, the British Council in Paris helped me to approach Lord Abinger in his manor house, Clees Hall in Bures (Suffolk). I was allowed one day of study in his library, during which time I took down nearly a hundred pages of notes! Seven years later, I was granted another day's study at Bures, when I saw such treasures as a copy of *The Fortunes of Perkin Warbeck* containing autograph notes and corrections by the author, a copy of *Lodore* bearing the date of 1834, an anomaly still unexplained to this day, and a copy of *Rambles in Germany and Italy* inscribed to her son. The first two copies seem to have disappeared since then, perhaps lost during the removal of Lord Abinger's library to London.

Another 'family' element had to be taken into account, namely William Godwin's editorial activity and its possible influence upon Mary's education and thought. Godwin, as is known, had opened a small publishing house called the 'Juvenile Library' in Hanway Street (opposite Soho Square), whence he moved to 41, Skinner Street and, later on, 195, St. Clement's, Strand. He published a large number of schoolbooks under various pseudonyms (Edward Baldwin, Theophilus Marcliffe). The greatest success, *Fables Ancient and Modern* (1805), were said to be 'Adapted for the Use of Children from Three to Eight Years of Age'. They went through ten editions at least, the last one appearing in 1824 with a variant title. Godwin was known to test the pedagogical value of his books on his own children: 'I am accustomed to consult my children in this humble species of writing in which I have engaged.'[16] Mary and her stepsister Claire Clairmont were no doubt among his first readers! Mary presumably became familiar with mythology at an early age through her father's *Pantheon* (1806), the seventh edition of which came out in 1828; and perhaps the first hint for her novel *The Fortunes of Perkin Warbeck* arose from an early reading of her father's *History of England*,[17] which boasted 15,000 copies sold at that time. Godwin even introduced one of his fables into his translation of L. F. Jauffret's *Dramas for Children* (1817), in which Mrs Mildmay, the governess in charge of the children's education, sings the praise of the author: 'What I propose reading to you is one of Baldwin's Fables, a book that is, I know, highly approved of by parents of understanding and discrimination.'[18] I succeeded in gathering ten of these volumes covering about a quarter of a century (1805–28).

All these bibliographical and bibliophilic investigations were necessary steps, allowing, for instance, the perusal at the same time of Mary's novel *The Last Man* and Godwin's treatise *Of Population*, so as better to perceive how far the former was an answer to the latter. Such investigations, however, were made difficult through the scarcity of the books, particularly Godwin's schoolbooks, clumsily handled by children's fingers, and failing to survive.

After fourteen years (1955–69) spent upon this work, the reviews of the book when published showed that the unfair prejudice towards Mary's right to be taken seriously had far from abated. The book incurred judgments both courteous and reserved in France and in England as well. The same doubtfulness was felt in every quarter. In the *Keats-Shelley Journal*, the late Alice Green Fredman wrote: 'Such preliminary protests may call undue attention to the question that must underlie any investigation with such proportions as Palacio's: does its subject warrant it?'[19] After some customary compliments, Peter Butter wrote in the *Yearbook of English Studies*: 'The only doubt is whether the subject deserves such elaborate treatment.'[20] And Professor Jacques Voisine, who acted as chairman at my viva, in *Revue de littérature comparée*:

> Il était hardi de choisir Mary Shelley — écrivain mineur malgré le succès (toujours vif) des adaptations (de moins en moins fidèles) de son *Frankenstein* — pour le sujet d'une grosse et riche thèse de doctorat. J. de Palacio n'a sans doute pas fini de se le voir reprocher; à suivre, comme c'était son propos, un 'itinéraire spirituel' (p. 594), il risquait sans doute, en toute bonne foi, d'attribuer à l'auteur une grandeur qui appartient indubitablement à la femme.[21]

> [Choosing Mary Shelley — a minor writer despite the continuous success of the adaptations (less and less faithful) of *Frankenstein* — as the subject of a rich and hefty doctoral thesis was a bold move. Jean de Palacio will no doubt have been told so; his aim to follow her 'spiritual itinerary' [...] risked claiming for the author the importance that certainly one should acknowledge for the woman.]

'Œuvre intéressant, surtout pour un comparatiste', Béatrice Micha remarked in *Arcadia*, 'mais non de grande qualité' ['Mary Shelley's work is interesting, especially for a scholar in comparative literature, but is not of a great quality.'].[22]

No such reproach is levelled at me nowadays; and my most hearty thanks are tendered to Antonella Braida and the Université de Lorraine for giving evidence of the change. In 2016, she organized in Nancy the first colloquium in France exclusively devoted to Mary Shelley. I also thank Professor Nora Crook for her kind words in *The Cambridge Quarterly* (1990) under a felicitous title:

> In 1969 Jean de Palacio's *Mary Shelley dans son œuvre* (Paris: Éditions Klincksieck) was considered too specialized a study to merit publication in the English-speaking world; hence the most comprehensive account to date of Mary Shelley's sources and intellectual milieu remains untranslated (and unsuperseded).[23]

Indeed, Mary is no longer on the wane. In the course of half a century, I saw her reputation and condition change, passing over from 'écrivain mineur' ['minor writer'] to a 'major writer'. She was thus characterized in a recent volume: 'Major writers such as William Wordsworth, De Quincey and Mary Shelley [...] are treated in this exploratory mapping of the field.'[24] Seeing Mary on a par with Wordsworth and De Quincey was formerly quite unthinkable. In Maria Schoina's work, *Romantic 'Anglo-Italians': Configurations of Identity in Byron, the Shelleys, and the Pisan Circle*, we read: 'Mary Shelley is given a prominent role as retrospective constructor of the Anglo-Italian group.'[25] That was emphasizing the *comparative* character of Mary's thinking, who occasionally affixed 'Anglo-Italicus' to her signed name (in her paper in the *Examiner* on the Italian castrato Velluti). Mary Shelley was bilingual, she spoke, read, and wrote Italian, with a thorough knowledge of Italian literature, as exemplified in her *Lives of the most Eminent Literary and Scientific Men of Italy, Spain, and Portugal* for Dionysius Lardner's *Cabinet Cyclopædia* (1835). Her achievement as a whole is now available in the eight-volume and four-volume editions published by Pickering & Chatto in 1996 and 2002.[26] The late Betty T. Bennett was responsible for an epoch-making edition of Mary's correspondence (3 vols, 1980–88). Readers who cannot afford to buy expensive books may now find cheap scholarly editions of all her novels. One of her most neglected novels so far has just been translated into French.[27] It is now gratifying that Mary Wollstonecraft Shelley increasingly receives unstinted acknowledgments.

1.2 *The Last Man*: An Answer to Malthus?[28]

On 6 February 1962,[29] I was lucky enough to be able to purchase a copy of William Godwin's *Of Population* (1820) at Sotheby's through Maggs's exertions. On 26 January, W. Maishman, the then assistant in the firm, had written to me: 'Although the binding is in poor condition, we do not think this will come through at a reasonable price, as it is a work much sought after. It might fetch in the neighbourhood of £40.'[30] This was a large sum at that time!

After the bidding had proved successful, Maishman wrote again on 6 February: 'Although we wrote to you on January 26th, that we were afraid this would not come through at a reasonable price, we were very surprised to secure it to-day for as low as £22.' It was a poor copy indeed, bound in old half-calf, worn, with backstrip missing. But I was so happy to be able to read it 'in my own chamber', as Godwin himself put it in the preface to his *Life of Geoffrey Chaucer*, when he complained about the necessity 'to yield to an assiduous and almost daily attendance at the British Museum', adding: 'This has been productive of great loss of time and many disadvantages. No studious man can collate authorities and draw his inferences satisfactorily, except in his own chamber.'[31] After I had the book carefully rebacked, a close reading suggested the idea of a study of Mary Shelley's novel *The Last Man* in its possible counter relationship with Thomas Malthus's tenets. I wrote that a few months later.

★ ★ ★ ★ ★

The sixth edition of Malthus's *Essay on Population* came out in 1826, the same year as Mary's novel. Her aversion to Malthus's theories is well-documented.[32] Godwin's answer, *Of Population: An Enquiry Concerning the Power of Increase in the Numbers of Mankind. Being an Answer to Mr. Malthus's Essay on that Subject*, had appeared in 1820. He derided Malthus's 'prophetic conception', which consisted in seeing the United States of America 'some centuries hence, full of human inhabitants, even to overflowing'.[33] In her novel *The Last Man*, Mary seemed to endorse her father's view, according to which any ominous prospect would derive from 'depopulation' rather than 'overpopulation'. Her own prophecy goes the same way: that of a nightmarish world, becoming 'a wilderness, a wide and desolate place', 'a universe of death',[34] emptied of its human population by plague. Plague, used either literally or antiphrastically, is a frequent argument in Godwin's book. With Montesquieu in mind,[35] he describes mankind as 'a race of beings, just escaped from the ravages of a universal plague'.[36] He moreover observes, that the vindication of Malthus's theories (which he calls 'his doctrine of depopulation') would make it necessary to fancy such infantile mortality in China as would fill the country with corpses: 'They must lie on heaps, like what we read of human bodies in the plague of Marseilles.'[37] In the conclusion to his book, Godwin also alludes to the 1348 great plague and quotes Boccaccio.[38]

Both major European epidemics, be they of the fourteenth or the eighteenth century, are present in *Of Population*. Plague even becomes metonymic of Malthus's theories: 'I can liken Mr. Malthus's world to nothing but a city under the severe visitation of a pestilence.'[39] Plague as a motif crops up too often in his book to be considered as a mere haphazard. Godwin had read Boccaccio; he had read some of the many reports and testimonies left of the 1720 plague in France. His idea of a pestiferous city may have been suggested or strengthened by John Wilson's dramatic poem *The City of the Plague* (1816), a copy of which is contained in the holograph catalogue of Godwin's library which he drew up on the following year. Mary was conversant with the same sources and read, of course, her father's work: Godwin wrote to his daughter on 30 January 1821: 'I am at the present moment very anxious about the success of the "Answer to Malthus", into which I put all my strength, and employed about it a labour that I never underwent before.'[40] *The Last Man* to *Of Population* seems to be what *Caleb Williams* was to *Enquiry Concerning Political Justice*.

The argument of the novel in a nutshell is often to be found in the treatise. Thus, Godwin expatiates upon 'the depopulation of the world' and the fact that 'the human species is hastening fast to extinction',[41] somewhat harping upon Benjamin Franklin's hypothesis, according to which 'the human species were *by some tremendous casualty* swept from any part of the globe, except this island'.[42]

In Godwin's treatise and Mary's novel as well, what lies at the core of the question is a keen sense of the eminent dignity of man under adverse circumstances, 'a deep feeling of the worth and estimation of man in the abstract', a wish 'to make much of this precious creature, man',[43] whose exalted value is still enhanced by the frailty and precariousness of the human condition. What is at stake is both beauty[44] and freedom, a vindication of the rights of man. 'The sentiment that teaches us to hold the life of man at a cheap rate, has been the source of all the crimes of statesmen and warriors.'[45] The purport of the sentence seems still true in our time; so was it in the fictitious twenty-first century of Mary's novel. Plague at least did remind us that 'one living beggar had become of more worth than a national peerage of dead lords'.[46] Indeed, she saw eye to eye with her father when she wrote: 'now man had become a creature of price; the life of one of them was of more worth than the so-called treasures of kings.'[47] Percy Shelley would not have disowned such a bold statement.

1.3 Percy Shelley and Decadence

In 1971, more than forty years ago, I contributed a paper to the Festschrift in honour of Professor Louis Bonnerot.[48] My contribution was entitled 'Shelley et D'Annunzio: Motifs rapportés ou influence créatrice?', and it was a comparison between an English Romantic poet and an Italian 'decadent' novelist, taking for its object the latter's novel *Il Piacere* (1889). I contended there were no fortuitous analogies, but deep affinities between them both. The survey may now be extended to the turn of the century in general. How can Percy Shelley befit that critical period? How can a poet, who was born at the very end of the eighteenth century, embody the taste and thought of the twentieth century at its very beginning? And how can Shelley be a sign and symptom of a change in appreciation, throwing, for instance, Byron and Byronism into shade?

As could be expected, the connection between Shelley and Decadence rests almost wholly on *The Cenci*. The play had been translated into French by Tola Dorian in 1883.[49] It is the subject matter of the chapter Gabriel Sarrazin devoted to Shelley in his book *Poètes modernes de l'Angleterre* (1885).[50] A review of Dorian's translation in *Le Zig-Zag* of 18 November 1883, is quite significant in this respect: the Marquis de Sade is silently called forth, and the play as a whole appears as 'une suite de meurtres, de viols et d'incestes' ['a series of murders, rapes and incests'].[51] The same reviewer still insists in 1884, when accounting for Dorian's translation of Percy's *Hellas*: 'On voit que Shelley affuble toujours ses héros de tous les crimes. Il aime à présenter l'homme chargé de forfaits, reproduire ses remords, ses colères, ses épouvantes.' ['One sees that Shelley loves to saddle his heroes with all kinds of crimes. He loves to portray a man full of infamy, to reproduce his remorse, wrath, and terror.'].[52] In 1890, Jules Bois wrote his sonnet 'Baiser rouge' under Shelley's influence, and quotes several lines of the play as a motto to the poem. He chose Count Cenci's words in I. I. 81–83 (in Felix Rabbe's translation):

> I love
> The sight of agony, and the sense of joy,
> When this shall be another's, and that mine.[53]

Ten years later, he will quote the selfsame lines again as an epigraph to his short story 'L'Amante de douleur' (contained in *Le Mystère et la volupté*).[54] Percy Shelley's most baleful passages seem then to attract particular attention. Nonce Casanova, as 'decadent' an author as may be, still borrows from (or ascribes words to?) Shelley for his late novel *La Libertine* (1923): 'Oh! Cette beauté d'abjection, cette beauté d'abîme, ce gouffre adorable et immonde dans lequel, parfois, nos pauvres cœurs naïfs s'écroulent à jamais! ...' ['Oh! This beauty of abjection, this sublime beauty, this adorable and foul abyss in which our poor naïve hearts sometimes collapse for eternity! ...'].[55] Other writers, such as Joséphin Péladan (1888), Alfred Vallette (1891), and Hugues Le Roux (1898) showed marked interest in Shelley's drama.[56]

Shelley is often associated with other writers pertaining to Decadence. Maxime H★★★, the main character in Hugues Rebell's novel *Baisers d'ennemi* (1892), thus sets Baudelaire, Swinburne, and Shelley side by side, and describes them as 'des maîtres de son époque, plus subtils encore dans leur manière de rendre l'effrayante torture de leurs frères' ['masters of his epoch, finer still in their ability to render the appalling torture of their brothers'].[57] Jean Lorrain introduces a poet called Sir Algernon Isburne (an obvious pseudonym for Swinburne) into his short story 'Esthéticité'.[58] Isburne agrees to the proposal of having 'les poètes anglais: Macpherson, Rosetti et Shelley' ['the English poets Macpherson, Rosetti [sic], and Shelley'] translated for the sake of a fashionable marchioness: a scheme or device to carry the conviction that Shelley's verse is consistent with such poetry as is replete with 'de perversités mystiques, d'énervements lents, d'ardeurs inassouvies, de chastes infamies, de corruptions tristes et de caresses étranges' ['mystical perversities, slow irritations, unfulfilled fervours, chaste infamies, sad corruptions, and strange caresses'].[59]

Epipsychidion is often quoted or commented upon (by Pierre Louÿs, André Gide, Louis Gillet, Paul Tenarg). 'Shelley m'attire infiniment' ['I feel immensely attracted to Shelley.'] (André Gide, letter to Pierre Louÿs, 1 October 1889); 'Dès que je suis moi-même, je pense à l' "*Epipsychidion*" de Shelley, et je me récite les vers' ['When I am being myself, I think about Shelley's *Epipsychidion* and recite the lines to myself.'] (Pierre Louÿs, letter to Paul Valéry, 29 May 1890).[60] In Tenarg's *Cahiers d'un faux Don Juan* (1898), Maxime Villeneuve reads *Epipsychidion* and extols Shelley's idealism as opposed to 'volupté morbide' and 'nausée d'amour' ['morbid voluptuousness' and 'nausea of love'].[61] Shelley is frequently mentioned or even made part of the plot in fiction (Félicien Champsaur,[62] Jean Lorrain, Marcel Batilliat). He is Madame de Ceyneste's favourite poet in Batilliat's *La Beauté* (1900), the poet with whom she whiles away the time and beguiles her melancholy.[63] In another short story by Lorrain, 'Ferme d'autruches' (*L'École des vieilles femmes*), Shelley is reckoned among 50-year-old Mrs Burton's readings together with Tennyson and Rossetti.[64] In fact, Shelley may be in turn satanic or divine. The adjective 'divine' is frequently applied to him (Charles Morice, Georges Rodenbach).[65] Poets celebrate him: Charles Rouvin (1892), Robert d'Humières (1902),[66] Albert Reggio (c. 1905), Henri Beslais (1913). He is now the poet 'dont la pensée est toujours triste' ['whose mind is always sad'] and whom 'jamais le bonheur n'assiste' ['never accompanied by joy'] (Reggio); now 'le messie du monde émancipé' ['the messiah of the emancipated world'] (Rouvin); showing '[le]s splendides beffrois de la Cité future' ['the splendid belfries of the future City'] (Beslais).[67] In Beslais' words, the end of the nineteenth century makes amends to Shelley for undue neglect in his lifetime.

Conclusion: 'Hereafter'

The point of union between the Shelleys and Decadence may possibly, and somewhat unexpectedly, be found in the ill-reputed Victorian novelist Marie Corelli. Among the few scholars who cared to investigate Corelli's case, some of them (Jessica Amanda Salmonson, Annette R. Federico)[68] have laid emphasis upon the close relationship between her novels and the so-called 'Gothic' spirit and 'Decadent' style. Such a relationship, however, is not wholly devoid of ambiguousness, since Corelli, although she avails herself of the main decadent archetypes (the occultist and satanic vein, such characters as the fateful woman and the evil monk), occasionally inveighs against the end-of-the-century 'prurient novels' containing 'a judicious mixture of Zola, Huysmans, and Baudelaire'.[69] A third source of Corelli's inspiration would be a fantastic disposition with a scientific undercurrent, often embodied in a sorcerer, magician, or mad scientist. Such indeed is Corelli's art as a novel writer, impersonated in such characters as El-Râmi-Zaranos, 'a sort of magician, — a kind of private conjuror'[70]; Lucio Rîmanez, who is in fact a namesake of Satan; or Feodor Dimitrius, 'a scientist engaged in very important and difficult work'[71], unless he is 'some wealthy "crank" who fancies himself a scientist', somebody, at any rate, having 'something about him more than mere appearance'.[72] When Corelli states that the subject matter of her novel consists in 'tak[ing] risks in the inventions and discoveries of modern science'[73], she is not very far from another novel of another woman writer, as Salmonson noticed:

> She developed the theme of eternal youth in a weird scientific femme fatale adventure, the comparatively scarce *The Young Diana* reworking themes from *Frankenstein* when youth regeneration results in monstrous, soulless immortality.[74]

As the author of *Frankenstein* and another fantastic tale, 'The Mortal Immortal',[75] Mary Shelley was one among 'those', as Corelli puts it elsewhere, 'who were interested in the unseen "possibilities" of the Hereafter',[76] and could rightly be counted as Corelli's forerunner, for she too has intercourse with monsters and even Satan! 'When Cornelius came and offered me a purse of gold if I would remain under his roof, I felt as if Satan himself tempted me.'[77]

★ ★ ★ ★ ★

Corelli also partakes in the interest Percy Shelley aroused at the turn of the century. In a pamphleteering book, anonymously published in 1893, she composed a pungent satirical poem entitled 'English Scribes and Small Reviewers', in imitation of Byron's famous title 'English Bards and Scotch Reviewers'. Shelley takes a prominent place there, curiously associated with Corelli's own name; she calls upon the publisher Richard Bentley to refrain from publishing rubbish:

> Excellent Bentley! stay thy lavish hand,
> Continuous trash were more than we could stand;
> Give us good authors who deserve their name,
> And save thy once distinguished house from shame;
> Give prominence to Genius — publish less,
> Or rivals new thy 'house' will dispossess,
> In spite of folks who think the works of Shelley
> Inferior to romances by Corelli.

Corelli's mock self-praise is pleasantly associated with some encomiastic lines extolling Shelley's poetry on the occasion of the centenary of his birth (1792), meanly celebrated by such unworthy penmen as William Sharp and Edmund Gosse:

> See where at Horsham, Shelley's muse is crown'd!
> Two Parsons and a Justice on the ground!
> What glorious homage doth 'Prometheus' win! —
> [...]

> O Shelley! My companion and my friend
> Brother in golden song, is this the end?
> Is this the guerdon for thy glorious thought,
> Thy dreams of human freedom, lightning-fraught?[78]

Thus were both Shelley and Mary still alive in the nineties through Marie Corelli's exertions.

Notes to Chapter 1

1. Besides memories of things past (what was Mary Shelley scholarship some fifty years ago) (1.1.), the reader will find here some hints about Mary, Thomas Malthus, and *The Last Man* (1.2.), and a few words on the 'fortune' (or ill fortune) of Percy Shelley and the spirit of the time at the turn of the century (1880–1910) (1.3.).
2. Mary Shelley, *Frankenstein, ou, Le Prométhée modern*, trans. and with an introduction by Germain d'Hangest (Paris: La Renaissance du livre, 1922).
3. Percy Bysshe Shelley, *Epipsychidion*, in *Shelley's Poetry and Prose: A Norton Critical Edition*, 2nd edn, ed. by Donald H. Reiman and Neil Fraistat (London: Norton, 2002), p. 381.
4. Ibid.
5. Ibid.
6. *MWS Journals*, II, 561.
7. *Shelley's Poetry and Prose*, ed. by Reiman and Fraistat, p. 273.
8. Newman Ivey White, *Shelley*, 2 vols (New York: Knopf, 1940), II, 255.
9. *Relics of Shelley*, ed. by Richard Garnett (London: Moxon, 1862).
10. De Palacio, 'Shelley and Dante: An Essay in Textual Criticism'.
11. Private conversation between de Palacio and a professor at the Faculté des Lettres et Sciences Humaines at the Sorbonne, in Paris.
12. All translations in this article are by the editor, unless otherwise stated.
13. Robert Browning expressed this view in a letter to Elizabeth Browning, on 11 September 1845. Cited in *Mary Shelley*, Bloom's Classic Critical Views, ed. with and introduction by Harold Bloom (New York: Infobase Publishing, 2008), p. 30.
14. A copy on Abebooks recently sold for €12,000.
15. Holst's plate is the frontispiece of the 1831 edition of Mary Shelley, *Frankenstein; or, The Modern Prometheus [...]* (London: Colburn and Bentley, 1831).
16. Edward Baldwin [William Godwin], *The History of England for the Use of Schools and Young Persons* (London: printed for Baldwin, Cradock and Joy, 1807), p. v.
17. Ibid., pp. 113, 115–16.
18. 'The Dangers of Gossiping', in Louis François Jauffret, *Dramas for Children; or, Gentle Reproofs of their Faults, Imitated from the French of L. F. Jauffret by the Editor of Tabart's Popular Stories* (London: for Godwin, at the Juvenile Library, 1817), p. 19. Although this translation is now generally attributed to M. Jane Godwin, the author felt that William Godwin's contribution can be identified.
19. Alice Green Fredman, review of Jean de Palacio, *Mary Shelley dans son œuvre*, in *Keats-Shelley Journal*, 23 (1974), 129–38 (p. 130).
20. Peter Butter, review of Jean de Palacio, *Mary Shelley dans son œuvre*, in *The Yearbook of English Studies*, 2 (1972), 300 (ibid.).
21. Jacques Voisine, review of Jean de Palacio, *Mary Shelley dans son œuvre*, in *Revue de littérature comparée*, 45 (1971), 284–87 (pp. 284–85).
22. Béatrice Micha, review of Jean de Palacio, *Mary Shelley dans son œuvre*, in *Arcadia*, 8.2 (1973), 228–30 (p. 230).
23. Nora Crook, 'Mary Shelley: A Waxing Moon', *The Cambridge Quarterly*, 19.1 (1 January 1990), 47–52 (p. 47).
24. *Romantic Autobiography in England*, ed. by Eugene Stelzig (Farnham, Surrey: Ashgate, 2009), cover blurb.

25. Schoina, *Romantic 'Anglo-Italians'*, p. 5.
26. *The Novels and Selected Works of Mary Shelley*, 8 vols, and *Mary Shelley's 'Literary Lives' and Other Writings*, 4 vols.
27. Mary Shelley, *Les Aventures de Perkin Warbeck*, trans. and with an introduction by Anne Rouhette-Berton, Collection Littératures du Monde (Paris: Classiques Garnier, 2014).
28. Written forty years ago. See the more recent paper by Lauren Cameron, 'Mary Shelley's Malthusian Objections in *The Last Man*', *Nineteenth-Century Literature*, 67.2 (September 2012), 177–203.
29. The introduction to this section provides the context for de Palacio's interest in William Godwin's essay *On Population*. The editor thanks Jean de Palacio for this addition.
30. Author's private correspondence.
31. William Godwin, *Life of Chaucer, The Early English Poet [...]*, 4 vols (London: printed by Davison, for Phillips, 1804), p. xix.
32. De Palacio, *Mary Shelley dans son œuvre*, pp. 227–31.
33. William Godwin, *Of Population: An Enquiry Concerning the Power of Increase in the Numbers of Mankind, Being an Answer to Mr. Malthus's Essay on that Subject* (London: printed for Longman, Hurst, Rees, Orme & Brown), p. 14.
34. Ibid., pp. 21, 33.
35. *Esprit des Lois*, XIV. 11, in Montesquieu, *Œuvres complètes*, ed. by Roger Caillois, Bibliothèque de la Pléiade, 2 vols (Paris: Gallimard, 1951), II.
36. Godwin, *Of Population*, p. 39.
37. Ibid., p. 51.
38. Ibid., p. 620.
39. Ibid., p. 620.
40. *Shelley and Mary*, ed. by Lady Jane Shelley, 3 vols (London: privately printed, 1882), II, 580 C.
41. Godwin, *Of Population*, p. 100.
42. Ibid., p. 125.
43. Ibid., p. 112, 115.
44. Ibid., p. 114.
45. Ibid., p. 113.
46. Mary Shelley, *The Last Man*, in *The Novels and Selected Works of Mary Shelley*, IV, 229.
47. Ibid., p. 189.
48. Jean de Palacio, 'Shelley et D'Annunzio: Motifs rapportés ou influence créatrice?', in *Le Romantisme anglo-américain: Mélanges offerts à Louis Bonnerot*, Études anglaises, 39 (Paris: Didier, 1971), pp. 180–200. Reprinted in Jean de Palacio, *Figures et formes de la décadence* (Paris: Séguier, 1994), pp. 233–51.
49. Percy Bysshe Shelley, *Les Cenci: Drame de Shelley*, trans. by Tola Dorian (Paris: Lemerre, 1883).
50. Gabriel Sarrazin, *Poètes modernes de l'Angleterre* (Paris: Ollendorff, 1885), pp. 65–127.
51. Aymé Delyon, review of Percy Bysshe Shelley, *Le Cenci*, in *Le Zig-Zag* (18 November 1883).
52. Aymé Delyon, review of Percy Bysshe Shelley, *Hellas*, in *Le Zig-Zag* (23 November 1884).
53. Jules Bois, 'Baiser rouge', *Le Courrier français*, 5 October 1890, p. 8. Percy Bysshe Shelley, *Œuvres poétiques complètes de Shelley*, trans, by Félix Rabbe, 3 vols (Paris: Savine, 1885–87).
54. Jules Bois, *Le Mystère et la volupté* (Paris: Ollendorff, 1901), pp. 109, 117.
55. Nonce Casanova, *La Libertine* (Amiens: Bibliothèque du hérisson, 1923).
56. Joséphin Péladan, *A Cœur perdu* (Paris: Edinger, 1888), p. 260; Alfred Vallette, 'Les Cenci au Théâtre d'Art', *Mercure de France*, 1 March 1891, pp. 181–82; Hugues Le Roux, 'La Cenci', *Le Journal*, 18 September 1898.
57. Hugues Rebell, *Baisers d'ennemi* (Paris: Sauvaitre, 1892), p. 173.
58. Jean Lorrain, 'Esthéticité (Scènes de la vie anglaise)', in *Très Russe* (Paris: Giraud, 1886), p. 319.
59. Ibid, p. 315.
60. André Gide, Pierre Louÿs, and Paul Valéry, *Correspondance à trois voix*, ed. by Peter Fawcett and Pascal Mercier, with a preface by Pascal Mercier (Paris: Gallimard, 2004), p. 104 (André Gide to Pierre Louÿs) and p. 179 (Pierre Louÿs to Paul Valéry).
61. Paul Tenarg, *Cahiers d'un faux Don Juan* (Paris: Antony, 1898), pp. 89–93.

62. Félicien Champsaur, *Paris. Miss América* (Paris: Ollendorff Éditeur, 1885), p. 55.
63. Marcel Batilliat, *La Beauté* (Paris: Mercure de France, 1900).
64. Jean Lorrain, *L'École des vieilles femmes* (Paris: Ollendorff, 1905), p. 247.
65. Charles Morice, *La Littérature de tout à l'heure* (Paris: Libraire académique Perrin et Co., 1889), p. 123; Georges Rodenbach, *L'Art en exil* (Paris: Librairie moderne, 1889), p. 76.
66. Robert d'Humières, 'Les Funérailles de Shelley', in *Du Désir aux destinées* (Paris: Mercure de France, 1902), p. 142.
67. Albert Reggio, *La Sonate des heures* (Paris: Perrin, [n.d.; *c.* 1905]), pp. 277–78; Charles Rouvin, 'Shelley', in *Poésie de l'art et de des lettres* (Montmorency: Imprimerie Gaubert, 1892), p. 136; Henri Beslais, *Le Plectre*, (Paris: Jouve, [1913]), pp. 237–39.
68. Annette R. Federico, *Idol of Suburbia: Marie Corelli and Late-Victorian Literary Culture* (Charlottesville: University of Virginia Press, 2004).
69. Marie Corelli, *The Sorrows of Satan* (London: Methuen, 1895), pp. 61, 305.
70. Marie Corelli, *The Soul of Lilith*, 3 vols (London: Bentley, 1892), I, 19.
71. Marie Corelli, *The Young Diana* (London: Hutchinson, 1918), p. 34.
72. Ibid., pp. 95, 105.
73. Ibid., p. 35.
74. Jessica Amanda Salmonson, 'Marie Corelli and her Occult Tales', *The Victorian Web* (12 August 2012) <http://www.victorianweb.org/authors/corelli/salmonson1.html> [accessed 15 January 2020].
75. Mary Shelley, 'The Mortal Immortal', *The Keepsake for 1834* (1833), pp. 71–87.
76. 'Introductory Note' to Corelli, *The Soul of Lilith*, online edition, *Victorian Women Writers Project* <http://webapp1.dlib.indiana.edu/vwwp/view?docId=VAB7163&chunk.id=d1e431&toc.id=&brand=vwwp;query=#docView> [accessed 27 March 2020].
77. Shelley, 'The Mortal Immortal', p. 72.
78. [Marie Corelli], *The Silver Domino* (London: Lamley, 1893), pp. 342, 347–48.

CHAPTER 2

But How Do We Know that It Is by Mary Shelley?

Nora Crook

One of the important contributions of permanent value made by Professor Jean de Palacio, Mary Shelley's first true bibliographer, results directly from his active participation in canon establishment. His immersion in Mary Shelley's writing during the 1950s and 1960s, his archival work, his bibliophilic activities, his attributive skill, and his sensitivity to the qualities of Mary Shelley's individual style added twenty-two uncollected letters to the tally of her writings, most of them previously unknown and unpublished, the surviving portion of the *Valperga* draft, and a superior version of one of Mary Shelley's best lyrics, 'The Tide of Time Was at my Feet'. He confirmed the previously doubtful attribution of 'A Night Scene', a tender and voluptuous poem published in the Christmas annual *The Keepsake,* now known to have been addressed to Mary Shelley's friend Isabel Baxter Booth, by discovering a sales record of the manuscript. This evidence showed that the manuscript undoubtedly existed in 1885 (and may still exist, though untraced).[1] He identified verse translations that Mary Shelley had made from the Spanish.[2] Two of his attributions, Mary Shelley's reviews of Prosper Mérimée's *1572: Chronique du règne de Charles IX*, and of her father's novel *Cloudesley*, have been accepted and securely canonized. (This list is not exhaustive.)

The effect of his attributive work was to sharpen the portrait of Mary Shelley as a professional writer and commentator on cultural life and politics, engaged in the public sphere, though veiled by anonymity. It identified her as having a personal style and a poetic voice, though Professor de Palacio was too judicious to inflate her lyric gift into the expression of a major poetic talent. It filled out the contours of the figure of Mary Shelley as a European — a traveller and sojourner in Europe, a reader of European literature, and a writer on the literature of Southern Europe and France. While disattribution was not his primary purpose, he was also the first to cast doubt on Elizabeth Nitchie's attribution to Mary Shelley of a review of Thomas Moore's *The Life and Death of Lord Edward Fitzgerald* (in the *Westminster Review*).[3] It is sobering to reflect how few people have actually been involved in this work of attribution (and disattribution) over the last fifty years since, after having contributed so much, de Palacio passed the baton over to others, and of those few how many have sadly died within the last fifteen: Emily Sunstein, Betty Bennett (who never actually made a canonical list of her own, but who was the adviser to many), Arnold Markley, and Charles Robinson. This is not a healthy state of affairs. The fewer scholars involved in attribution, the greater the risk that one of them will end up being both judge and jury. But no single expert is infallible or has access to all relevant facts — or is free from bias.

To sum up the present state of play: there is a solid core of works where Mary Shelley's authorship — or co-authorship, in the case of *History of a Six Weeks' Tour* (1817) — is secure. These works include the six novels, *Mathilda* (1819; pub. 1959), *Rambles* (1844),[4] and, with one exception, a number of published tales and poems signed 'The Author of Frankenstein' or 'Mrs Shelley'. A few of these are gift items in manuscript, discovered or rediscovered during the last thirty years. There are literary biographies written for Dionysius Lardner's *Cabinet Cyclopædia* between 1835 and 1839. These have been identified by her letters and by consulting the archive of the publisher Longman. There are works anonymously published during the 1820s and 1830s in major periodicals such as the *Liberal*, the *London Magazine*, the *Westminster Review*, and Christmas gift-book annuals, notably the *Keepsake*. In every case there is external evidence of her authorship — surviving press copies, letters or diary entries, advertisements, or a publisher's ledger recording payment — as well as internal evidence. For a very few items, the internal evidence of authorship alone is strong enough for a secure attribution (as when, for instance, Mary Shelley repeats material almost verbatim from her other attested work in a publication to which she was a known contributor). Outside these secure items are manuscripts in her autograph, some of which, it has been suggested, may be by, or partly by, Percy Shelley,[5] or be translations rather than original works.[6] Then come anonymous published works where the internal and circumstantial evidence so far uncovered is inconclusive, but which are sometimes included in collections, bibliographies, and list of works by her, sometimes as *dubia*, sometimes as definite attributions. And then there is outright *spuria*, material which is dead but won't lie down.

None of the main canonical lists or bibliographies (Elizabeth Nitchie's, de Palacio's, W. H. Lyles's, Emily Sunstein's, the current Wikipedia 'List of Mary Shelley's Writings')[7] is complete, yet a conflation of them into a grand union list would be seriously inaccurate. At present there is no current bibliography that is reliable and comprehensive. Lyles's 1975 bibliography still has its uses, but is irrevocably out of date. It is still the first port of call for many and is the basis of the Wikipedia 'List'. This is a 'featured article', i.e. rated among the best of Wikipedia, but could be very much better. Since its creation in 2008 it has not radically changed. Its original compiler, the late Adrianna Wadewitz, was an energetic and much valued contributor to Wikipedia, particularly on women writers, but not a Mary Shelley specialist. She supplemented Lyles with items in *MWS Literary Lives*, which came out nearly twenty years ago and is itself in need of updating.

Here are a few examples of the current (June 2020) inadequacies of the 'List', by way of illustration. Two spurious items are entered without warning or qualification: 'Narrative of a Tour Round the Lake of Geneva' (1823) and 'Recollections of the Lake of Geneva' (1829), attributed by Nitchie, and accepted by Lyles. Although the titles are suggestive, and the second is signed 'M. W. S.', their content does not mirror Mary Shelley's itineraries or (in the second case) her opinions. Both were rejected by Sunstein in 1989 for good reasons.[8] On the other hand, some secure items are absent from the Wikipedia 'List', such as 'The Smuggler and his Family' (1834), discovered by Bennett and included in *MWS Tales* (1976).[9] The Wikipedia 'List' records as uncertain the authorship of some of the *Literary Lives* (1835–39) written for Lardner's *Cabinet Cyclopædia*, despite Mary Shelley's letters specifying which were hers and corroboration by Longman's ledgers, as documented in 2002.[10] The Spanish verse translations identified by de Palacio are not included, nor those that Lisa Vargo was able to add to his tally.[11] Mary Shelley's review of J. P. Cobbett's *Tour of Italy* (1831), notable for her perspectives of the Masi affair in Pisa in 1821, of William Cobbett, and of Jews of the Roman Ghetto, is likewise absent.[12]

Does this matter? Certainly. The present situation, with some long-verified items still in the penumbra of needless doubts and some long-disattributed items continuing to be cited as hers, particularly impinges on Mary Shelley's life-writing and journalism, and discourages students and critics from venturing off the beaten track into these lesser-known areas of her work. No one wants to waste time building a case on doubtful attributions. Thanks to the *Frankenstein* phenomenon, Mary Shelley now belongs to the pantheon of authors whose name in itself makes headlines and whose autograph manuscripts, together with association copies of her printed works, command high prices. Anyone may claim to have retrieved a lost work and be fairly sure of publicity. It is a two-edged sword. On the one hand, genuinely new material is more than ever likely to come to light. On the other, the same process is equally likely to raise the ever-growing pile of her *dubia* and *spuria*.

The purpose of the above examples is not to cane the Wikipedia list, currently probably the most consulted list of Mary Shelley's works, but to advocate for its improvement. Wikipedia encourages readers to edit its pages in the idealistic hope and faith that the good will drive out the bad. Indeed, some small improvements have taken place recently. Until mid-2019 the Wikipedia list included the lyric 'Song: When I'm no more, this Harp that Rings', first published in the *Keepsake* and in Lyles. It was identified as Mary Shelley's on the basis of the signature, 'Mrs Godwin', speculatively deemed a pseudonym of hers, and speculation hardened into fact, as speculation tends to do. But as it is included in the 1854 posthumous *Poetical Works* of Catherine Grace Godwin (no relation of Mary Shelley), it can now be jettisoned from the canon. By the time this essay is published, it is possible that the 'List' will have been improved still further. However, tinkering is not enough. A makeover of the site is needed with new categories for doubtful and disattributed items and more accurate annotations and links. In the absence of such a radical move, it is pleasing to find that a recently published (2019) *Dictionary* of Mary Shelley's work[13] is both reliable and up to date. Readers consulting it to discover the canonical status of any particular work will receive accurate information. But the purpose of the *Dictionary* (and that of other literary handbooks and encyclopaedias) is not and cannot be primarily bibliographical. Moreover, such works capture the situation only as it exists at the time of publication.

There is, then, a need for a collaborative forum within which to discuss the pros and cons of Mary Shelley's authorship of any proposed lost or not-so-lost work, and to exchange and update fragmented and dispersed information. Without constituting itself as an authority on the lines of (say) the Rembrandt Research Project, such a forum could draw together many international scholars, including those who may not be primarily Mary Shelley specialists, but who have expertise in, for instance, writers active in the 1820s and 30s, publishing archives, memoirs, and letters. This forum may prove part of a permanent legacy of the conferences at the University of Nancy in 2016. It would publicize new discoveries in an appropriate way. One goal might be a regularly updated *Mary Shelley Index* on the model of *The Curran Index* (http://curranindex.org) though more limited in scope. It would, ideally, engage the help of computer-assisted stylometry, which, as I understand, has not yet arrived at a point where it can reliably prove or disprove authorship, but can indicate probabilities.[14] Members of such a forum could monitor websites of auction houses, antiquarian booksellers, and autograph dealers, and search special collections in libraries to trace MSS, association copies, and previously unnoticed reviews, as Jean de Palacio has done. It would be a practical way of building on his legacy.

Where might such a forum begin? One obvious place might be with examining Mary Shelley's *dubia* afresh, to see whether any items might be released from the limbo to which they have been consigned by fragmented information or its absence, complicated by the tussle between excessive scrupulousness and excessive enthusiasm. Some attributers are dogged goalkeepers, blocking every proposed new attribution. Others are incautious kite-flyers. I have been both in my time, as I will now proceed to illustrate with a few admonitory examples, dredged from the murky but fertile hinterland of *dubia*.

An example of my overcaution concerns 'Modern Italian Romances', which appeared in the *Monthly Chronicle* in 1838.[15] A newspaper advertisement listed Mary Shelley among its contributors, and Emily Sunstein had flagged up this long and significant review essay on the subject of the Risorgimento novel as likely. In 1996, I excluded this work from *The Novels and Selected Works of Mary Shelley* as insecure (1, p. 240). This was a case of 'a little learning' on my part; closer and wider reading showed that Sunstein was right, and the situation was remedied in the *Literary Lives* in 2002.[16] But elsewhere I was insufficiently cautious, as in the case of 'Lacy de Vere' in the *Forget-Me-Not*, earliest and most prestigious of the Christmas annuals. A letter by Mary Shelley thanking Rudolf Ackermann, the *Forget-Me-Not*'s proprietor, for accepting her 'story' for the 1827 number (published in late 1826), suggested 'Lacy de Vere' as a possibility to Bennett and her colleague Alice G. Fredman. It contains themes common in Mary Shelley's other fiction: 'sibling devotion and unmotivated, fatal hatred', as well as 'the last-of-the-line figure'.[17] It is set in the era of the Wars of the Roses, which Mary Shelley was researching for her historical novel *Perkin Warbeck* (1830). But although later privately warned by a now sceptical Bennett, I persuaded myself and Arnold Markley that it should be included in *MWS Literary Lives*. Bennett's chief objection was that the villain is named Lionel, a favourite name with both Shelleys, whose Lionels are otherwise heroic or at least sympathetic. Other warning bells should have rung in my head. Mary Shelley wrote from the point of view of the White Rose faction, the Yorkists; the author of 'Lacy de Vere' from that of the Red Rose faction, the Lancastrians; the phrase 'the relative love which God hath planted in the human heart'[18] sounds untypical of her. While one cannot always say *why* a phrase strikes a wrong note, one should always listen with the inner ear for such alerts. In this case, the orthodox religious register invoked by 'God hath', and the term 'relative love'[19] inserted a wedge of doubt, which kept on pushing until it finally broke through, decisively ruling out her authorship. The breakthrough came upon my discovering an article published in 1999 quoting from a letter by Maria Jane Jewsbury in which she reported receiving £6 from Mr Ackermann for her 'Lucy de Vere', 'Lucy' patently being the transcriber's error for 'Lacy'.[20] Jewsbury, who met and was fascinated by Mary Shelley, was almost her contemporary, and an attested contributor to the *Forget-Me-Not*.[21] This is a good illustration of how easy it is to screen out counterevidence and, with one's eyes focused on thematic congruency, look only at what supports one's case.

But as one door closes, another opens. Which story, then, did Mary Shelley send Ackermann? Almost all the short fiction in the 1827 *Forget-Me-Not* is either signed by known authors or by their pseudonymous personae. There are only two remaining anonymous ones: 'The Red-Nosed Lieutenant' and 'The Attacked Escort: A Spanish Scene'.[22] In 2002 neither seemed characteristic to me nor to Arnold Markley, but with 'Lacy de Vere' now eliminated, they must be reconsidered. 'The Red-Nosed Lieutenant' has proved to be authored by Byron's 'Rowley-Powley', the Revd George Croly.[23] This attribution leaves 'The Attacked Escort' as the only possible contender. However, it needs to be shown that the story has characteristics of Mary Shelley's other writing, that it is *like her*. Otherwise the possibility that she withdrew the story for some unknown reason remains open.

The plot is slightly unusual for Mary Shelley. The narrator (a French officer) describes a violent ambush in a Spanish forest during the Peninsular War (1807–14). Filled with compassion for a proud Spanish nobleman and his son, who die when their chateau is stormed, the narrator renounces soldiering. The tale evinces no obvious peculiarity of her style and contains a few words (admittedly from a specialized vocabulary — 'guerillas', 'voltigeurs')[24] found nowhere in her other writings to date. No other story of hers is set in Spain during the Peninsular War or has a Frenchman as its narrator. (Frankenstein is not French, though he is a French-speaking citizen of Geneva.) There is no love interest and no female character. These unusual features would make it unique in her known works of fiction. There is, however, a dead mother, visible as a marble funereal monument only. The final tableau (the Spanish family, noble in death, marble-like forms laid on marble in their family chapel) is reminiscent of the burial of Idris in St George's Chapel, Windsor, in *The Last Man*. Mary Shelley frequently adopted the persona of a male narrator and was fascinated with Spain. *Perkin Warbeck* is partly set in Spain and contains several battle scenes. Indeed, it is surprising how many battles and skirmishes, including two ambushes in a forest, are to be found in her fiction. It would be worth investigating how typical this was of early nineteenth-century female authors. The anonymity of 'The Attacked Escort' is not, in itself, counterevidence of her authorship. Until 'The Sisters of Albano' and 'Ferdinando Eboli' appeared in the *Keepsake for 1829* (1828), her short fiction was published unsigned. This profile makes 'The Attacked Escort' a very suitable case for closer scrutiny.[25]

Another case demonstrating that attribution by elimination should be attempted with extreme caution concerns the sketch 'Rome in the First and Nineteenth Centuries', a jaunty double dialogue in which two dandies and two reanimated ancient Romans carry on parallel conversations while walking around Rome, each pair unaware of the other's existence. It appeared in the March number of the 1824 *New Monthly Magazine*. It was first suggested tentatively by Robinson, is attributed as 'Mary Shelley, prob.' in the *Wellesley Index*,[26] doubtfully by Sunstein, and, also with a query, on the Romantic Circles website.[27] On 13 December 1823 William Godwin wrote to Henry Colburn, proprietor of the *New Monthly*, to recommend his daughter, Mrs Shelley, as a contributor, Colburn having previously invited him to suggest suitably qualified writers. Colburn's reply is lost, but he evidently welcomed Godwin's initiative, for on 13 January 1824 Godwin, on Mary Shelley's behalf, enclosed an 'article' intended for the next number.[28] As 13 January was probably too late to catch the February number, it is likely to have appeared in the March one. (In any case, none of the three articles in the February number that the *Wellesley Index* editors failed to identify is, on internal evidence, at all plausible.)[29] Although the theme of the reanimated Roman is found in Mary Shelley's work (as in her unfinished tale 'Valerius', commenced probably in 1819), Bennett rejected 'Rome in the First and the Nineteenth Centuries' outright. She considered it decisive against Mary Shelley's authorship that Constantine is classed with Titus, Trajan, and Antoninus as a 'virtuous' Roman emperor by one of the dandies;[30] Mary Shelley thought him a 'hateful wretch'.[31] A scatter of facetiously 'vulgar' phrasing in 'Rome' is unmatched elsewhere in Mary Shelley's work ('thinks I', 'Mistress Rome', 'noddle'). There are at least two other possible authors: Thomas Medwin, who had visited Rome in 1822, and contributed a translation from Calderón in the same number, and Horace Smith, a frequent contributor of facetious articles to the *New Monthly*, who had never been to Rome, but who was perfectly capable of constructing the piece out of his reading, though it lacks his characteristic 'H' signature.

Unlike 'Lacy de Vere', Arnold Markley and I did not include 'Rome' in the *Literary Lives*. But if it was not the article sent by Godwin, which one was? It is possible that the article was rejected, but given that it seems to have been solicited, this seems unlikely. There are only two remaining unattributed possibilities in the March number (and none in the April one). One is a review of James Morier's *The Adventures of Hajji Baba of Ispahan* (1824). Content and style are neither strongly indicative nor totally contraindicative of Mary Shelley's authorship. Like her, the reviewer has read Thomas Hope's *Anastasius* and Alain-René Lesage's *Gil Blas of Santilane*, but all other located reviews of *Hajji Baba* also mention them. In 1832 Mary

Shelley asked Charles Ollier to send her, as a treat, the '[n]ew book by the Author of Hadji Baba' (referring to *Zohrab the Hostage*), which suggests that at some previous date she had read *Hajji Baba* and that Morier's fiction interested her.[32] The other is 'The Crown of Victory: A Tale from La Motte Fouqué', a story about Benvenuto Cellini and a dying painter, translated from Friedrich de la Motte-Fouqué's 'Der Kranz am Ziele' (1823).[33] The translator cannot have been Mary Shelley, who had little German in 1824, nor have I found an early translation of 'Der Kranz am Ziele' into French or Italian from which she might have made a translation into English. It seems safe to assume that the translator could read German. Yet the translation might still have been the product of a member of Mary Shelley's circle. Claire Clairmont, then in Vienna, had translated Goethe's *Dichtung und Wahrheit*, and read La Motte-Fouqué in English. She was later to read Goethe's German translation of Benvenuto Cellini's memoirs.[34] Godwin's finances were, as usual, in a dire condition. Claire might have sent the translation to her stepsister from Vienna in 1823 before moving to Moscow, asking her to find a publisher, and both Godwin and Mary Shelley might have let Colburn suppose that it was by the famous Author of *Frankenstein*. This last possibility, though the most complicated, has some merit, if only because she was to do something comparable eight years later. The short story 'The Pole' (1832), despite being signed 'The Author of Frankenstein' was actually written by Claire Clairmont, being edited (probably lightly) by Mary Shelley.[35] As for 'Rome', the fact that two possible alternatives exist makes it more dubious than it was before.

If attribution by a process of elimination is fallible, so is the use of initials as an authorship indicator. The initials 'M. W. S.', as implied above, cannot be totally trusted; still less can the initials 'M. S.', a signature that Mary Shelley used occasionally to identify her own editorial notes in her editions of Shelley's works between 1840–47, but not before that, and never, as far as is known, to mark her own fiction or journalism. A group of poems translated from the German and Italian, signed M. S. and attributed by Sunstein in 1989, proved to be by the young Margaret Scott, later to achieve fame as Mrs Gatty, the Victorian children's author.[36] In 2018 the author Adam Newell followed up a suggestion of Charles Robinson, made in 1976, that 'The Ghost of the Private Theatricals', a story in the *Keepsake for 1844* (1843) signed 'M. S.', was worth further investigation.[37] Convinced that this was indeed a lost work by Mary Shelley, he reissued it in a (very affordable) limited edition, attributing it to her but stopping short of claiming that he had found conclusive proof of authorship.[38] What impressed him most was the congruency between passages describing mountainous scenery in 'The Ghost' and in the German portion of *Rambles*, which Mary Shelley was working on during this period. He drew attention to their common elements: abrupt, rent, wooded crags produced by convulsions of nature, alternating with spots of soft green turf.

> Opposite the castle rose another tall and precipitous crag, and the chasm between which, though deep, was exceedingly narrow, was clothed with luxuriant wood, carpeted in some parts by the greenest and softest turf, and at others diversified by the huge fragments of dark gray rock, which had either

been scattered there by Nature, or rent from their elevated stations, and plunged into the valley below by some of those convulsions common to mountainous regions.³⁹

He juxtaposed it with the following passage from *Rambles*:

As we proceeded through the narrow ravine, the rocks rose perpendicularly on each hand, and shut us in as with walls, but not walls as in Via Mala, abrupt and bare. The precipices are broken into a thousand fantastic shapes, and formed into rough columns, pillars, and peaks numberless; with huge caverns, mighty portals, and towering archways; the whole clothed with pines, verdant with a luxuriant growth of various shrubs [...]; there are little verdant spots in the midst, too, where the turf was green and velvetty. [...] The scene is inconceivably wild. Earth looks rent, convulsed, shattered — isolated, disjointed mountains, rising abruptly from the plain, their sides clothed by firs, are spread around.⁴⁰

But while the verbal parallels are striking at first sight, the phrases and words that Newell singled out as characteristic, such as 'clothed with luxuriant wood', are staples of topographical writing of the first half of the nineteenth century. The narrator tells readers that the privately performed play within the story is based on Franz Grillparzer's play *Die Ahnfrau* (1817). The allusion is certainly significant, and relates to the figure of the paternal grandmother, whose violent prejudices frame the story and whose implacable hatred (it is hinted) may have somehow unleashed the catastrophe. But Mary Shelley is not known to have read Grillparzer. By late 1839 she had read Thomas Carlyle's *Critical and Miscellaneous Essays*⁴¹ in the first volume of which the plot of *Die Ahnfrau* is (dismissively) recounted, but it is quite unlike the plot of the fictional play. The author of 'The Ghost' was evidently steeped in German ghost stories like those in *Fantasmagoriana* (1812) that inspired *Frankenstein*; like Mary Shelley, the author also has a relish for the world of theatre. But there are many writers of the 1830s and 1840s of whom the same could be said.

Nevertheless, Newell has done a service to Mary Shelley studies by resurrecting the story and placing it before the public. The plot involves, like the 1818 *Frankenstein*, the frustration (by apparently supernatural means) of a very discreetly intimated quasi-incestuous marriage between first cousins brought up in the same household, and on the impersonation of a living person by a ghost, a device also found in M. G. Lewis's *The Monk* (read by Mary Shelley in 1814) and in *Fantasmagoriana*. Mary Shelley had previously contributed to *Heath's Book of Beauty*, which, like this number of *The Keepsake*, had been edited by Lady Blessington. She had visited romantic Gothic Germany and Austria in 1840 and 1842 and had made some progress in learning German. If she wrote this 'German' ghost story, the year 1843 was a plausible one for her to have done so. It was also the year before her son inherited the Shelley baronetcy and thereby ended any incentive for her to write for money. Anonymous publication is less easy to explain, given that Lady Blessington would have regarded the celebrated Mrs Shelley as adding lustre to her production,⁴² but Mary Shelley may have thought the story fell below her own standards (the denouement is predictable although one reviewer called the tale 'so well told that we incline to ask whether it be original or a translation').⁴³ While these considerations still do not, in my opinion, add up to a compelling attribution, there is a prima facie case for further investigation. A record of a payment at the relevant time to Mrs Shelley by the firm of Longman, which published the *Keepsake*, may yet survive, overlooked, in its archive, despite the loss of many records during the London Blitz. Nor has the work yet been the subject of computer-aided stylometric analysis.

Sleuthing for new Mary Shelley work can be highly enjoyable, as Charles Robinson attested,[44] and it continues to yield new finds. A group of previously unknown poems was published by Bennett in 1997, two of which had been found in special collections of public or university libraries. Serendipitous discoveries also continue to be made. The short story 'Maurice' was discovered in 1997 in Italy in a locked box among the papers of the family to whom it had come by descent. Online catalogues of special collections in libraries and public bodies offer tools unavailable to our predecessors and have democratized the science and art of attribution. An archive of letters to the Horace Smith family swam unexpectedly into my ken in 2012.[45] The catalogue description of the last had been on the website of the Essex Records Office since 2006; anyone might, with equal luck, have come upon it. Online digitized images of nineteenth-century texts on such sites as HathiTrust Digital Library, Google Books, and Internet Archive have opened up the possibilities to search journals and periodicals to which Mary Shelley submitted anonymous articles. Another task suitable for a Mary Shelley forum is an investigative search through periodicals of the 1820s, 1830s, and even the early 1840s for material that might have escaped the eyes of earlier scholars.

Foremost among the periodicals worth searching is the *New Monthly* between 1824 and 1831. Cyrus Redding, the editor, named Mary Shelley among the contributors.[46] However, the only certain item found is 'Roger Dodsworth, the Reanimated Englishman', not published until 1863 (*MWS Tales*, pp. 43–50, 377). Three other *New Monthly* articles, companions in limbo, have been attributed to her.[47] Possibly others exist that have never been noticed at all. The next most promising location is the *Westminster Review*, a radical journal to which Mary Shelley contributed between 1826 and 1832. Apart from *Rambles*, it contains her most overtly political non-fiction writing. Three of the seven reviews attributed to her to date are of books on travelling and living in Italy. So are two short anonymous pieces, both from 1831, which have not previously been considered for attribution.

The first is a short (*c.*1000 word) review of William Brockedon's *The Passes of the Alps* and his *Italy: A New Illustrated Road-Book*,[48] that I circulated at the 2016 Nancy conference 'Beyond Frankenstein's Shadow', inviting discussion. It needs, of course, to be read as a whole, but these extracts give some idea of its style and content. The reviewer begins with a general reflection arising out of personal experience (one of Mary Shelley's ways of starting an essay, but hardly exclusive to her), part of which is as follows:

> We have usually found [...] that it requires a thorough acquaintance, and considerable habit, to feel the sublime. The first view of the sea for instance —

> a sheet of dusky water, as little admirable as a Russian steppe or our English downs. The superior sublimity of the waste of waters over the barren plains of earth is at first sight by no means obvious; nor, while standing on the beach, do you dwell on the vast immensity of waters, poured forth from the Atlantic and Pacific, to pause, tremble, and retire from our feet, like a stricken dog. By degrees its wild and gloomy changes, its awful and its placid beauty, its terror and its docility, unfold themselves. And thus it is in most cases.[49]

After giving two other instances of self-unfolding into sublimity (St. Peter's, Rome, and the Bay of Naples), the reviewer exempts 'the first view of the Alps' from this stricture:

> Whether from the heights of Jura we behold Mont Blanc lifting its proud head to the sky, or from the ravine which leads from Pontarlier to Neufchâtel, we discover the vast range of Saint Bernard, we at once acknowledge, with extacy and enthusiasm, the novelty, the magnificence, and the wonder of the sight. [...] There above, that white ridge, darkly flecked with shadows, which has usurped the place of the clouds, and which with more pride than Babel invades the wastes of air, that also is the earth.[50]

The Swiss people, however, are less sublime, because of their isolation:

> there is a stultified manner, awakened only by the love of gain, and a cheerless sloth about their inhabitants, by no means inviting. We knew some young people who, desirous of living in Switzerland, eagerly sought the wildest and most secluded retreat, as being the most romantic and delightful. Looking over maps of the country in which the mountains of eternal snow were distinctly marked, they selected the district where the Alps looked highest and whitest — the lake of Lucerne: its verdurous isles, its giant barriers, its wild vallies, invited them. We are ashamed to say in how short a time the mists, rains, storms, the patois and the slow stupidity of the peasants, destroyed the charm.[51]

Brockedon's *Passes of the Alps* is then recommended to the armchair traveller and prospective visitor to Switzerland: 'We mention the Pass of the Splugen [...] as being the Pass usually selected by English travellers, who, preferring the romantic beauties of the Rhine, to the cultivated desarts of France, enter Italy by the Austrian territory.'[52] The review closes with the prediction that Brockedon's forthcoming book on Italy, when complete, 'will present a perfect guide to the classic land, which so many among us are now happily in the habit of visiting'.[53]

The conference audience immediately noticed similarities between this text and Mary Shelley's *Six Weeks' Tour*, including the route to Switzerland taken via Pontarlier. The anecdote of the naive 'young people' who went to the Lake of Lucerne struck them as highly indicative of Mary Shelley's authorship. However, they were rightly cautious, pointing out that being staggered by the Alps, the scenic descriptions, and first impressions of Rome and Naples, are staples of tourist narratives of the period. The reviewer recommends Brockedon's engraving of the Pass of the Splügen, a route that Mary Shelley took only in July 1840. She was to write in *Rambles* of having 'studied' Brockedon's prints 'with such longing to really see' the actual scenery,[54] but many others must have done the same.

A more detailed vocabulary search, however, finds more correspondences between the review and other writings of Mary Shelley: 'Russian steppe', 'downs', and 'waste of waters' turn up close together in her sprightly sketch, 'A Visit to Brighton' (*London Magazine*, 1826). The downs (the chalk landscape behind Brighton) are pronounced barren, and the sublimity of the sea, on first viewing, is similarly questioned:

> I see only the vast waste of waters [...]. The sea is called immense, sublime, the best created image of space and eternity. I do not perceive the sensible type of these ideas in it. It is bounded narrowly by the horizon, and the uniformity of its surface is no more sublime than a Russian steppe.[55]

The Swiss are called 'stultified' in 'The Swiss Peasant' (1830; published in the *Keepsake for 1831*): 'Perpetual hardship and danger, however, rather brutify than exalt the soul of man; and those of the Swiss who are most deeply planted among the rocky wilds are often stultified and sullen.'[56] The coincident wording across these quoted passages is distinctive, even a little eccentric, unlike the topographical clichés singled out in the case of 'The Ghost of the Private Theatricals'.

The second short, unattributed, anonymous *Westminster* article is a joint review of Josiah Conder's *Italy* and James Johnson's *Change of Air; or, Pursuit of Health: An Autumnal Excursion through France, Switzerland, and Italy, in the Year 1829*.[57] The reviewer refers to J. P. Cobbett's *Tour of Italy* (reviewed by Mary Shelley for the *Westminster Review* in 1831), admires the beauty of Naples and the Bagni di Lucca, and appears to have resided in Tuscany (all these square with Mary Shelley's movements in Italy). The reviewer advises readers to collect 'a few English comforts' which 'are easily to be procured at Leghorn, and transported up the Arno'.[58] The focus on domestic affairs in the review suggests female authorship. To James Johnson's complacent assertion that 'few people who remain a whole year in Italy escape the "germs of disease, which are afterwards to take activity and growth"', the reviewer retorts that she (or he) 'passed six summers and five winters consecutively in Italy and the germ of disease gathered there, still slumbers undeveloped'.[59] This period tallies precisely with Mary Shelley's stay in Italy (from March 1818 to July 1823), and the dry, ironic wit is very much in her style.

The reviewer then bursts into a brief digressive rhapsody on the theme of Niccolò Paganini, who had taken London by storm in the spring and summer of 1831:

> In Paganini we recognize one of the magicians, the 'Ut Magii' of the olden times; and the rapture with which we hang upon his melodious eloquence, is near akin to the worship which would have made a demigod of him in the days of the antique world.[60]

But, the reviewer concedes, Paganini possesses '"a solitary and selfish advantage;" he cannot perpetuate his talent; [...] it cannot be transmitted'.[61] An almost exact match of the quotation appears in William Godwin's *St Leon*, republished in Colburn's Standard Library in the same year (1831).[62] I have found nothing resembling it anywhere else; Mary Shelley frequently quotes inaccurately from memory. She did everything she could to get tickets for a Paganini concert in the summer of 1831. His performance threw her into hysterics (*MWS Letters*, II, 136, 210).

Style, content, tone, vocabulary, the periodical, and the year (1831, one in which

Mary Shelley had no major project in hand) cumulatively make it extremely likely that this article, also, is hers. But many others were similarly enraptured by Paganini, who had acquired the sobriquet 'The Modern Orpheus' by the summer of 1831. The article contains a few loose ends. The reviewer declares: 'It is a curious fact, that the Russians are especially susceptible of the fleeting but poignant inconveniences of an Italian winter; and that the natives themselves feel them less than any of their visitants from the north.'[63] Wherever did Mary Shelley observe Russians in Italy? An answer is not beyond conjecture: possibly the observation came from Claire Clairmont, who was *persona grata* with members of an aristocratic expatriate Russian colony in Florence in 1821. But the necessity for explanatory conjecture here and elsewhere suggests that it would be premature to canonize either of these reviews unless and until they have been scrutinized by many knowledgeable eyes.

If they were to be accepted as canonical, these additions would not place Mary Shelley in a startlingly new light, but, for all their brevity and offhand quality, each would cut, as it were, a new facet for existing light to shine on. They would offer tantalizing glimpses of how she remembered her European adventures during the years 1814 to 1823: a delightful image of the Shelley party looking over maps in order to work out which Swiss mountains were the most remote; the poignancy of the designation of Italy as the land 'which so many among us are now happily in the habit of visiting' — a wistful aspiration for Mary Shelley in 1831. They would underscore what is known about her passionate response to Italian music and to certain performers. They would confirm that she had a special place among the *Westminster*'s contributors, and establish her as the author of every single review of books on the scenery, manners, and culture of contemporary Italy published in the *Westminster Review* during the period 1826–31.

Notes to Chapter 2

1. De Palacio, *Mary Shelley dans son œuvre*, pp. 482–86; hereafter De Palacio.
2. Mary Shelley, *Lives of the Most Eminent Literary and Scientific Men of Spain and Portugal*, in the *Cabinet Cyclopædia of Biography*, ed. by Dionysius Lardner, 3 vols (London: Longman, 1837).
3. De Palacio, p. 684.
4. Mary Shelley, *Rambles in Germany and Italy in 1840, 1842 and 1843*, 2 vols (London: Moxon, 1844).
5. For example, 'Address to the Duchess of Angoulême', included with a query in volume IV (*Life of William Godwin, Poems, Uncollected Prose, Translations, Post-Authored and Attributed Writings*, ed. by A. A. Markley and Pamela Clemit) of *Mary Shelley's 'Literary Lives' and Other Writings*, hereafter *MWS Literary Lives*. Arnold A. Markley was the editor of volume IV items except for 'Life of William Godwin'. Michael Rossington, at the conference 'Beyond Frankenstein's Shadow', argued cogently for her authorship, and I am now persuaded. As for *Frankenstein*, my position squares with that of Charles E. Robinson: that *Frankenstein* is a collaborative work, but falls short of being co-authored. Arguments so far advanced for Percy Shelley's *sole* authorship have been too thin and ill-reasoned to amount to a proper contestation of the existing consensus, but an article explaining why the surviving *Frankenstein* manuscript is authorial work in progress and not, as has been alleged, a work of amanuensis would be worth having.
6. For example 'History of the Jews', in *MWS Literary Lives*, IV. Markley set out the case for its being original (IV, pp. lxxii–lxxvi). Conversely, another fragment, 'Cecil', attributed by de Palacio and accepted by Robinson, Sunstein, and Bennett, was included by Markley and myself as original work in *MWS Literary Lives* IV, but turned out to be a translation from the first two chapters of

a novel by Ida von Hahn-Hahn (Nora Crook, 'Germanizing in Chester Square: Mary Shelley, Cecil, and Ida von Hahn-Hahn', *TLS*, 6 June 2003, p. 14). The error was not obvious from the content of the translation. Mary Shelley had evidently chosen to translate that novel precisely because the early chapters, at least, mirrored her interests and views. The correction was made as a result of my chance discovery, early in 2003, that Hahn-Hahn had written an untranslated novel called *Cecil* (1844), and my awareness, through *MWS Letters*, that Mary Shelley had been impressed by Hahn-Hahn's *Gräfin Faustine* and had met the author in the 1840s.

7. Elizabeth Nitchie, *Mary Shelley, Author of Frankenstein* (New Brunswick, NJ: Rutgers University Press, 1953), pp. 205–10; de Palacio, pp. 643–78; *Mary Shelley: An Annotated Bibliography*, comp. by W. H. Lyles (New York: Garland, 1975), pp. 3–44; Emily W. Sunstein, *Mary Shelley: Romance and Reality* (Baltimore, MD: Johns Hopkins University Press, 1991 [1989]), hereafter Sunstein (pp. 409–19); 'List of Works by Mary Shelley', *Wikipedia* <https://en.wikipedia.org/wiki/List_of_works_by_Mary_Shelley> [accessed 24 May 2020]. To these may be added the list of *dubia* and *spuria* in *The Novels and Selected Works of Mary Shelley*, I, 234–340.
8. Sunstein, pp. 412, 440, 446.
9. Charles E. Robinson, *Mary Shelley: Collected Tales and Stories* (Baltimore, MD: Johns Hopkins University Press, 1976), hereafter *MWS Tales*.
10. *MWS Literary Lives*, I: *Italian Lives*, ed. by Tilar J. Mazzeo, pp. xxiii–xxiv, xxxvii, xl. The Wikipedia 'List' is at odds in this respect with the more accurate Wikipedia page on *Lives of the Most Eminent Literary and Scientific Men* <https://en.wikipedia.org/wiki/Lives_of_the_Most_Eminent_Literary_and_Scientific_Men> [accessed 24 May 2020]. This page also appears to be basically the work of Wadewitz.
11. De Palacio, pp. 522–59; further verified and augmented by Vargo, editor of the Lardner *Spanish and Portuguese Lives* (*MWS Literary Lives*, II, p. xxvii and n.).
12. As the one who made the attribution, I declare an interest; see Nora Crook, 'Counting the Carbonari: A Newly Attributed Mary Shelley Article', *Keats-Shelley Review*, 23 (2009), 39–50. It was accepted by the late Eileen Curran for the *Curran Index to Victorian Periodicals* <http://victorianresearch.org/curranindex.html> [accessed 24 May 2020].
13. Martin Garrett, *The Palgrave Literary Dictionary of Mary Wollstonecraft Shelley*, Palgrave Literary Dictionaries (London: Palgrave Macmillan, 2019).
14. So far, computer-assisted attribution has been applied, in Mary Shelley's work, to *Frankenstein* only, but Pamela Clemit has used it to attribute two articles by Godwin; see Pamela Clemit and David Wools, 'Two New Pamphlets by William Godwin: A Case of Computer-Assisted Authorship Attribution', *Studies in Bibliography*, 54 (2001), 265–84; the attribution is accepted by the *ODNB*.
15. [Mary Shelley], 'Modern Italian Romances, I', *Monthly Chronicle*, 2 (November 1838), 415–28, and 'Modern Italian Romances, II', *Monthly Chronicle*, 2 (December 1838), 547–57.
16. Nora Crook, 'Sleuthing towards a Mary Shelley Canon', *Women's Writing*, 6 (1999), 417–24; *MWS Literary Lives*, IV, p. lvii.
17. *MWS Letters*, I, 526–27.
18. [Maria Jane Jewsbury], 'Lacy de Vere', in *Forget-Me-Not for 1827* (1826), 275–94 (p. 279).
19. Mary Shelley's religious beliefs, insofar as they can be deduced, have affinities with Unitarianism. They were never orthodox, whereas 'relative love' is a doctrinal term, encountered chiefly in eighteenth- and nineteenth-century sermonizing. It is an antithesis of divine love. God permits a proportion of human love to be diverted from absolute and total love of himself towards family, country, and other created entities, though on a subordinate, unequal basis. Mary Shelley shows no interest in the issue and never uses the term. On her Romantic deism, see Maurice Hindle, *Mary Shelley: Frankenstein*, Penguin Critical Studies (Harmondsworth: Penguin, 1994), pp. 173–76.
20. Harriet Devine Jump, '"My Dearest Geraldine": Maria Jane Jewsbury's Letters', *Bulletin of the John Rylands Library*, 81.1 (1999), 63–74 (p. 66).
21. Sunstein, p. 305.
22. 'The Attacked Escort: A Spanish Scene', *Forget-Me-Not for 1827*, 333–43.
23. It was collected by Croly as 'The Captain's Tale' in his *Tales of the Great St Bernard*, 3 vols (London: Colburn, 1828), II, 315–21.

24. 'The Attacked Escort', *Forget-Me-Not for* 1827, pp. 333, 337.
25. For a more extended account of 'The Attacked Escort', see Nora Crook, 'Mary Shelley: Geology, Statuary, and "The Attacked Escort"', *The Wordsworth Circle*, 50.3 (Summer 2019), 348–69 (pp. 363–67).
26. *MWS Tales*, p. xviii; *Wellesley Index of Victorian Periodicals, 1824–1900*, ed. by Walter E. Houghton and Esther Rhoades Houghton, 5 vols (Toronto: University of Toronto Press, 1966–89), III, 187. Full text in *New Monthly Magazine*, 10 (March 1824), 217–22.
27. 'Rome in the First and Nineteenth Centuries', *Romantic Circles* <http://www.rc.umd.edu/editions/mws/lastman/rome.htm> [accessed 27 February 2020].
28. London, National Art Library, Victoria and Albert Museum, MS, MSL/1876/Forster/228. I am grateful to Pamela Clemit, editor of Godwin's letters (in progress), for supplying me with copies of the texts of these two items.
29. These are 'Sneezing', 'On Keeping in Costume', and 'On Corpulence'.
30. Private email communication from Betty Bennett, 2 July 2001. For 'Valerius', see *MWS Tales*, pp. 332–46. For a detailed description of the notebook containing Mary Shelley's 'Valerius' fragment, see Rossington, 'Mary Shelley's Short Stories Notebook', pp. 113–17.
31. *MWS Journals*, I, 239.
32. *MWS Letters*, II, 174–75. *Blackwood's Magazine* reported *Hajji Baba* as forthcoming in December 1823, and a review by one of *Blackwood*'s regulars appeared in its January 1824 number. There was time for Mary Shelley to have read the book and submitted an *uncommissioned* review to the *New Monthly Magazine* by 13 January. That the article submitted by her to the *New Monthly* was done in some haste is indicated by a curious detail in Godwin's submission letter: Mrs Shelley would supply two missing words at proof stage.
33. *Wellesley Index*, III, 187. The *Index* does not identify the original German title or the translator.
34. Claire Clairmont read other works by La Motte-Fouqué and his wife in English and German, see *Journals of Claire Clairmont*, ed. by Marion K. Stocking and David M. Stocking (Cambridge, MA: Harvard University Press, 1969), pp. 202, 278–83, 309–10, 353–54.
35. Rosalie Glynn Grylls, *Claire Clairmont, Mother of Byron's Allegra* (London: Murray, 1939), pp. 190, 202, 241.
36. Christabel Maxwell, *Mrs Gatty and Mrs Ewing* (London: Constable, 1949), p. 32.
37. See *MWS Tales*, p. xviii. Full text of 'The Ghost of the Private Theatricals' in *Keepsake for 1844* (1843), 9–34.
38. *The Ghost of the Private Theatricals: A True Story. By M. S. Now Attributed to Mrs Shelley with [...] an Afterword by Adam Newell* (Penrith: printed for Newell and Newell, 2018).
39. 'The Ghost of the Private Theatricals', p. 16.
40. *Rambles*, I, 262, 263, 273–74.
41. Thomas Carlyle, *Critical and Miscellaneous Essays [...]* (Boston: Munroe, 1839); for documentation of her reading this work, see Nora Crook, 'That Crabbed German', in *Romantic Dialectics: Culture, Gender, Theater: Essays in Honor of Lilla Maria Crisafulli*, ed. by Serena Baiesi and Stuart Curran (Bern: Lang, 2018), pp. 81–97 (p. 88).
42. I owe this suggestion to Miranda Seymour (private communication).
43. 'The Annuals for 1844', *The Athenæum*, 838 (1 November 1843), 1026.
44. *MWS Tales*, pp. xviii–xix.
45. Nora Crook, 'Fourteen New Letters by Mary Shelley', *Keats-Shelley Journal*, 62 (2013), 37–61.
46. Cyrus Redding, *Fifty Years Recollections, Literary and Personal*, 3 vols (London: Skeet, 1858), II, 331.
47. 'Byron and Shelley on the Character of Hamlet'; 'Living Literary Characters' (I and IV), all in Sunstein (p. 414), with a query.
48. Full text in *Westminster Review*, 15 (July 1831), 177–80.
49. Ibid., p. 177.
50. Ibid., p. 178.
51. Ibid., p. 178.
52. Ibid., p. 179.
53. Ibid., p. 180.
54. *Rambles*, I, 56–57, 134.

55. *The Novels and Selected Works of Mary Shelley*, II, 167, 170.
56. *MWS Tales*, p. 138.
57. Review of Josiah Conder's *Italy* and James Johnson's *Change of Air; or, Pursuit of Health: An Autumnal Excursion through France, Switzerland, and Italy, in the Year 1829*, in *Westminster Review*, 15 (October 1831), 335–38.
58. Ibid., p. 338
59. Ibid., p. 336.
60. Ibid., p. 337.
61. Ibid., p. 337. Compare Mary Shelley's use of the Horatian tag in 'Shakspeare [...] was still "Ut magus" the wizard to rule our hearts and govern our imaginations' (*The Last Man*, in *The Novels and Selected Works of Mary Shelley*, IV, 219).
62. William Godwin, *Travels of St Leon* (London: Colburn, 1831): 'you present me with a projector and a chemist, a cold-blooded mortal, raking in the ashes of a crucible for a selfish and solitary advantage' (p. 210).
63. Review of Josiah Conder's *Italy* and James Johnson's *Change of Air; or, Pursuit of Health*, p. 338.

CHAPTER 3

Mary Shelley as Editor, Translator, and European: A Tribute to the Scholarship of Jean de Palacio[1]

Michael Rossington

It is an honour to be asked to offer an appreciation of Jean de Palacio's scholarship. Now, more than ever, it seems urgent to follow his example of promoting dialogue about Mary Shelley's works amongst scholars in Europe and beyond. My welcome task is to consider his pioneering research into Mary Shelley as editor of her husband's writings. I also address, selectively, his commentary on her learning of languages and her translations, his comparative critical approach to her oeuvre, and his appreciation of her lifelong regard for continental Europe, especially Italy.

3.1

Before discussing the originality of de Palacio's research into Mary Shelley's editing, I shall suggest some contexts for understanding the history of Percy Shelley's texts, while conscious that two other contributors to this volume, de Palacio himself and Nora Crook, are authorities in this regard, having played leading roles in the publication of satisfactory texts of Percy Shelley's writings in our time.[2] Editing Percy Shelley's works has been a fraught exercise for the past two centuries. I have discussed elsewhere the reasons that led until recently to an unreliable canon of his writings and one that has been alarmingly unstable in textual terms.[3] The cause of such a state of affairs is that for nearly a century after Mary Shelley's death in 1851 the public appetite for her husband's works exceeded the possibility of a rational way of presenting them satisfactorily.

Two contexts seem pertinent to emphasize when situating de Palacio's Mary Shelley scholarship. Firstly, he may be seen as part of a continental European tradition of editing Percy Shelley (in some cases translating him, too) that goes back to the nineteenth century especially in Italy and France (in the latter regard, one thinks of André Koszul's scholarly editing of both Shelleys in the early twentieth century).[4] That de Palacio himself was aware of this tradition, still insufficiently acknowledged in Britain and North America, is evident in the consideration he gives to Italian editions and translations of Shelley between 1858 and 1926 in his article on Percy Shelley as self-translator.[5] Secondly, de Palacio's earliest publications on Shelley, in which his characteristic emphasis on the primacy of accurate manuscript readings and evidence-based arguments about the dating of manuscripts are to the fore, emerge out of a significant epoch in the development of an understanding of Shelley's text.[6] Between the publication of book-length studies by Neville Rogers in 1956 and Donald Reiman in 1965 that focused on parts of Percy Shelley's manuscript corpus then only relatively recently in the public domain, scrutiny of Mary Shelley's key role in the printed texts of Percy Shelley's posthumous poems was treated by Charles H. Taylor in his still invaluable book of 1958.[7] Since the first of de Palacio's Shelleyan publications appeared in 1961, it is worth considering why the early 1950s, when his graduate research on Mary Shelley began, marked the beginning of a fertile period of endeavour regarding Percy Shelley's text.[8]

In an article published in 1946, Edmund Blunden, the biographer of Shelley, announced the gift of the second part of the Shelley family collection of manuscripts and relics to the Bodleian Library by the poet's great-nephew, noting that '[t]he possibilities which SIR JOHN SHELLEY-ROLLS has opened to Shelleyans are indeed striking'.[9] Further accessions were added by bequest after the death of Shelley-Rolls's wife in 1961 such that just over fifteen years after the end of World War II a large tranche of manuscripts, additional to those given to the Bodleian by Jane, Lady Shelley, in 1893, became available for study.[10] It is the 1946 'MS. Shelley adds.' material that fuelled the original work of Rogers and Reiman as well as articles by Geoffrey Matthews in the early 1960s which provided new texts of major poems including 'The Triumph of Life' and 'Lines Written in the Bay of Lerici'.[11] De Palacio may thus be seen as a key member of an international group of scholars who at this time were dedicated to research into these newly accessible manuscripts of Percy Shelley's poems. He stands out not only because he is (to my knowledge) the only academic based in continental Europe who published on the recent Bodleian accessions, but also because his interest in the light they cast on Mary Shelley as an editor is virtually unique. His emphasis on manuscript sources complement Taylor's account of the history of the printed text of Percy Shelley's poems between Mary Shelley's editions of 1824 and 1839. I say 'virtually' because the pioneering work of Irving Massey must also be acknowledged: his research into Mary Shelley's two copybooks of Percy Shelley's poetical works (Bodleian MS. Shelley adds. d. 7 and Bodleian MS. Shelley adds. d. 9) in the 1960s culminated in editions of each.[12]

The obstacles to de Palacio's access to primary resources in the course of his Mary Shelley research provide a further perspective on the working conditions of his generation.[13] Today, when facsimiles and diplomatic transcriptions are available in print in Donald Reiman's 'Bodleian Shelley Manuscripts' and 'Manuscripts of the Younger Romantics: Percy Bysshe Shelley' series, and online through 'The Shelley-Godwin Archive' (http://shelleygodwinarchive.org/), curated and edited by Neil Fraistat, Elizabeth Denlinger, and Raffaele Viglianti, it is sobering to learn of the challenges faced by those, including de Palacio, who worked on the manuscripts and lifetime editions of the Shelleys' writings prior to the mid-1980s.

3.2

De Palacio's 'Shelley and Dante: An Essay in Textual Criticism' culminates in the first scholarly edition of Mary Shelley's transcription of Percy Shelley's translation of the opening canzone of Dante's *Convivio*.[14] His approach to establishing a text is characteristically to the point: 'we limit our purpose to textual criticism, with a view to giving a correct text of what Shelley actually wrote.'[15] Comparing Percy Shelley's original manuscript with Mary Shelley's transcription which she prepared in later life, possibly, as de Palacio points out, for the first collected edition of 1839 (although it did not appear there), and the first publication of a text based on Percy Shelley's manuscript (by Richard Garnett in 1862), de Palacio notes that 'her version is much truer to Shelley's own words than Garnett's is, showing that her achievement as an amanuensis is most reliable as usual'.[16] In 1951, Neville Rogers had noted that in the Shelley-Rolls gift to the Bodleian '[s]ometimes Mary appears; there are transcripts in her hand of Shelley's poems'.[17] A decade later, this, the first of de Palacio's Shelleyan articles, salutes Mary Shelley's skills as editor by demonstrating the many flawed readings in the *textus receptus*. De Palacio thereby enhances our understanding of how writing by Percy Shelley unpublished until after the death of Mary Shelley was frequently mediated in inferior texts and, along the way, implicitly acknowledges her proficiency in Italian, a subject to which I shall return.[18]

In reviewing de Palacio's assessment of Mary Shelley as editor, the insights of Chapter 8 of his book *Mary Shelley dans son œuvre*, 'Le travail d'édition', demand particular attention. Since the last decade of the twentieth century, appraisals of Mary Shelley's editorial achievement have largely concurred with Michael O'Neill's sensitive and informed judgement that her 'labors represent a heroic attempt to undertake a virtually impossible task to the best of her abilities'.[19] But de Palacio was right to claim in *Mary Shelley dans son œuvre* that her editing had hitherto been given little, if any, serious consideration:

> on ne s'est presque jamais attaché à scruter cette tâche dans le détail, à tenter d'analyser la méthode suivie, à jeter les fondements d'une étude critique des principes d'édition qui furent ceux de Mary et la guidèrent dans l'établissement du texte, la classification, le choix des leçons, la prise en considération des variantes.[20]
>
> [almost never has anyone applied themselves to examine this task in detail, to attempt to analyse the method followed, to lay the foundations for a critical study of the principles of Mary's edition and how they guided her in the establishment of the text, the arrangement, the choice of readings, the taking into account of variants.]

'Le travail d'édition' is exemplary in its assessment of Mary Shelley's editorial corpus. On the one hand, de Palacio shows due respect for her labours, understanding her desire to promote her husband's reputation and sympathizing with the difficult circumstances in which she had to work. On the other, he does not gloss over the serious problems with some of her texts that are obvious to later editors who have considered them alongside the evidence of the holograph manuscripts. In short, his approach allows for even-handed, sensibly nuanced judgements to be arrived at without defensiveness or the overlooking of Mary Shelley's deficiencies. In the chapter's opening section, he comments: 'On se limitera [...] à l'intérieur des poèmes posthumes, à certains cas qui nous ont semblé particulièrement caractéristiques, et font à des degrés divers ressortir les traits principaux et aussi les carences de Mary Shelley dans sa tâche d'édition' ['We limit ourselves to the inner workings of the posthumous poems, to certain cases which seem to be particularly characteristic, and bring out in varying degrees the principal traits and also the defects of Mary Shelley in her task of editing.'].[21] His focus is upon her treatment of three poems: 'Summer and Winter', first published in *The Keepsake for 1829*, an annual edited by Frederic Mansel Reynolds, and 'Fiordispina' and 'The Boat on the Serchio', which both appeared first in her *Posthumous Poems of Percy Bysshe Shelley* (1824). As de Palacio puts it, these printings 'ne sont pas à proprement parler représentatifs de la méthode suivie par Mary, mais formeraient plutôt des cas extrêmes, des exemples originaux' ['are not, strictly speaking, representative of the method followed by Mary, but rather form extreme cases, eccentric examples'].[22] Certainly her 'Summer and Winter' is a clear example of faking it. Without any authority, she combines together two unconnected manuscript verse fragments of Percy Shelley for publication, adding a line 'de son cru' ['of her own invention'].[23] De Palacio summarizes her edition of this poem thus: 'Le bilan, on le voit, semble ici particulièrement lourd pour Mary Shelley, et son intervention désastreuse. Mais il s'agit d'un cas limite, extrême sinon exceptionnel, assez aisément explicable par les circonstances de la publication' ['The toll, one can see, seems here particularly heavy for Mary Shelley, and her intervention disastrous. But this is a matter of a limited case, extreme if not exceptional, fairly easily explained by the circumstances of publication.'].[24] Notwithstanding such problems, his judgement of her overall achievement is fair and measured: 'Mary Shelley, répétons-le, a fait œuvre louable dans son ensemble, et le texte procuré par elle, bien que non exempt d'erreurs, est à tout prendre fort honorable' ['Mary Shelley, we repeat, produced altogether commendable work, and the text she established, although not exempt from errors, is on the whole creditable'].[25]

Finally, de Palacio's treatment of 'Orpheus' (in Chapter 9, 'La poésie dramatique', of *Mary Shelley dans son œuvre*) must be mentioned in this brief account of his assessment of Mary Shelley as editor of Percy Shelley.[26] This blank verse fragment is a special, difficult case in the Shelleyan canon. While the sole manuscript witness is some pages of fair copy in Mary Shelley's hand in Bodleian MS. Shelley adds. e. 17 and what appears to be some rough draft of it on the remaining stubs of pages torn out of this notebook, its authorship is not easy to attribute with certainty to either her or Percy Shelley.[27] Garnett first published a text in 1862, conjecturing that it was, on Percy Shelley's part, 'an attempt at *improvisation*' and adding '[i]t *may* be a translation from the Italian'.[28] But, according to Koszul's introduction to his edition of Mary Shelley's dramas *Proserpine* and *Midas* (1922), he later changed his mind: 'Dr. Garnett in 1905 inclined to the view that *Orpheus* was the work not of Shelley, but of his wife.'[29] Further to Koszul's publication, a new explanation was given in *The Times Literary Supplement* by an unidentified correspondent ('J. E. R.') — that, '[p]erhaps the most we can say, and this could account for her exclusion of it from the "Posthumous Poems" of 1824, is that the respective shares of herself and her husband are inextricably mingled.'[30] De Palacio published his consideration of the evidence after reviewing Glenn O'Malley's *Shelley and Synesthesia* (1964). In this book O'Malley asserted unhesitatingly that 'Orpheus' was 'so characteristically Shelleyan [i. e. Percy Shelleyan] as to make question of its true authorship appear idle'.[31] In his review, 'The Shelley Studies' (1966), de Palacio rebuked O'Malley's failure to give due weight to the manuscript evidence that Mary Shelley's involvement in the poem may have been more than that of a transcriber of the words of her husband:

> The authorship of the poem, as is known, is still uncertain, and its ascription to Mary Shelley more than a probability. Anyway, it may seem both impertinent and rash to dismiss previous conjectures in this respect as having 'little or no plausibility'.[32]

De Palacio's detailed assessment of the evidence regarding 'Orpheus' in *Mary Shelley dans son œuvre* constitutes a unique and original contribution to our understanding of the poem, as has been acknowledged in two recent editions of it.[33] Here he reworks and refines J. E. R.'s hypothesis, suggesting how authorship may have been broadly divided:

> L'absence de tout manuscrit corrigé des vers 1–34 peut enfin suggérer une dernière conclusion, celle d'une collaboration possible entre Shelley et sa femme. Celui-là apporta-t-il son aide à Mary pour tout ou partie du poème, notamment le début, Mary ayant plus spécialement fait porter son effort sur les vers 35–124? On ne saurait l'affirmer, mais l'idée d'un travail 'en commun' ne peut malgré tout être totalement éliminée.[34]

> [The absence of a fair copy of lines 1–34 may in fact suggest one last conclusion, that of a possible collaboration between Shelley and his wife. Did he supply help to Mary for the whole or part of the poem, notably the start, Mary having more especially contributed her efforts to lines 35–124? It cannot be confirmed, but the idea of a work 'in collaboration' nevertheless cannot be completely ruled out.]

Such a notion, advanced with due circumspection but nevertheless grounded in knowledge of the manuscript sources, was entirely original in its day. Moreover, in retrospect, de Palacio's tentative theory about 'Orpheus' now appears to be a relatively early example of an area of inquiry — the extent of co-creation in the writings of Mary Shelley and Percy Shelley — that is now receiving due attention in Shelley studies.[35]

3.3

In concert with his skill in scholarly editing is de Palacio's expertise in the study of translation. Moreover, his evaluation of Mary Shelley as a translator sheds light on her editorial practice. Necessarily overlooking his assessments of Byron and Percy Shelley as translators,[36] I here touch on his careful treatment of Mary Shelley's 1817 translation from Books IV and V of Apuleius's *Metamorphoses* (later known as *The Golden Ass*) in a manuscript notebook acquired by the Library of

Congress in 1941 (MSS. 13, 290). As de Palacio observes in his 1964 article on this translation, its existence had then only quite recently been made known to the scholarly community[37] (and it did not receive full editorial treatment — in which the findings of de Palacio's article are acknowledged — until 2002).[38]

In addressing the question of why Mary Shelley omits to translate certain passages from Apuleius, de Palacio adopts a comparative method, in one instance setting her translation of a passage alongside that of Walter Pater in *Marius the Epicurean* (1885) to show his to be 'definitely more poetic and felicitous'.[39] He also contrasts Mary Shelley's outright omission of the complaint of one of Psyche's sisters that her elderly husband 'rarissimo Venerem meam recolentem sustineo' ['hardly ever pays homage to my Venus'] with William Adlington's diplomatic rendering, 'paying the debt of love', in his 1566 translation.[40] However, while de Palacio's analysis of her translation (or non-translation) alongside the original Latin is rewarding and his juxtaposition of it alongside those of others illuminating, his ultimate goal is to answer a more fundamental question, namely: how are occasional reticences of Mary Shelley's Apuleius translation to be viewed in light of her wider practice as a writer?

> [T]his 'minimising of naturalism' to which she too was brought as later on Pater, aimed at nothing less than restoring to the tale its ideal poetic quality. Mary's constant effort throughout her literary achievement was directed towards giving 'ideality to that, from which, taken in naked truth, the soul would have revolted'.[41]

In this article, de Palacio shows not only the lasting importance to Mary Shelley of *Metamorphoses* (long acknowledged as a significant work for Byron, Percy Shelley, and John Keats), but also how translation is a creative act, always underestimated if considered only as a secondary activity for a major writer. Moreover, he enables us to see parallels between Mary Shelley's editing and her translating. Editing involves the requisites of literary knowledge, scholarly accuracy, and linguistic aptitude but is also, like translation, a creative intervention, and in her case, she felt, one that obliged her to shape her husband's oeuvre for posterity. For his synthesis of continuities across the entire corpus of Mary Shelley's writings (which he mastered like no previous scholar), as well as innumerable local insights of value, students of de Palacio's work are lastingly indebted.

In conclusion, de Palacio's understanding of the fundamental importance of Mary Shelley's continental European, in fact particularly Italian, identity must be emphasized. Here is her account of visiting the bay of Naples in June 1843:

> It seems to me as if I had never before visited Italy — as if now, for the first time, the charm of the country was revealed to me. At every moment the senses, lapped in delight, whisper — this is Paradise. Here I find the secret of Italian poetry: not of Dante; he belonged to Etruria and Cisalpine Gaul: Tuscany and Lombardy are beautiful — they are an improved France, an abundant, sunshiny England — but here only do we find another earth and sky. Here the poets of Italy tasted the sweets of those enchanted gardens which they describe in their poems — and we wonder at their bright imaginations; but they drew only from reality — the reality of Sorrento.[42]

In this passage, her literary sensibility is heightened through direct experience of the unfamiliar 'South' and she shows herself willing to be enriched by a 'foreign' physical environment, much as her mother, Mary Wollstonecraft, had done in her travel narrative to the European 'North': *Letters Written during a Short Residence in Sweden, Norway, and Denmark* (1796). The passage thus evidences a point made in the opening of the first chapter, 'L'Italianisme' (Italianism), in 'Livre I' of *Mary Shelley dans son œuvre* ('Les intérêts profonds de Mary Shelley: les éléments de la formation d'une romancière' ['The underlying interests of Mary Shelley: factors in the making of a novelist']) where de Palacio asserts Mary Shelley's residence in Italy to have been fundamental to her formation as a writer:

> La langue italienne lui était une seconde langue maternelle; la péninsule, une seconde patrie préférée à l'ancienne et regrettée ensuite à l'égal d'un paradis perdu; Dante enfin, pour ne citer que lui, imprègne son œuvre littéraire qui sans lui ne serait pas ce qu'elle nous a été léguée. Il a semblé opportun, dans ces conditions, de placer tout ce qui touche à l'Italie au centre même des éléments qui ont contribué à la formation de Mary Shelley.[43]

> [The Italian language was, for her, another mother tongue; the peninsula a second native land, preferred to the former one and regretted afterwards as much as a lost paradise; lastly Dante, to make mention only of him, saturates her literary oeuvre such that without him it would not be what has passed down to us. It has seemed advisable, in these circumstances, to position all that touches on Italy at the very centre of the factors which contributed to the making of Mary Shelley.]

De Palacio's sensitivity to Mary Shelley's writing about the physical and cultural environments of continental Europe, to her interest in languages other than English, to her engagement, as a humane, enlightened intellectual with causes beyond Britain, all these matters are as important to recognize today as they were fifty years ago when his remarkable monograph was first published.

Notes to Chapter 3

1. This is a revised version of a paper given at the invitation of Antonella Braida on 30 September 2016 at the 'Atelier en hommage à M. Jean de Palacio', Université de Lorraine, Nancy. Unless otherwise indicated, translations from the French and Latin are the author's.
2. Nora Crook's distinguished publications concerning Mary Shelley's editing of Percy Shelley are too extensive to list here. For an example of their originality and value, see her 'Mary Shelley's Concealing "To ——": (Re)addressing Poems', *The Wordsworth Circle*, 43 (2012), 12–20.
3. Michael Rossington, 'Editing Shelley', in *The Oxford Handbook of Percy Bysshe Shelley*, ed. by Michael O'Neill and Anthony Howe, with the assistance of Madeleine Callaghan (Oxford: Oxford University Press, 2013), pp. 645–56.
4. See, for example, Percy Bysshe Shelley, *The Poetical Works of Percy Bysshe Shelley*, with an introduction by A. H. Koszul, 2 vols (London: Dent, 1907), and Mary Shelley, *Proserpine & Midas: Two Unpublished Mythological Dramas by Mary Shelley*, ed. by A. Koszul (London: Milford, 1922).
5. Jean de Palacio, 'Shelley traducteur de soi-même', *Revue des Sciences Humaines*, 40.158 (April–June 1975), 223–44 (pp. 232–33, n. 2).
6. De Palacio, 'Shelley and Dante: An Essay in Textual Criticism', pp. 105–12, and his 'Shelley's Library Catalogue: An Unpublished Document', *Revue de littérature comparée*, 36.2 (April–June 1962), 270–76.

7. Neville Rogers, *Shelley at Work: A Critical Inquiry* (Oxford: Clarendon Press, 1956); Donald H. Reiman, *Shelley's 'The Triumph of Life': A Critical Study* (Urbana: University of Illinois Press, 1965); Charles H. Taylor, Jr, *The Early Collected Editions of Shelley's Poems: A Study in the History and Transmission of the Printed Text* (New Haven: Yale University Press, 1958).
8. The period of de Palacio's research on Mary Shelley is given as '1953–1968' in his *Mary Shelley dans son œuvre*, p. 11.
9. [Edmund Blunden], 'An Oxford Poet', *TLS*, 2332, 12 October 1946, p. 493; see also R. W. H., 'Gift of Shelley Manuscripts', *Bodleian Library Record*, 2 (1946), 144–45.
10. See B. C. Barker-Benfield, *Shelley's Guitar* (Oxford: Bodleian Library, 1992), pp. xvi–xvii.
11. G. M. Matthews, '"The Triumph of Life": A New Text', *Studia Neophilologica*, 32 (1960), 271–309, and his 'Shelley and Jane Williams', *Review of English Studies*, n.s., 12 (1961), 40–48.
12. Percy Bysshe Shelley, *Posthumous Poems of Shelley: Mary Shelley's Fair Copy Book*, ed. by Irving Massey (Montreal: McGill-Queen's University Press, 1969); *Bodleian MS. Shelley adds. d. 7: A Facsimile Edition with Full Transcription and Textual Notes*, ed. by Irving Massey, The Bodleian Shelley Manuscripts, II (New York: Garland, 1987).
13. De Palacio, 'Avant-propos', *Mary Shelley dans son œuvre*, pp. 9–11.
14. De Palacio, 'Shelley and Dante', pp. 110–12. Mary Shelley's transcription is in Oxford, Bodleian Library, Bodleian MS. Shelley adds. c. 5, fols 157ʳ–158ʳ.
15. De Palacio, 'Shelley and Dante', p. 109.
16. *Relics of Shelley*, ed. by Garnett, pp. 53–55; de Palacio, 'Shelley and Dante', p. 107.
17. Neville Rogers, 'The Shelley-Rolls Gift to the Bodleian: I — Shelley at Work', *TLS*, 2582, 27 July 1951, p. 476.
18. The most recent scholarly edition of Mary Shelley's transcription is by Alan M. Weinberg in his edition of *Bodleian MS. Shelley adds. c. 5*, The Bodleian Shelley Manuscripts, XXII/2 (New York: Garland: 1997), pp. 53–54, 362–67, 444–46.
19. Michael O'Neill, '"Trying to make it as good as I can": Mary Shelley's Editing of P. B. Shelley's Poetry and Prose', in *Mary Shelley in her Times*, ed. by Betty T. Bennett and Stuart Curran (Baltimore: Johns Hopkins University Press, 2000), pp. 185–97 (p. 186).
20. De Palacio *Mary Shelley dans son œuvre*, pp. 401–02.
21. De Palacio, *Mary Shelley dans son œuvre*, p. 405.
22. Ibid.
23. De Palacio, *Mary Shelley dans son œuvre*, p. 408.
24. Ibid., p. 410.
25. Ibid., p. 405.
26. *Mary Shelley dans son œuvre*, pp. 464–72.
27. See *The 'Charles the First' Draft Notebook: A Facsimile of Bodleian MS. Shelley adds. e. 17*, ed. by Nora Crook, The Bodleian Shelley Manuscripts, XII (New York: Garland, 1991), pp. xli, 14–27, 50–53.
28. *Relics*, ed. by Garnett, p. 20.
29. *Proserpine & Midas*, ed. by Koszul, p. xi.
30. J. E. R., 'Mary Shelley and "Orpheus"', *TLS*, 1102, 1 March 1923, p. 143.
31. *Mary Shelley dans son œuvre*, p. 465.
32. Jean de Palacio, 'The Shelley Studies', *Les Langues modernes*, 9.5 (September–October 1966), 69–73 (p. 71).
33. See Nora Crook's in *The Novels and Selected Works of Mary Shelley*, II, 439–47; and Percy Bysshe Shelley, *The Poems of Shelley*, ed. by Kelvin Everest and others (London: Longman, 1989–), IV: *1820–1821*, ed. by Michael Rossington, Jack Donovan, and Kelvin Everest with the assistance of Andrew Lacey and Laura Barlow, Longman Annotated English Poets (London: Routledge, 2014), pp. 379–87.
34. De Palacio, *Mary Shelley dans son œuvre*, p. 467.
35. See Anna Mercer, *The Collaborative Literary Relationship of Percy Bysshe Shelley and Mary Wollstonecraft Shelley* (London: Routledge, 2019).
36. Jean de Palacio, 'Byron traducteur et les influences italiennes', *Rivista di Letterature Moderne e Comparate*, 11.3–4 (December 1958), 209–30, and his 'Shelley traducteur de Dante', 571–78.

37. Frederick L. Jones, 'Unpublished Fragments by Shelley and Mary', *Studies in Philology*, 45 (1948), 472–76 (p. 472, n. 1); Jean de Palacio, 'Mary Shelley's Latin Studies: Her Unpublished Translation of Apuleius', *Revue de littérature comparée*, 38.4 (October–December 1964), 564–71 (p. 565, n. 3).
38. Mary Shelley, 'Cupid and Psyche', ed. by A A. Markley, in *Mary Shelley's 'Literary Lives' and Other Writings*, IV, pp. lxii–lxv, 282–95. For Markley's acknowledgement of de Palacio's identification of omissions and alterations in Mary Shelley's translation, see p. lxiv.
39. De Palacio, 'Mary Shelley's Latin Studies', p. 568.
40. Apuleius, *Metamorphoses*, ed. and trans. by J. Arthur Hanson, 2 vols (Cambridge, MA: Harvard University Press, 1989), I, 268–69. For the signalling of the omission in Mary Shelley's translation, see 'Cupid and Psyche', ed. by Markley, p. 293 and n. c.
41. De Palacio, 'Mary Shelley's Latin Studies', p. 570. The quotation is from Mary Shelley, *The Last Man*, 3 vols (London: Colburn, 1826), II, 17.
42. Shelley, *Rambles*, II, 262.
43. De Palacio, *Mary Shelley dans son œuvre*, p. 23.

CHAPTER 4

Mourning in Mary Shelley's 'The Choice', and the Work of Editing

Valentina Varinelli

Soon after Shelley's death on 8 July 1822, Mary Shelley imposed on herself the 'task' of collecting, arranging, and transcribing all his manuscripts, with a view to publication.[1] First announced in December of the following year, *Posthumous Poems of Percy Bysshe Shelley* appeared in June 1824, with a preface signed 'Mary W. Shelley'.[2] Just as, during their life together, Shelley's encouragement and example had prompted Mary Shelley to experiment with different genres, so her immersion in his poetry in her new role as editor must have acted as a creative stimulus, for at this time she also began to write poetry. But Mary Shelley's parallel efforts to edit Shelley's posthumous works and compose her own poems are even more closely interrelated: they constitute two forms of a dialogue with her late husband's poetry central to her work of mourning. Nowhere is this dialogue more sustained than in 'The Choice'. In this poem, Mary Shelley appropriates Shelley's language and imagery to come to terms with the memory of their Italian years, and with the losses that marked them. Her many allusions to Shelley's works of that period can tell us something about the way she interpreted them, and the value they had for her. More importantly, reading 'The Choice' as a response to Percy Shelley's Italian production can help make sense of some of Mary Shelley's most puzzling editorial 'choices', as I intend to show in this essay.

'The Choice' is the earliest and longest of Mary Shelley's poems. It is unique among them in having a colloquial tone, which results from its being written in heroic couplets, as prescribed by the subgenre to which it belongs, that of the 'choice poem', in which an ideal mode of life is envisioned. The text is available to us in two versions. The earlier one, first published by Harry Buxton Forman as *The Choice: A Poem on Shelley's Death, by Mary Wollstonecraft Shelley* (London: printed for the editor for private distribution, 1876), is based on a holograph fair copy Mary Shelley left with Leigh Hunt in Genoa when she departed for England, on 25 July 1823.[3] She later transcribed it with some minor alterations and the significant omission of the last fourteen lines at the end of the so-called 'Journal of Sorrow' — spanning the years 1822 to 1825 — and she dated it 'July 1823 Genoa',[4] most likely its date of composition. Mary Shelley's probable source of inspiration was Hunt's own poem entitled 'The Choice', which had been modelled, in turn, on the poem by John Pomfret (1667–1702) of the same title and appeared in the fourth and last issue of *The Liberal* (published on 30 July 1823). Pomfret's poem does not figure in Mary Shelley's reading, but it is unlikely that she did not know it, since it was quite popular at the time and Godwin, too, had written an imitation of it in his youth.[5]

Like Mary Shelley's, Hunt's poem was presumably composed at some point towards the end of their forced cohabitation at Casa Negrotto, in Albaro near Genoa. However, the two works could not be more different. A thorough comparison of them is beyond the scope of this essay. I shall confine myself to noting that Hunt's poem is a faithful imitation of its model although one may well suspect that the dream life it depicts is but a thinly veiled recollection of the period he and his family spent at Albion House, the Shelleys' residence at Marlow, in 1817. By contrast, Mary Shelley's poem is largely retrospective. In the state of desolation she has been in since her 'Choice' was 'gone', 'Lost in that deep wherein he bathed his head',[6] the poet looks back at her past life, especially to the time she spent in Italy. Despite (or because of) the sorrowful recollections it evokes, Mary Shelley identifies Italy with the 'Choice' of her title, and, at the very moment of her departure, she elects it as her 'adopted land' (l. 60). The contradiction is apparent only, for Italy represents Mary Shelley's *literary* choice, the 'exhaustless theme'[7] — as she terms it in a review written three years later — around which her future productions will revolve.

Only towards its conclusion does 'The Choice' align itself with its models. Addressing her 'dearest, widowed friend' (i.e. Jane Williams, l. 143), the poet recounts a dream she had prophesying a future life in Italy for them both.[8] While the journal transcription stops here, the earlier version of the poem goes on to re-enact cyclically the tragic loss of the beginning, and finishes remembering Edward Williams, who drowned with Shelley. But the mourner's last thought is always for her husband, whom she envisions waiting for her in his 'far home' (l. 159).[9] Perhaps not particularly original in itself, this image is the only explicit allusion to Hunt's poem in 'The Choice', a reply to his lament for his 'dearest friend', 'gone to his great home, over the dreadful sea',[10] which must have induced his widow to assert her superior right to grieve.[11]

I will now look more closely at the passages in 'The Choice' which echo Shelley's poems, relating them to Mary Shelley's corresponding choices as editor. In the opening lines of the poem, Italy is depicted as a sepulchre, the vault of its sky having turned into the 'fitting charnel-roof'[12] of *Adonais*. This image also occurs in the preface to *Posthumous Poems*, where Mary Shelley writes that Shelley's death 'made [her] loved and lovely Italy appear a tomb, its sky a pall':[13]

> A wanderer here, no more I seek a home,
> The sky a vault, and Italy a tomb. (ll. 5–6)

Mary Shelley's self-definition as a 'wanderer' does more than simply voice her disorientation. A traditional (and very Shelleyan) epithet of the moon, the term signals her acceptance of the symbol of the 'cold chaste Moon' from Shelley's *Epipsychidion* (l. 281), in which she seems to have first recognized herself after his death. Writing to Byron on 21 October 1822, in fact, she affirmed: 'now I am truly *cold moonshine*'.[14]

As generations of Shelley scholars have reproachfully remarked, *Epipsychidion* is the only major poem Mary Shelley did not even mention in her notes on *The Poetical Works of Percy Bysshe Shelley*,[15] where she published it. Perhaps, as Newman Ivey White put it, she did not want to 'completely "remove a veil" which [she] was willing only to touch for one brief moment'.[16] But why should she pass over in silence a poem she had openly associated with herself only a few months after Shelley's death? A simpler, yet more probable explanation is that she acted in accordance with Shelley's opinion as much as with her own when she decided not to allude to Teresa Viviani ('Emily' in the poem), who had greatly disappointed him by turning out to be 'a cloud instead of a Juno'.[17] Mary Shelley's identification with the moon in 'The Choice' is symptomatic of her sense of guilt for the coldness Shelley attributed to her in *Epipsychidion*. At the same time, she charges this unflattering metaphor with a positive meaning, by complementing it with her own symbol for Shelley, whose 'companionship and love' she remembers to have illuminated her 'young life's cloud like sunlight' (ll. 11–12).[18] Her sun being set, the poet is saved from darkness by 'one star' (l. 16), which can be identified with her sole surviving son, Percy Florence (born on 12 November 1819). I owe to Nora Crook the identification of an antecedent for this metaphor, which complements Mary Shelley's familial cosmology, in Shelley's letter [of 11 January 1822?] to Thomas Love Peacock, whom he asks about his 'little star', i.e. his baby daughter.[19]

In the following lines, Mary Shelley first gives voice to her uncertainties about the future:

> Since I must live, how would I pass the day,
> How meet with fewest tears the morning's ray,
> How sleep with calmest dreams, how find delights, (ll. 17–19)

and then expresses her determination to go on living 'As fire flies gleam through interlunar nights' (l. 20).[20] The adjective *interlunar* (indicating the time between a waning and a waxing moon) frequently recurs in Shelley's poetry, but Mary Shelley may be directly echoing a passage from Milton's *Samson Agonistes* describing the moon 'Hid in her vacant interlunar cave' (l. 89), which she quoted from memory in an early entry of her 'Journal of Sorrow'.[21] The previous pages of the journal present the same cosmic imagery later employed in 'The Choice':

> [5 October 1822] I shall commence my task, commemorate the virtues of the only creature on earth worth loving or living for, & then maybe I may join him, Moonshine may be united to her planet & wander no more, a sad reflection of all she loved, on earth. [...]

> [10 October 1822] I would endeavour to consider my self a faint continuation of his being, & as far as possible the revelation to the earth of what he was.[22]

In light of these resolutions, it is not going too far to see the image of the fireflies illuminating the night in the absence of the moon in 'The Choice' as a figure for Mary Shelley dedicating her widowed life to keeping her husband's memory alive through the publication of his works. In the fireflies, which Shelley famously loved,[23] Mary Shelley found a more congenial symbol for herself, while preserving her association with the moon, for it is more than likely that while in Italy she had been told one of the many legends explaining the gleam of the fireflies as a reflection of moonlight.

From its first lines, 'The Choice' suggests that Mary Shelley's editorial work was primarily meant as an antidote to sorrow, at once preventing her from wasting away in grief, and enabling her to follow in her husband's footsteps and achieve something that would make her worthy to join him.[24] This purpose is especially true of *Posthumous Poems*, as revealed by an epigraph from Petrarch intended for the volume, but later discarded, which still survives in one of Mary Shelley's copybooks (Bodleian MS. Shelley adds. d. 9): 'Ma ricogliendo le sue sparte fronde | Dietro lo vo pur così passo passo' ['But gathering his scattered leaves | I still follow him thus step by step'].[25] It has already been noted that Petrarch's importance for Mary Shelley consisted chiefly in his being 'one of the supreme poets of grief'.[26] Through his words, Mary Shelley could also express her feelings in the language of the country she associated most with Shelley's memory, and which (language and country) they both loved. As for this quote, its significance extends beyond the limits of the work for which it was chosen. In describing a lover collecting scattered leaves, it seems to anticipate the 'Introduction' to *The Last Man* (1826), in which the narrator remembers gathering and deciphering a heap of leaves found in the Sibyl's Cave near Naples — a scene which I interpret as an allegorization of Mary Shelley's editorial activity. Like the narrator's reconstruction of the Sibyl's prophecy, Mary Shelley's work on Shelley's papers may well 'have cheered long hours of solitude, and taken [her] out of a world, which ha[d] averted its once benignant face from [her], to one glowing with imagination and power'.[27]

However, her work was not painless, as reading through 'The Choice' makes clear. While the past is looked back to as a 'race of joy' (l. 62), which associates the poet with Percy Shelley's skylark, flying and singing 'Like an unbodied joy whose race is just begun' ('To a Sky-Lark', l. 15), now she needs him to sustain her in a life of 'lonely pain, | As link by link she weaves her heavy chain' (ll. 49–50). Such a life is as starkly in contrast to the song of the skylark as is the madman's speech in 'Julian and Maddalo' echoed in these lines.[28] On the other hand, the quintessentially female, mythical gesture of weaving which oxymoronically mitigates this fate suggests that, heavy as it is, it is Mary Shelley's own 'Choice'. Thus, her poem proves to be more than a declaration of poetics: it is her promise that she will 'earn', by 'suffering and by patience, a return | Of [Shelley's] companionship and love' (ll. 9–11).

The allusion to 'Julian and Maddalo' also sheds light on the immediately preceding lines, in which Shelley is addressed:

> Oh, gentle Spirit! thou hast often sung,
> How fallen on evil days thy heart was wrung;
> Now fierce remorse and unreplying death
> Waken a chord within my heart, whose breath,
> Thrilling and keen, in accents audible
> A tale of unrequited love doth tell.
> [...]
> It speaks of cold neglect, averted eyes,
> That blindly crushed thy soul's fond sacrifice. (ll. 23–34)

The first two lines of this key passage clearly allude to Shelley's 'saddest verses', a handful of poems he had fleetingly contemplated collecting in one volume.[29] In her 1839 'Note on Poems Written in 1818', among which she published some of these texts, Mary Shelley explains that he had kept them hidden from her in order not to wound her feelings; she then expresses 'regret and gnawing remorse', as she had done in 'The Choice', and admits 'that had one been more alive to the nature of his feelings and more attentive to soothe them, such would not have existed',[30] implicitly assuming for herself at least part of the responsibility for Shelley's sadness. The actual cause of the latter, and the exact date of composition of his 'saddest verses' have been the subject of much debate; what is relevant here is how Mary Shelley read them. Her comments suggest that she related them to the deep depression into which she sank after her son William's death, in Rome on 7 June 1819, which estranged her from her husband. Her publishing them among the poems of the year before, when, as explained in her note, Shelley suffered from bad health, may therefore look like an attempt to conceal any connection she might have had with them. Nobody seems to have conceived the all too human possibility that, twenty years later, Mary Shelley mistakenly thought that her depression had begun after Clara's death, on 24 September 1818.[31] This idea would also explain why 'Julian and Maddalo', which in *Posthumous Poems* was dated 'Rome, May, 1819', and in the first edition of *Poetical Works* figured among the 1820 poems, in the second edition was moved to 1818.

Even more than the distinct echo already highlighted, the passage from 'The Choice' quoted above indicates that Mary Shelley especially associated 'Julian and Maddalo' with her depression: the madman's story can indeed be defined as a 'tale of unrequited love', speaking of 'cold neglect' and 'averted eyes'. If, as I believe, Mary Shelley interpreted the madman's ravings as Shelley's own laments for her estrangement, and in her poem she repented of it, her choice of 'Julian and Maddalo' as the opening poem in *Posthumous Poems* cannot but surprise. My supposition is that she intended it as a tribute to Byron, who had died two months before the publication of the volume, and whom readers would easily recognize in the character of Maddalo.[32] After all, she might have thought, the madman's identity could hardly be as clear to others as it was to herself, 'the unconnected exclamations of his agony' being, as Shelley suggested in his 'Preface', 'a sufficient comment for the text of every heart'.[33]

Whatever passed between Percy Shelley and Mary Shelley after the death of their children, in 'The Choice' she fondly remembers him as the 'Companion of [her] griefs' (l. 103), previously enumerated. Mary Shelley's first thought is for Clara, her 'sweet girl' lying 'on bleak Lido, near Venetian seas' (ll. 63–64). This passage symmetrically corresponds to the lines dedicated to the memory of Allegra, 'whose deep lucid eyes, | Were a reflection of these bluest skies' (ll. 97–98). By paraphrasing Shelley's description of Byron's daughter in 'Julian and Maddalo',[34] Mary Shelley identifies Allegra with the sky — a move parallel to her previous association of Clara with the sea, which also invests the Shelleys' nickname for Allegra, 'Alba' (the Italian for 'dawn'), with a quasi-prophetic meaning. The lines dedicated to the little girls of the Shelley household encompass a long passage remembering William, at the end of which the image of the 'evening star', central to Shelley's *Adonais*, is combined with the 'bright spirit' Shelley alludes to in the fragment dedicated to his son, beginning 'My lost William, thou in whom':

> The image shattered, the bright spirit fled,
> Thou shin'st the evening star among the dead. (ll. 95–96)

The dialogue with *Adonais* becomes more sustained in the lines that follow, as the poet commemorates her husband. Questioning Rome's 'ancient walls, and weed grown towers' its 'airs and brightly painted flowers' (ll. 113–14), she finds confirmation that, like Adonais, 'he is not dead', but 'is made one with Nature' (*Adonais*, ll. 343, 370):

> My trembling hand shall never write thee — dead —
> Thou liv'st in Nature, Love, my Memory, (ll. 118–19)

Thus she can declare herself 'The wife of Time no more, I wed Eternity' (l. 121), a line which Jean de Palacio aptly reads as a reply to Urania's words: 'But I am chained to Time, and cannot thence depart!' (*Adonais*, l. 234).[35] *Adonais* would for his widow always be Shelley's 'own elegy';[36] as such, the poem is pivotal for her work of mourning through poetic writing and editing. Understandably, when she published it in 1839, she could not bring herself to comment on it, but she gave it prominence, nonetheless, quoting it at large in the last, most personal of her notes. If, as variously exemplified above, a continuity with the tone and images of 'The Choice' is already present in the editor's preface to Shelley's *Posthumous Poems*, Mary Shelley's concluding 'Note on Poems Written in 1822' reproduces the very mingling of voices that characterizes her poem. The note is introduced by another of Mary Shelley's attempts in the lyric genre, a revised version of the lines she had published in the *Keepsake for 1831* (1830) with the title 'A Dirge'. De Palacio, whose book contains the most exhaustive analysis of the lyric to date, was the first to consider it within the context of *Poetical Works*, and to read it as an integral part of Mary Shelley's elegiac, critical biographical prose.[37] As de Palacio observes, her decision to use 'A Dirge' as an epigraph to her 'Note on Poems Written in 1822' indicates that her lyric had a similar purpose to that of Shelley's *Adonais*, the final, prophetic stanza of which closes the same editorial note.

A few years before de Palacio's groundbreaking study, Mary Shelley's 1839 edition of *Poetical Works* (including the dedication to Percy Florence and William Finden's engraving on the frontispiece) met the praise of Sylva Norman, who honoured Mary Shelley 'for submerging her own literary egotism [...], in the recognition that it could be more valuable to edit than to create'.[38] But Norman seems to have missed the point here: Mary Shelley's editorial achievement is as much an expression of her own authorial voice as a celebration of her late husband's poetry. That her task is twofold, and is equally concerned with his and her original work, is clearly stated in the preface, where she announces that her duty will consist in 'giving the productions of a sublime genius to the world', and, '*at the same time*, detailing the history of those productions' (my italics).[39] As we know, she plays no minor role in that history, and, for all her professed desire to 'abstain from any remark on the occurrences of his private life',[40] her notes contain a lot more than they promise. In a sense, *Poetical Works* represents the last of the Shelleys' joint efforts, the culmination of a literary collaboration which began in the summer of 1814, when on the shores of Lake Lucerne Shelley dictated his unfinished novel 'The Assassins' to Mary, who proudly recorded the feat in the plural.[41] Three years later, the same collaboration produced *History of a Six Weeks' Tour*, where we first hear the duet of voices that resonates in Mary Shelley's last editorial note. In the latter, however, it fulfils a more specific aim. By incorporating Shelley's voice in her own narrative, Mary Shelley resuscitated him, as it were. Thus, she refined a mourning strategy she had first employed in 'The Choice'.

The closer the poem gets to its end, the more audible Shelley's voice becomes. Having memorialized her dead husband and children, Mary Shelley declares:

> 'Tis thus the Past — on which my spirit leans,
> Makes dearest to my soul Italian scenes. (ll. 122–23)

Italy is no longer the realm of death of the beginning: it turns into her own land of memory, an idealized projection of her landscape of the mind, in which the past relives as in a diorama (to use a favourite image of hers) with a specific set of natural figures. 'The pools reflecting Pisa's old pine wood, | The Fire flies' beams, the aziola's cry' (ll. 131–32) identify Mary Shelley's ideal of Italy with the environs of Pisa, where the Shelleys resided more or less permanently from early 1820. Given the optimistic tone of the following lines, in which the poet tells her prophetic dream, these elements also acquire auspicious significance, contrasting with the sadness conveyed by the song of Shelley's 'Aziola'.[42] I suspect, however, that Mary Shelley had another of her husband's poems in mind. 'The Choice' is much indebted for its colloquial tone to Shelley's 'Letter to Maria Gisborne', which Mary Shelley urged her friend to send her as early as 20 September 1822.[43] In his verse epistle (which is also, in a sense, a 'choice poem'), Shelley delineates his own version of the Tuscan idyll, where the fireflies figure alongside an unidentified 'bird | Which cannot be the Nightingale', yet 'sings so sweet as it' (ll. 287–89), implying either a seasonal incongruity or, more likely, an altogether different song. Percy Shelley's description is not incompatible with the singing habits of the *assiolo*, for which at the time he had no name, if we are to rely on his eponymous poem (written a year later). Considering the peculiar resonance that the semi-serious final line of Shelley's rural sketch ('Now Italy or London — which you will!', l. 291) must have had for his widow, I suggest that she identified the mysterious bird in 'Letter to Maria Gisborne' with the *assiolo*, and then transposed its imagery to her own poem.

'Letter to Maria Gisborne' was published in *Posthumous Poems*, in the preface to which the editor writes: 'Such was his love for nature, that every page of his poetry is associated in the minds of his friends with the loveliest scenes of the countries which he inhabited.'[44] These include the scenes of Shelley's verse epistle, which return in his last, perfect lyrics dedicated to Jane Williams.[45] By reproducing the distinctive elements of Shelley's 'Italian scenes' in 'The Choice', Mary Shelley kept his memory alive; at the same time, she exorcized the most painful of her recollections. Not only did she attain an idealized view of Italy through Shelley's poetry, which reconciled her to the country where he and her children had died. As she assimilated it into her own verse, she also learned to accept his weaknesses, from his infatuations with other women to his inability to cope with her depression. Her choice to publish the poems related to those aspects of her life with Shelley without a word of comment can only be understood in light of this symbolic appropriation of their language and imagery, which she knew how to appreciate. Mary Shelley's double sanction as editor and writer suggests that, if in her commentary she passed over some of Shelley's poems in silence, she did so out of discretion rather than a sense of guilt, or even jealousy.

All Percy Bysshe Shelley editors need to take Mary Shelley's editorial decisions into account, from her sometimes bold interventions in the unpublished texts to the unobvious arrangement of major and minor poems in both the 1824 and the 1839 collections. But these decisions should not be isolated from their context. Pamela Clemit's intelligent inclusion of the list of contents of each collection in her critical edition of Mary Shelley's prefaces and notes rests upon the conviction that 'Mary Shelley's selection and arrangement of P. B. Shelley's works are central to her editorial achievement'.[46] They are central, too, to an understanding of her attitude to Shelley's poetry after his death. We may never know the reasons behind certain choices Mary Shelley made when editing her late husband's works. Yet de Palacio showed us that we can try to get a glimpse of them by setting her editorial activity against the backdrop of her own literary production. Thus, relating 'The Choice' to Mary Shelley's various 'choices' as editor has led to a reconsideration of her response to some of Shelley's major poems, and has permitted us to follow her as she worked through her mourning by editing and absorbing them.

Notes to Chapter 4

1. *MWS Journals*, p. 434. See also *MWS Letters*, I, 252, 262, 292.
2. The volume was originally intended as a collection of poetry, prose, and letters (see Roger Ingpen, *Shelley in England: New Facts and Letters from the Shelley-Whitton Papers* (London: Kegan Paul, Trench, Trubner, 1917), p. 577, n.). It was published by John and Henry L. Hunt, London. All references are to this edition.
3. The manuscript, which contains corrections in Leigh Hunt's hand, is now in the Carl H. Pforzheimer Collection of Shelley and his Circle at the New York Public Library (MWS 0203 *Pforz 558L 11). Dr Elizabeth Denlinger, who kindly confirmed this information, explained to me that the manuscript was purchased by Carl Pforzheimer in March 1920 at the Buxton Forman sale (email communication, 11 October 2017). Arnold A. Markley's statement that 'its present whereabouts are unknown' in his introduction to the latest edition of the poem (*Mary Shelley's 'Literary Lives' and Other Writings*, IV, pp. i–xciii (p. xxx), hereafter *MWS Literary Lives*) is therefore incorrect.
4. *MWS Journals*, p. 494.
5. *MWS Literary Lives*, IV, 6.
6. Mary Shelley, 'The Choice' [Hunt/Forman version], in *MWS Literary Lives*, IV, ll. 1, 3. The pun on Shelley's name (here as at l. 21, 'lost' translates the Italian *perso*, which sounds like Percy) is already implicit at the beginning of *Epipsychidion*. (All further references to 'The Choice' are to this edition.)
7. 'The English in Italy', in *The Novels and Selected Works of Mary Shelley*, II, 159.

8. Poetic convention and autobiography merge here, for this dream was a real one (*MWS Letters*, I, 329).
9. However incomplete, Mary Shelley's later version reflects the optimism expressed in her last entry in 'The Journal of Sorrow', written at some point in the summer of 1825: 'Winter passed, and summer brilliant as if it had been Italian, awoke — & raised me from desperation to happiness — [...] for the first time since that fatal day life was not a burthen — I hailed the Morn with smiles, the hours passed placidly' (*MWS Journals*, pp. 489–90). Although this tonal continuity is no proof that 'The Choice' was transcribed in the journal at that time, it seems to confirm the fact, based on external evidence, that the omission of its closing lines was not accidental. On the other hand, since back in England Mary Shelley insistently requested Marianne Hunt to send her a copy of the second half of her poem (*MWS Letters*, I, 399, 404), it cannot be ruled out that the missing conclusion is Marianne's fault.
10. Leigh Hunt, 'The Choice', in *The Selected Writings of Leigh Hunt*, ed. by Robert Morrison and Michael Eberle-Sinatra, The Pickering Masters, 6 vols (London: Pickering and Chatto, 2003), VI, ll. 132, 237. The editors' introductory note makes no mention of Mary Shelley's work.
11. Mary Shelley's strained relationship with Leigh Hunt at the time of their residence in Albaro originated from their altercation over the remains of Shelley's heart, which Edward John Trelawny had snatched from his funeral pyre. Hunt's accusations that her coldness had been the cause of Shelley's unhappiness further exacerbated their tensions and may have led Mary Shelley to exaggerate her sense of guilt in 'The Choice'.
12. Percy Bysshe Shelley, *Adonais*, in *Shelley's Poetry and Prose*, ed. by Donald H. Reiman and Neil Fraistat, 2nd edn (New York: Norton, 2002), l. 60. All quotations from Shelley's poems are from this edition.
13. P. B. Shelley, *Posthumous Poems*, p. vii.
14. *MWS Letters*, I, 284. See also note 22 below. While Mary Shelley's interpretation of the symbol of the moon in *Epipsychidion* is supported by both internal and external evidence, it should be remembered that in the same passage Shelley praised her for the love and tenderness she hid under her cold appearance (Kenneth Neill Cameron, 'The Planet-Tempest Passage in *Epipsychidion*', *PMLA*, 63 (1948), 950–72). Shelley discussed this contrast between love and apparently cold attitude with Teresa Viviani, who reported his words to Mary Shelley in her letter of 24 December 1820: 'tuo Marito disse bene, allorchè disse: *che la tua apparente freddezza, non è che la cenere che ricuopre un cuore affettuoso*' ['your Husband said well, when he said *that your apparent coldness is but the ash which covers a tender heart*'] (my translation) (Oxford, Bodleian Library, Bodleian MS. Abinger c. 45, fols 50^v–51^r). I am grateful to Dr Christopher Fletcher and Dr Bruce Barker-Benfield of the Bodleian Library for permission to access, and cite from, Teresa Viviani's correspondence in the Abinger Collection.
15. Published by Edward Moxon in 1839 in four octavo volumes. A one-volume in-quarto second edition appeared later the same year with the date 1840. All references are to the former.
16. White, *Shelley*, II, 55.
17. *PBS Letters*, II, 434.
18. See also Mary Shelley's references to Shelley as 'the sunshine of my life' and 'the sun of my existence' in *MWS Journals*, pp. 436, 452.
19. *PBS Letters*, II, 374.
20. I follow the editors' suggestion that a question mark is required at the end of line 19.
21. *MWS Journals*, p. 437.
22. Ibid., pp. 434–36.
23. See Leigh Hunt's recollections in the fourth of his 'Letters from Abroad', *The Liberal*, 2 (1823), 251–64.
24. This does not mean that she did not also aim to grant Shelley the fame that had eluded him in his life. As for the possibility of gaining renown, or even wealth, for herself, what she wrote to Maria Gisborne [on *c*. 27 August 1822] about her own writings can be applied to her editorial work too: 'were it not for the steady hope I entertain of joining him what a mockery all this would be. Without that hope I could not study or write, for fame & usefulness (except as far as regards my child) are nullities to me' (*MWS Letters*, I, 254).

25. *Posthumous Poems of Shelley*, ed. by Massey, p. 17 (my translation). Mary Shelley substituted the feminine indirect object pronoun *le* of the original (Sonnet CCLXXXVII) with the masculine direct object pronoun, *lo*, to adapt Petrarch's words to her male subject. Her inability to find a grammatically acceptable solution might account for the eventual omission of the epigraph.
26. Tilar J. Mazzeo, 'Introduction' to *Italian Lives*, in *MWS Literary Lives*, I, pp. i–lviv (p. xlviii). Mary Shelley used quotes from Petrarch's *Canzoniere* as epigraphs to *Posthumous Poems* and to *Poetical Works*, as well as at the end of her preface and her 'Note on Poems Written in 1818' in the latter collection. Two lines by Petrarch function as the title (or motto) of her poem beginning 'Sadly borne across the waves', and a locket bearing an inscription from Petrarch, and containing locks of Shelley's and Mary Shelley's hair, is among the family relics at the Bodleian (see 'Locket Containing Shelley's and Mary's Hair', *Shelley's Ghost: Reshaping the Image of a Literary Family* <http://shelleysghost.bodleian.ox.ac.uk/locket-containing-shelleys-and-marys-hair> [accessed 2 March 2020].
27. Mary Shelley, *The Last Man*, in *The Novels and Selected Works of Mary Shelley*, IV, 8.
28. Cf. P. B. Shelley, 'Julian and Maddalo', ll. 302–03: 'To drag life on, which like a heavy chain | lengthens behind with many a link of pain!'
29. On 10 November 1820, Shelley wrote to his publisher: 'The Julian & Maddalo & the accompanying poems are all my saddest verses raked up into one heap' (*PBS Letters*, II, 246). The projected volume and the poems it might have included are discussed by Neil Fraistat in *The Prometheus Unbound Notebooks: A Facsimile of Bodleian MSS. Shelley e.1, e.2, e.3*, ed. by Neil Fraistat, The Bodleian Shelley Manuscripts, IX (New York: Garland, 1991), xlvii–lx.
30. P. B. Shelley, *Poetical Works*, III, 162. Mary Shelley alluded to some or all of the following poems, which fit in the definition of 'saddest verses': 'The Past' ('Wilt thou forget the happy hours'), 'Stanzas, Written in Dejection, near Naples', 'Misery. — A Fragment', 'On a Faded Violet', 'Sonnet' ('Lift not the painted veil'), to which in the second edition 'Julian and Maddalo' was added. All but 'Misery. — A Fragment' had already appeared in *Posthumous Poems*, but not grouped together — as, in fact, any of the 'Miscellaneous Poems' with analogous theme, source of inspiration, or date of composition.
31. Clara Shelley died aged one during the Shelleys' residence in Este, the very recollection of which in 'The Choice' (ll. 77–78) proves it was not a period of depression for its author.
32. It is perhaps worth remembering that Mary Shelley's press copy is entitled 'Maddalo and Julian' (see *Shelley and his Circle: 1773–1822*, ed. by Kenneth Neill Cameron and Donald H. Reiman, 10 vols (Cambridge: Harvard University Press, 1961–2002), VI (1973), 860, n.). Reiman insightfully relates the process of composition of Shelley's poem to his marital problems.
33. *Shelley's Poetry and Prose*, ed. by Reiman and Fraistat, p. 113.
34. At ll. 147–48, Julian (Shelley) says of the eyes of Maddalo (Byron)'s daughter that they 'seem | Twin mirrors of Italian Heaven'.
35. De Palacio, *Mary Shelley dans son œuvre*, p. 388.
36. *MWS Letters*, I, 249.
37. De Palacio, *Mary Shelley dans son œuvre*, pp. 476–78.
38. Sylva Norman, *Flight of the Skylark: The Development of Shelley's Reputation* (London: Max Reinhardt, 1954), p. 145.
39. P. B. Shelley, *Poetical Works*, I, p. vii.
40. Ibid.
41. Her journal entry of 25 August reads: 'We arrange our appartments [*sic*] — & write part of Shelleys Romance.' Two days later she wrote: 'Dine Then we write a part of the Romance' (*MWS Journals*, pp. 19–20).
42. Mary Shelley seems to have known the Italian saying according to which the *assiolo*'s song announces fine weather for the next day ('Quando canta l'assiolo, contadin, semina il fagiolo'); cf. *Valperga*, in *The Novels and Selected Works of Mary Shelley*, III: *Valperga; or, The Life and Adventures of Castruccio, Prince of Lucca*, ed. by Nora Crook, 108. Mary Shelley invariably spelled 'aziolo', unlike Shelley, whose use of the Italian feminine ending Forman probably followed in his edition of 'The Choice'.
43. *MWS Letters*, I, 262.

44. P. B. Shelley, *Posthumous Poems*, p. vi.
45. See especially 'To Jane. The Invitation' and 'To Jane. The Recollection', first published in *Posthumous Poems* as a single poem entitled 'The Pine Forest of the Cascine, near Pisa'.
46. Pamela Clemit, 'Introductory Note' to 'Prefaces and Notes', in *The Novels and Selected Works of Mary Shelley*, II, 231–35 (p. 231).

PART II

Mary Shelley across Languages and Cultures

CHAPTER 5

'Sa "lutte solitaire"':
Mary Shelley's Liberal Authority
and the Philosophic Radicals

Lisa Vargo

Jean de Palacio's groundbreaking monograph, *Mary Shelley dans son œuvre*, is invaluable for understanding the subtleties and nuances of the writings of the 'later Mary Shelley' with respect to her social and political thought. One particularly significant contribution is what de Palacio locates as 'le liberalisme de Mary Shelley'; he carefully parses her politics as neither radical nor revolutionary but nevertheless based on the notion of liberty and of equality and defined in her writings through her abiding interest in and advocacy for reform in Italy and Greece. While her work from the late 1820s and 1830s has been characterized as falling off into literary mediocrity and political conservatism, de Palacio points the way to a narrative of a public intellectual and woman of letters who adopts what I will call a 'liberal authority', a sense that literature can advance an awareness among its readers of the value of liberty. His perspective on Shelley's political thought is carefully parsed: 'Et si son libéralisme pâlit un peu avec le temps, on ne saurait pourtant exagérer ce recul, ni oublier la part qui en revient à vingt-cinq années de lutte solitaire' ['And, although her liberalism weakens a little with time, one should not exaggerate this shift, or forget the part played by twenty-five years of solitary struggle.'].[1] Accordingly, Shelley's writings offer continuity with her earlier works: 'ses divers écrits sont pour elle autant d'occasions d'affirmer discrètement ses idées libérales' ['Her various works are, for her, different occasions to affirm discreetly her liberal ideas.'].[2] De Palacio's belief that her liberalism 'weakens a little' needs to be balanced with his affirmation of her beliefs. Edward and Eleanor Marx Aveling's 1881 statement attributed to Karl Marx that had Byron lived 'he would have become a bourgeois reactionary' whereas Percy Shelley was 'a revolutionary through and through, and would always have been in the vanguard of socialism' must ever be a matter of speculation.[3] Mary Shelley is the survivor judged by the beliefs of her parents (although she never knew her mother, her father lived to 1834) and her husband. Part of her 'lutte solitaire' was to resist the assumptions of others, and de Palacio's perceptive reading of her later liberalism forms the basis for this essay.[4] Her contributions to *The Westminster Review* and 'Euphrasia', a work of short fiction, offer examples of her ongoing allegiance to liberal values.

It is important to remember that Mary Shelley herself had a role in the formation of British liberalism. She contributed to the journal that Leigh Hunt founded with Percy Shelley and Lord Byron, *The Liberal: Verse and Prose from the South* (1822–23), a venture that actively contributed to the definition of liberalism during the early part of the nineteenth century. Jonathan Gross argues that Byron chose the title for its associations with Spanish and Italian liberation movements.[5] Beyond these transnational matters, the English use of 'liberal' shifts in meaning during the period, from being associated with 'persons of superior social station' and with connotations of generosity and licentiousness, to have specific political associations that make it synonymous with the word 'radical'.[6] An example is the Dissenting periodical *The Monthly Review* founded by Richard Phillips in 1796 and edited by John Aikin whose purpose was 'the propagation of those liberal principles respecting some of the most important concerns of mankind' opposed by other periodicals.[7] These connections with British and Continental writing and cosmopolitan intellectual currents are made clear in the preface that Leigh Hunt wrote for the first issue of *The Liberal*:

> The object of our work is not political, except inasmuch as all writing now-a-days must involve something to that effect, the connexion between politics and all other subjects of interest to mankind having been discovered, never again to be done away. We wish to do our work quietly, if people will let us, — to contribute our liberalities in the shape of Poetry, Essays, Tales, Translations, and other amenities, of which kings themselves may read and profit, if they are not afraid of seeing their own faces in every species of inkstand.[8]

It is clear that Mary Shelley did not abandon the ideals of liberalism. During the 1830s her circle included individuals associated with the Philosophic Radicals, a group of liberal intellectuals affiliated with Utilitarian thinkers James and John Stuart Mill and Jeremy Bentham, and her literary activities included writing for their journal, *The Westminster Review*.[9] At the same time this relationship was a rather fraught one and with the help of de Palacio's scholarship it is possible to understand how her sense of what it is to be a liberal is defined as much against the Philosophical Radicals, as it is by the ideas she shared with them. Key to this difference is her appreciation of Hunt's 'wish to do our work quietly' as well as a belief in the close connection between politics and literature.

Some further elucidation of de Palacio's reference to twenty-five years of solitary battle is relevant to understanding her liberalism in the years preceding and following the Reform Act of 1832 and the era of Chartism. As the daughter of two radical thinkers from an earlier generation, Shelley chafed against those who expected her to back their causes because of her parents and her husband rather than for her own convictions. These associations made some, like Lucy Aikin, unwilling to meet her, while Frances Wright wanted the daughter of Mary Wollstonecraft to join her utopian community in Nashoba, Illinois, and included Edward Trelawny and the Philosophical Radicals.[10] Mary Shelley's reticence is a register of her lack of ease with the rise of the author as a marketable public celebrity balanced with a need to support herself and her surviving son with literary work. When she responded to the wishes of the publishers of the Standard Novels 'that I should furnish them with some account of the origin of the story', she prompted readers of her 1831 preface to *Frankenstein*:

> It is true that I am very averse to bringing myself forward in print; but as my account will only appear as an appendage to a former production, and as it will be confined to such topics as have connection with my authorship alone, I can scarcely accuse myself of a personal intrusion.[11]

It is not authorship from which Shelley demurs, but writing about herself, entering in a public manner into forms of excessive introspection and a sense of the artist's life as inextricably bound up in his or her works that increasingly accompanied literary celebrity during the nineteenth century and which she witnessed first-hand through her association with Lord Byron. In her 1829 review of Anna Jameson's *Loves of the Poets* she seems to be thinking of her own experience as she mentions the modern tendency 'of dragging into undesired publicity the modest and retiring'.[12] How someone averse to bringing her private self into the literary public sphere nevertheless finds a means to play an active role in cultural and political debates is a struggle for Mary Shelley. A form of literary authority defined through the principles of liberalism offers her a means to preserve a sense of personal privacy while engaging in public discourse. Shelley's version of liberal authorship espouses egalitarianism and liberty and above all encourages others to engage with such values by thinking for themselves rather than being told what they should espouse.

Shelley's negotiation of her liberal authority is illustrated in a long journal entry composed in 1838 in which she reflects upon her failures in the eyes of her 'pretended friends'. The diary entry takes the form of a kind of imaginary conversation, a combination of giving oneself a talking to and rehearsing what one might hope to say in ideal conditions. It commences by laying out the 'charges' brought against her: 'I have been so often abused by pretended friends ~~as to~~ ↑for↓ my lukewarmness in the "Good Cause", that though I disdain to answer them, I shall put down here a few thoughts on this subject. I am much of a self examiner.'[13] However, the discontent is not only with herself: 'And if I use the word disdain — it is that I think my qualities — such as they are — [are] not appreciated ↑from unworthy causes↓.'[14] It needs be asked who those friends are and what the nature of the 'Good Cause' is. Mary Shelley answers this in the next paragraph of the entry, though in a manner that is not completely straightforward: 'In the first place with regard to the "good Cause" — the cause of the advancement of freedom & knowledge — of the Rights of Women &c — I am not a person of Opinions.'[15] Her claim that she is 'not a person of Opinions' requires some careful parsing. In the nineteenth century, 'opinions' can mean a specific political belief along with our contemporary understanding of 'opinion' as a more general matter of what or how one thinks (*OED*). Given the contexts of her comments and the capital 'O', it is likely that she uses the word to signify a particular political position. A number of suggestions have been made about the identity of the 'good Cause', including the Chartist Movement. William St Clair offers the most helpful lead in mentioning that in July 1838 Edward Trelawny asked Mary Shelley to write a pamphlet on women's rights for the Philosophic Radicals, which she declined to undertake.[16] Reference to the Radicals likely accounts for why 'Good Cause' is given quotation marks and capitals for importance. While it is a long-standing phrase with respect to politics that goes back at least to the time of English Commonwealth, it is specifically associated in the 1830s with the Philosophic Radicals. Harriet Grote's *Philosophical Radicals of 1832* contains a helpful gloss: 'In the early part of this year (1837) I received a letter from Molesworth, dictated with some acerbity it is true, but replete with hearty zeal for "the good cause", as it used to be termed amongst our party.'[17] In her journal entry Shelley is being careful to define her liberal political beliefs as distinct from those held by a particular group whom she felt were pressuring her to advance their own causes.

Given her ongoing connections with liberal views, Mary Shelley might be expected to have allegiance with the Philosophic Radicals.[18] Philosophically their Utilitarianism was allied to anti-aristocratic government and perfectibility, with which William Godwin and Mary Shelley's friend Robert Dale Owen had sympathies. In their rejection of class politics, the concept of 'the People' they adopted (a phrase that Shelley uses in connection with Percy Shelley's explicitly political poems) was significant.[19] William St Clair argues that with respect to Edward Trelawny and the Infant Custody Bill debated in 1838, 'Mary *ought* to have been sympathetic to the cause but she resented the presumption that she must necessarily share the views of the radicals in full' and embody the view of her parents and not have ideas of her own.[20]

If Trelawny is a likely catalyst for her journal reflections, Shelley's comments are not restricted to her difficult friend; nor should they be taken as an out and out rejection of liberal ideas as she makes emphatically clear in her journal: 'I have never written a word ~~that is not~~ in ↑dis↓favour of liberalism.'[21] As Shelley rehearses her beliefs, she demonstrates that her views are indeed close to those of the Radicals:

> For myself, I earnestly desire the good & enlightenment of my fellow creatures — & see all in the present course tending to the same, & rejoice — but I am not for violent extremes which only ~~tend to~~ ↑bring on an injurious↓ reaction.[22]

With respect to 'violent', she is referring to extremes and intensity; a lack of support from 'liberals' is a noticeable theme in her observations. Following the death of her father in 1836, she responded to Trelawny's accusation of her being afraid to publish Godwin's political views, by suggesting that it is his atheism about which she is concerned, adding, 'if I have ever found kindness it has not been from liberals — to disengage myself from them was my first act of my freedom — the consequence was that I gained peace & civil usage — which they denied me.'[23]

Some of the frustration she voices privately in 1838 is likely a legacy of her career with *The Westminster Review*, whose purpose was to counter the leading journals of the day — the Tory *Quarterly Review* and the Whig *Edinburgh Review*. Shelley's friend John Bowring was its first editor and her correspondence traces her proposals to him for reviews, the writing of which helped supplement her income; a letter to Bowring following the publication of her review of writings by her friend Prosper Mérimée suggests she was paid 5 pounds and 5 shillings.[24] In spite of this connection, writing for the *Westminster* did not lead to regular work — seven unsigned reviews between 1826 and 1832 have been identified as hers.[25]

While her reviews are in keeping with the expectations of the journal's readership, at the same time Shelley forges a perspective following her earlier association with *The Liberal* that art and literature necessarily play a role in political and social reform. In her witty review of three works of travel, 'The English in Italy', Shelley's authoritative narrative voice equates a love of 'the fine arts' and poetry with the means through which 'Italy possesses in her own bosom the germs of regeneration, which, in spite of their late overthrow, will in the end give birth to their emancipation', and she presents a portrait of the *improvvisatore* Tommaso Sgricci as an example of the variety and 'exhaustless fertility that makes Italy a paradise'.[26] She is critical of those English writers for whom 'the inferior classes of their fellow beings possess no interest [...]: and yet it is in the country of Italy that you see most of the true Italian character'.[27] In her review of writings by Mérimée she praises his *La Jaquerie*, which offers a portrait of a fourteenth-century peasant rebellion as an imagined ideal rather than a historical account, expressing her admiration for 'the imaginative writer, who deems that beyond the usual track he may find a fresh and untried ground, courageously launches forth, leaving the dull every-day earth behind him'.[28] While she offers praise for Louis Simond's *A Tour in Italy and Sicily*, she makes clear what would make his account all the more significant: 'Mr. Simond's book is no guide to works of art, nor is it of strong political tendency.'[29] She offered Bowring a review of Anna Jameson's *Loves of the Poets*, as the subject of love and poetry offers occasion to think about Percy Shelley's 'Essay on Love', which she had recently published in *The Keepsake*.[30] She is quite critical of James Cobbett's perspective on Italian politics and attacks his defence of the Italians' persecution of Jewish people, which leads to an observation that perhaps reflects her own experience: 'his reasoning displays the singular capacity the most acrimonious partisans of liberty have, of being the worst of tyrants when they choose.'[31]

In spite of opinions largely sympathetic to the journal's perspective, her work for *The Westminster Review* came to an end when Colonel Thomas Perronet Thompson, who bought the *Review* in 1830, forced her to change a review of James Fenimore Cooper's *The Bravo* for containing too much praise and declined to publish her review of Bulwer Lytton's *Eugene Aram* which he observed to Hunt 'could have been written by a girl of thirteen'.[32] If Thompson was not happy with Shelley's reviewing, Shelley herself could hardly be satisfied with its Utilitarian perspective on literature. Although John Stuart Mill famously describes his discovery of the importance of William Wordsworth's poetry in his *Autobiography*,[33] Jeremy Bentham's suggestions that the radical review would be one half 'consecrated to politics and morals, the other half left to literary insignificancies' locates a sense of division between her own values and those of the *Westminster*.[34] *The Edinburgh Literary Review* for 21 February 1829 pinpoints this division in perspective in a review, suggesting that the *Westminster*'s literary articles 'are mere political diatribes under the false colours of critical disquisition':

> This political tendency of the Westminster Reviewers has yet a more malign

> effect on their criticism. They are in the habit of praising or condemning a
> work, not on the ground of its literary merits, but according as it is favourable
> or unfavourable to their own moral and political tenets.[35]

Several reviews are criticized for their focus on politics rather than literary merit, while Mary Shelley's anonymous review of Mérimée's 'Illyrian Poems — Feudal Scenes' is mentioned as '[o]ne of the freest from this their besetting sin'.[36] But this freedom suggests how she is at odds with the Radicals in her conception of how literature can encourage liberty and egalitarianism.

A later work exemplifying Mary Shelley's liberal authority is 'Euphrasia: A Tale of Greece' (1838), which reflects her attempts to make readers think about the importance of reform and the role that art plays in the advancement of liberalism. A story in a gift book intended for woman readers offers an unusual venue to explore the matters that so distress her about the Philosophic Radicals; it seems particularly fitting that the story was told to Shelley by Edward Trelawny.[37] 'Euphrasia' was published in *The Keepsake* accompanied by a plate entitled *Constantine and Euphrasia* drawn by Edward Corbould and engraved by H. Robinson.[38] Its narrative of the war for Greek independence against the Turks and the deaths of a sister and brother is told by an Englishman named Harry Valency to entertain a young woman and another companion when they are stranded in a coach during a snowstorm in Sussex and waiting for rescue. Jean de Palacio's comments are key to understanding how the work demonstrates that 'à la base de toute la pensée politique de Mary Shelley, on retrouve la notion de liberté' ['underlying all Mary Shelley's political thinking is the notion of liberty'].[39] In a reading of the story, Gregory O'Dea suggests that 'implicit in the fractured, externally motivated structure of her tale is an ironic and confrontational critique of the reader'.[40] The engraving of a man rescuing a woman from a burning harem suggests that '[s]uch a tale could figure, allegorically, the heroism of the Greek freedom fighters as they liberated their beloved land from the invading Turks'.[41] Packaged between silk bindings and accompanied by its engraved plate, the tale is likely consumed by a female in comfortable circumstances reading by a fire. O'Dea argues: 'These ironic narrative reductions of the engraving's romantic content suggest that the particular power of a lived moment is often diminished by the context in which it is recounted and received.'[42] The story then in O'Dea's estimation is 'an implicit critique of the reader, who is made to feel most powerfully the difference between the active life of romantic heroism and the sedate life of home and hearth'.[43]

I will depart from this reading to offer one that echoes the issues discussed in the 1838 journal entry and suggest that the story is meant to educate English readers, especially the female audience of the gift book, about ideals of liberty and liberalism, albeit in different terms from those held by Trelawny. If Shelley objects to the violent attack against her on the part of the Philosophic Radicals, it seems unlikely that in turn she would create a critique of her readers. Accordingly, if irony exists in her story, it is not so much directed to the general reader as to its teller, Harry Valency who naively views Greece as a place he can use for his own selfish pursuit of a misguided form of liberty. Rather than critique the reader as O'Dea suggests,

Shelley wishes to make people think through the means of Valency's motive to 'divert the mind of the daughter and to lighten the slow pace of the hour'.[44]

Accordingly, 'Euphrasia' is a meditation on the means to liberty and a critique of the use of violence over culture in the story it tells about a brother and sister who are 'the last of their race' (p. 301). Their experiences are mediated by Valency, who is young and reckless and longs 'to have the pages of his young life written over by deeds that would hereafter be memories, to which he could turn with delight' (p. 296). His impressionable innocence makes him resemble the figures whose travel accounts of Italy Shelley critiques in *The Westminster Review*. The means to achieve his desire for memorable experiences is to fight against the Turks in Greece. He joins a band of Greek soldiers, led by the charismatic Constantine, and fights alongside them as they ambush a large group of advancing Turks. The battle leaves Valency severely injured and the leader dying. And before his death, Constantine relates his story and that of his sister Euphrasia. Valency's declaration in the final paragraph that '[t]he death of Constantine is the true end of the tale' (p. 307) seems a bleak statement about the tragedy of war.

But related to its critique of violence is a portrayal of the ideal liberal subject as it is especially embodied in women. Euphrasia, Constantine's sister, who is abducted into a harem and shot while attempting to flee with her brother, might be viewed — as is suggested in the engraving — as an image of Greece enslaved. But Shelley's focus seems to be self-enslavement as much as that imposed by the Turks. Brother and sister are orphaned and educated by an uncle who is 'more familiar with the deeds of men who had glorified his country several thousand years before, than with any more modern names' (p. 301). Accordingly, they become products of his ideas, which are noble but disengaged from the realities of the world (which might be a kind of reference to the Philosophical Radicals?). Convinced that Greece will benefit from 'the progress made in the science of politics all over the civilized world' (p. 301), Constantine is educated by his uncle to be a warrior: 'Had he believed that Greece would have continued hopelessly enslaved; he had brought him up as a scholar and recluse' (p. 302). Euphrasia's education is, the narrator suggests, all the more 'singular' because women

> cannot handle a sword nor endure bodily labor for their country, but they could refine the manners, exalt the souls — impart honor, and truth, and wisdom, to their relatives and their children. Euphrasia therefore he made a scholar. By nature she was an enthusiast, and a poet. The study of the classic literature of her country corrected her taste and exalted her love of the beautiful. While a child she improvised passionate songs of liberty; and as she grew in years and loveliness, and her heart opened to tenderness, and she became aware of all the honor and happiness that a woman must derive from being held the friend of man, not his slave. (p. 302)

This description presents a summary of what Shelley most values in her essays for *The Westminster Review*: scholarship, poetry, liberty, improvisation and enthusiasm, virtue, and the partnership of men and women. In fact the story is an indictment of male irresponsibility and powerlessness over learning the lessons represented by Euphrasia, whose name derives from the Greek word for 'happy and satisfied'. She holds the means to happiness and liberty, and it is significant that the story is told to an English woman described as having a high spirit and who is 'afraid of nothing' (p. 295).

A story in a gift book intended for woman readers offers an unusual venue to explore the matters that divide the author from the Philosophic Radicals while making clear her adherence to liberal politics. In 'Euphrasia' Shelley offers an implied critique of Philosophic Radical views through a meditation on the means to liberty, and a critique of the use of violence over culture. Shelley wants to offer a description of the lessons that might be considered as well as suggest women readers' ability to absorb them. If for the male teller of the tale, '[t]he death of Constantine is the true end of my tale', Shelley's liberal perspective authorizes another end, which lies not with the expression of her own opinions, but with what she might inspire in the minds of her readers.

Mary Shelley's practice of a form of literary authority that remains committed to principles of liberty and equality are exemplified by her essays for the *Westminster Review* and her tale of Greece. Jean de Palacio's valuable contribution to an understanding of Mary Shelley's social and political thought illuminates a commitment to these values while clearly recognizing the shaping force of her solitary struggle as the widow of Percy Shelley. She expresses her preference for what de Palacio calls occasions to 'affirmer discrètement ses idées libérales' ['affirm with discretion her liberal ideas'][45] while resisting what others would make of her. Leigh Hunt's 1837 poem 'The Blue-Stocking Revels' captures the complexities of her position:

> And Shelley, four-fam'd, — for her parents, her lord,
> And the poor lone impossible monster abhorr'd.
> So sleek and so smiling she came, people stared,
> To think such fair clay should so darkly have dared.[46]

De Palacio's reading of her continued allegiance to liberal politics is as a figure in her own right and not merely as a daughter of and wife of others, as well as suggesting that her daring as an author is not a product of the dark, but one that seeks to illuminate.

Notes to Chapter 5

1. All translations are by the editor, unless otherwise stated.
2. De Palacio, *Mary Shelley dans son œuvre*, pp. 185–86.
3. Edward B. Aveling and Eleanor Marx Aveling, *Shelley's Socialism* (London: Journeyman Press, 1975), p. 16.
4. For a reading of her exploration of issues of rights and political philosophy in *Frankenstein*, which forms the basis for beliefs held throughout her life, see Eileen Hunt Botting, *Mary Shelley and the Rights of the Child* (Philadelphia: University of Pennsylvania Press, 2018).
5. Jonathan Gross, 'Byron and *The Liberal*: Periodical as Political Posture', *Philological Quarterly*, 72 (1993), 471–72.
6. The *OED*, which gives the first citation to Robert Southey (writing in the *Quarterly Review* in 1816), also offers a contextual definition: 'Early in the 19th c. the n. occurs chiefly as applied by opponents to the advanced section of the Whig party: sometimes in Sp. or Fr. form, app. with the intention of suggesting that the principles of those politicians were un-English, or

akin to those of the revolutionaries of the Continent. As, however, the adj. was already English in a laudatory sense, the advocates of reform were not reluctant to adopt the foreign term as descriptive of themselves' (*OED Online* <https://www.oed.com> [accessed 30 March 2020]). The citation is from Southey in 'Art. I. La Roche Jaquelein — *La Vèndée*', *Quarterly Review*, 15 (1816), 1–69 (p. 69): 'These are the personages for whose sake the continuance of the Alien Bill has been opposed by the British *Liberales*.'
7. 'Preface', *The Monthly Magazine*, 1 (1796), iii–iv (p. iii).
8. Leigh Hunt, Lord Byron, and Percy Bysshe Shelley, *The Liberal: Verse and Prose from the South*, 2 vols (London: Hunt, 1822–23), I, p. vii.
9. The journal was founded in 1823. Its contributors included such figures as Sir William Molesworth (the cousin of Edward Trelawny), John Arthur Roebuck, Joseph Hume, George Grote, and Charles Buller.
10. See Lisa Vargo, 'Writing for *The Liberal*', in *Mary Shelley: Her Circle and her Contemporaries*, ed. by Mekler and Morrison, pp. 131–49, and 'The Aikins and the Godwins: Notions of Conflict and Stoicism in Anna Barbauld and Mary Shelley', *Romanticism*, 11.1 (2005), 84–98.
11. Shelley, *Frankenstein*, in *The Novels and Selected Works of Mary Shelley*, I, 175.
12. *The Novels and Selected Works of Mary Shelley*, II, 200.
13. *MWS Journals*, p. 553.
14. Ibid.
15. Ibid.
16. William St Clair, *Trelawny: The Incurable Romancer* (London: Murray, 1977), p. 159; Sunstein, *Mary Shelley: Romance and Reality* (1989), p. 341.
17. Harriet Grote, *Philosophical Radicals of 1832: Comprising the Life of Sir William Molesworth, and Some Incidents Connected with the Reform Movement from 1832 to 1842* (London: Savill and Edwards, 1866), p. 31.
18. Joseph Hamburger, *Intellectuals in Politics: John Stuart Mill and the Philosophic Radicals* (New Haven: Yale University Press, 1965). They include Aubrey Beauclerk, the MP for East Surrey 1832–37 and radical reformer, and Mr and Mrs Daniel Gaskell (he was the first MP from Wakefield near Manchester) who were described by Mary Shelley in an 1835 letter to Maria Gisborne as 'Liberals' who 'knew your friend Bentham & are allied to all the ultra Radical party' (*MWS Letters*, II, 259). Thomas Love Peacock was connected with Bentham and the Mills through his work at the East India Company; they dined together weekly. Likewise, Edward Bulwer was an admirer of Bentham and stood for parliament encouraged by William Godwin and John Bowring; in 1836 he was recruited by John Stuart Mill to write for the *Review* as well as support the Radical party (Hamburger, p. 221). However, Bulwer was not interested and in 1840 called them 'a small, conceited, and headstrong party' as well as 'the sect of the Impracticables' (Hamburger, p. 242).
19. It is unlikely that feminism and Chartism are the reference as the Chartists did not see women's rights as part of their cause. See Barbara Taylor, *Eve and the New Jerusalem* (London: Virago, 1983); Jutta Schwarzkopf, *Women in the Chartist Movement* (New York: St. Martin's Press, 1991), especially pp. 220–46.
20. St Clair, *Trelawny*, p. 159.
21. *MWS Journals*, p. 554.
22. Ibid., pp. 553–54.
23. Sunstein, *Mary Shelley: Romance and Reality*, p. 335; *MWS Letters*, II, 280–81.
24. *MWS Letters*, II, 70.
25. Mary Shelley, 'The English in Italy', *Westminster Review*, 6 (October 1826), 325–41; 'Illyrian Poems — Feudal Scenes', *Westminster Review*, 10 (January 1829), 71–81; 'Modern Italy', *Westminster Review*, 11 (July 1829), 127–40; 'Loves of the Poets', *Westminster Review*, 11 (October 1829), 472–77; '1572 Chronique du temps de Charles IX', *Westminster Review*, 13 (October 1830), 495–502; 'Journal of a Tour in Italy, and also in a Part of France and Switzerland. From October 1828, to September 1829', *Westminster Review*, 14 (January 1831), 174–80; and 'The Bravo', *Westminster Review*, 16 (January 1832), 180–92. For the most recent identification of a review see Nora Crook, 'Counting the Carbonari'.

26. *The Novels and Selected Works of Mary Shelley*, II, 152, 157–59.
27. Ibid., II, 155.
28. Ibid., II, 180.
29. Ibid., II, 194.
30. *MWS Letters*, II, 85.
31. Crook, 'Counting the Carbonari', p. 49.
32. Sunstein, *Mary Shelley: Romance and Reality*, p. 315.
33. John Stuart Mill, *Autobiography*, 3rd edn (London: Longmans, 1874), pp. 146–55.
34. G. L. Nesbitt, *Benthamite Reviewing* (New York: Columbia University Press, 1934), p. 34.
35. '*The Westminster Review*. No. XIX. January 1929 [...]', *The Edinburgh Literary Review; or, Weekly Register of Criticism and Belles Lettres*, 21 January 1829, pp. 205–06 (p. 205). Thanks to Nora Crook for directing me to this reference.
36. Ibid.
37. St Clair, *Trelawny*, pp. 136–37.
38. 'Euphrasia: A Tale of Greece', in Mary Shelley, *Collected Tales and Stories*, ed. by Charles Robinson (Baltimore, MD: Johns Hopkins University Press, 1976), p. 394. Hereafter 'Euphrasia'.
39. De Palacio, *Mary Shelley dans son œuvre*, p. 209.
40. Gregory O'Dea, '"Perhaps a tale you'll make it": Mary Shelley's Tales for *The Keepsake*', in *Iconoclastic Departures: Mary Shelley after Frankenstein*, ed. by Syndy M. Conger and others (Madison, NJ: Fairleigh Dickinson University Press, 1997), p. 75.
41. Ibid.
42. Ibid., p. 76.
43. Ibid., p. 77.
44. 'Euphrasia', p. 296. Further references are given in the main text.
45. De Palacio, *Mary Shelley dans son œuvre*, p. 186.
46. Leigh Hunt, *The Poetical Works of Leigh Hunt*, ed. by Thornton Hunt (London: Routledge, Warne, & Routledge, 1860), p. 212. Eileen Hunt Botting offers a reminder that the creature was associated throughout the nineteenth century with fears of revolt by the working classes (*Mary Shelley and the Rights of the Child*, p. 3).

CHAPTER 6

'Write my story and translate': Mary Shelley's *rambles* in the Italian Language, Literature, and Country

Maria Parrino

In her introduction to *European Gothic*, Avril Horner maintains that we need to challenge the 'tyranny of the Anglo-American narratives of the Gothic' and show the 'importance of translation and European writing in the development of the Gothic novel'.[1] Two questions emerge from such a consideration. First one must ask, whether the idea of Europe is the 'natural' result of geographical boundaries or the outcome of geopolitical and economic processes, a construction 'in theory', as Roberto Dainotto writes.[2] The second question concerns the issue of translation at large, both in terms of language and of migration of motives, themes, and imagery. David Punter refers to the 'uncanny of translation', a term related to the 'elsewhere', the otherness of experience, and underlines that alongside the benefit of sharing the experience of literatures in English from other parts of the world, 'there also lies a profound sense of the *unheimlich*, of all that is *not* told in English, of all that might be understood if only language were not a barrier as well as a facilitator.'[3]

This article intends to examine the issues of Anglo-centredness, foreign languages, and translations in Mary Shelley, the author of *Frankenstein*, unarguably one of the most translated novels in world literature. By analysing Mary Shelley's readings of Italian literature, her knowledge of the language, and her personal 'rambles' in Italy, this study aims to trace contaminations between her life and her writings. How was Mary Shelley's writing affected by her interpretations and her translations of Italian texts? Did she ever reflect on the issue of translation? How did she who made the most famous Gothic creature a multilingual traveller narrate her own migration into foreign countries and foreign languages?

Fifty years after Jean de Palacio's groundbreaking study, the importance of Mary Shelley's relation with Italy emerges once again as central to the understanding of the writer at large. As de Palacio writes in the first chapter of *Mary Shelley dans son œuvre*, entitled 'L'italianisme': 'cette compétence, et un ardent amour pour la langue italienne, constituent des traits distinctifs de la culture de Mary Shelley' ['This competence and ardent love for the Italian language are among the distinctive features of Mary Shelley's culture.'].[4]

In my approach to Mary Shelley's life story, I look at her relationship with foreign languages as a Gothic trope for otherness and multiple identities. After all, the woman who wrote *Frankenstein* must have had an interest in foreign languages if a number of characters in that novel are multilingual: Victor is French and speaks German and English; the Creature learns French and speaks English to Walton; Elizabeth is Italian and speaks French, Safie is Turkish and learns French. The author of *Frankenstein* must also have been aware of the importance of translations. As the Creature reminds us in one episode, the books he finds in the woods — which will be fundamental for his education — were 'luckily' written 'in the language, the elements of which I had acquired at the cottage',[5] which means that he read *Paradise Lost*, Plutarch's *Lives*, and the *Sorrows of Young Werther* in French translation.

Mary Shelley showed a remarkable interest in foreign languages at an early age. She was 11 years old when in 1808 she wrote the adapted version of the song 'Mounseer Nongtongpaw; or, The Discoveries of John Bull on a Trip to Paris', the humorous story of an Englishman who visits Paris and is unable to understand French. His questions in English concerning the ownership of everything he sees — houses, palaces, servants, pretty girls — all receive the same answer: 'Monsieur, je vous n'entends pas' ['Monsieur, I don't understand you'], which John Bull takes to be the name of a wealthy aristocrat, Mounseer Nongtongpaw. Although there are doubts whether this text was authentically produced by Mary Shelley, we know that, encouraged by her father William Godwin, she wrote a thirty-nine-quatrain expansion of Charles Dibdin's five-stanza song, and that her version became so popular that it was reissued in 1830 and illustrated by Robert Cruikshank. Whether Mary Shelley wrote a part or the whole text, she certainly showed an early pleasure in making fun of English people's ignorance of foreign languages.[6]

Mary's interest in foreign languages over the years was accompanied by a notable attention to the various aspects of languages. Unlike Victor who confesses in *Frankenstein* that he is not attracted by the 'structure of languages', Mary studied the lexicon, the morphology, the syntax, and the pronunciation, and, like Henry Clerval, wished to make herself 'complete master of the [...] languages'.[7] Thus, whereas Clerval 'turn[ed] his eyes toward East',[8] Mary directed her gaze toward Europe. Mary Shelley studied Latin, Greek, Spanish, French, and Italian, languages she first familiarized with by reading texts in the original version.[9] Among the European languages, Mary Shelley's main focus was on the Italian language, an interest which was manifested before she actually lived in Italy.[10] As early as 1815, in a letter to her friend Thomas Jefferson Hogg, she asked 'you are to teach me Italian'.[11] In the same year, she started to listen to her husband Percy and her stepsister Claire Clairmont read Italian aloud. Eventually she put herself at work on the Italian language in 1816 in Geneva and she read Latin and Italian with Percy, as she wrote to her half-sister Fanny Imlay.[12] In 1817 she told Leigh Hunt: 'you must either learn [French] or I Italian that we may not always shock one another with our vernacular tongue.'[13] Familiarity with the language certainly grew as Mary took to reading librettos and to attending Italian operas, an activity regularly performed by many middle-class English people, some of whom developed the ability of speaking what Nora Crook calls an 'operatic Italian'.[14] However, Mary's interest for the Italian language turned into a serious commitment as soon as it became certain in 1818 that she and Percy would move to Italy.

6.1. Italian Social Life, Writing, and Reading

In Italy, not only did Mary take Italian exercises and lessons under the supervision of an 'Italian Master', and regularly attend opera houses, but she also improved her language skills mainly because of the Italian social life she chose to participate in, mingling with natives from different social classes.[15] In Pisa, Mary befriended Francesco Pacchiani, a clergyman and professor at the university. In 1820, he introduced her to the actor Tommaso Sgricci, of whom she became particularly fond.[16] As she wrote in Italian, in a letter to Leigh Hunt on 3 December 1820, Sgricci was '[u]n'Improvisatore — un'uomo di gran talento — e molto forte nel Greco, e con un genio poetico incomparabile' ['an Improvvisatore — a man of great talent — and very strong in Greek, with an incomparable poetic genius'].[17] Pacchiani also introduced the Shelleys to Teresa Emilia Viviani, the woman Percy confessed was 'the only Italian for whom [he] ever felt any interest'.[18] Indeed, the ensuing love story between Percy and Emilia was satirized in Mary Shelley's shorter fiction *The Bride of Modern Italy* (1824), the story of an ill-fated young woman (Clorinda Saviani) who hopes she will be saved by her English lover.[19]

Mary Shelley was proud of her command of the Italian language and pleased to be able to participate actively in conversations and debates. In a note in her diary, Claire Clairmont contrasted the ease with which Mary Shelley and herself socialized with the natives and the awkwardness of the English people abroad who did not speak the language:

> In the Evening go to the Conversazione of the Signora Marianna Dionigi where there is a Cardinal and many unfortunate Englishmen who after having crossed their legs and said nothing the whole Evening, rose up at once, made their bows and filed off.[20]

Besides upper- and middle-class Italians, Mary Shelley had daily contacts with native servants. As she explained years later, practicing the language with Tuscan peasants and servants was useful to form one's speech without running the 'risk of falling into errors or vulgarisms'.[21] Confident in her language skills, she used the colloquial expressions she learned from her maid in a letter dated 13 November 1819 to her English friend Maria Gisborne:

> We have had for the last fifteen days a <u>tempo patetico</u> as Maria calls it — true enough, it is always crying, perhaps some little misfortune has happened <u>la su</u>, and that <u>il figlio</u> is <u>infreddato</u>, or the <u>padre</u> got a stroke of the palsy, and all the pretty angels and cherubs are weeping.[22]

In this description of bad weather, where the holy father is affected by palsy, the son is rather prosaically depicted as catching a cold, and the angels are weeping, the text shows the pleasure of a hybridization of the English language, a smooth merging of Italian words into the English narrative.

Thus, after a few years in Italy, Mary fulfilled her ambition and was able not only to speak but also to write in Italian. Along the years, she achieved an advanced level of knowledge as emerges in the twenty-one letters in Italian she wrote both to her Italian and English friends.[23] Moreover, familiarity with the Italian language and literature became explicit in her literary writings which frequently included foreign words, short sentences, exclamations, and popular expressions. In her novel *Valperga* (1823), the protagonist, Euthanasia, who is about to leave Tuscany, speaks in her 'beautiful Italian', a language 'whose soft accents and expressive phrases [...] so much transcended all other European languages'.[24] The text even reports a whole sentence in Italian: '*E' Bellissimo*, replied her guide, *ma figuratevi, Madonna, se è tanto bello sul rovescio, cosa mai sarà al dritto*'.[25] The sentence is not translated and in a footnote the reader is told that the author 'could not refrain from recording in their original language the words of a Florentine peasant', which, I believe, is a way of excluding the English reader who does not understand Italian from a full appreciation of the text.[26] Such literary device raises two issues: first, the question of the untranslatability of a foreign language, the inevitable loss that any attempt to transport one language into another causes; second, the question of the foreign language as an alterity which cannot be domesticated. I contend that Mary Shelley's untranslated Italian words in her text remind the English reader of the otherness of the foreign language, that something is told but *not* in English. Thus, instead of taming the foreign language, Mary Shelley incorporated it, made space in her Englishness and added her Italianness to her identity. She was a proud member of the 'Anglo-Italian', a new 'race' which, as she underlined in her article for the *Westminster Review*, 'The English in Italy' (1826), was different from the 'mere traveller, or true John Bull', the character she had made fun of as a child. For Mary Shelley, an 'Anglo-Italian' was one who understood Italian, and thus avoided the risk of getting involved in the 'ludicrous mishaps which occur to those who believe that a little Anglo-French is enough to communicate with the natives of Italy'.[27]

Mary Shelley was an avid reader of Italian authors, from Dante, Ludovico Ariosto, and Torquato Tasso to contemporary writers such as Vittorio Alfieri, Ugo Foscolo, Vincenzo Monti, Carlo Gozzi, and Alessandro Manzoni.[28] Her genuine interest in Italian literature combined with her attention to the language even led her to read Italian translations from English texts. As she recorded in her journal, she read Richardson's *Pamela* in Italian translation, following it with *Clarissa*.[29] If such a practice was most likely common among language learners, it tells us something about crossing language borders, and something of the *unheimlich*: a native English speaker deliberately reading in translation a text originally written in English occupies the space of liminality, the border between language familiarity and unfamiliarity. Furthermore, I believe, it challenges the issue of authorship by hiding the originator and foregrounding the translator.

6.2. Translating, Interpreting, and Becoming Anglo-Italian

Mary Shelley started translating at an early age. The entry for 12 August 1816 in her diary reads:

> Write my story and translate. Shelley goes to the town, and afterwards goes out in the boat with Lord B. — after dinner I go out a little in the boat, and then Shelley goes up to Diodati. — I translate in the evening and read *Le Vieux de la Montagne*. Shelley, in coming down, is attacked by a dog, which delays him; we send up for him, and Lord B. comes down; in the meantime, Shelley returns.[30]

Writing, reading, and translating are activities which Mary carried out at the same time in her daily routine. The 'story' mentioned in this journal entry is her first novel, *Frankenstein*, the writing of which was thus accompanied by translating and reading in a foreign language.[31] Not surprisingly, for Mary Shelley, whose mother was a professional translator and father a committed student of foreign languages, multilingualism marked her literary experiences, the result being a systematic intersection of languages, motives, and themes.[32]

Reading and translating had a direct effect on Mary Shelley's writings. In 1818, Percy Shelley in a letter from Padua encouraged Mary to 'be prepared to bring at least some of *Mirra* translated'.[33] The text Percy refers to is Vittorio Alfieri's play written in 1785, a tragedy of the incestuous love between a father and his daughter which became the source of Mary Shelley's *Mathilda* (1819).[34] Among the contemporary Italian writers who Mary Shelley particularly appreciated was Alessandro Manzoni, whose novel *I Promessi Sposi* (*The Betrothed Lovers*) she recommended to friends and promoted to English publishers. In a letter dated 20 June 1828 to Jane Williams, she suggested:

> Above all, dear, get the Promessi Sposi — at first you may lag a little, but as you get on the truth and perfect Italianism of the manners and descriptions — the beautiful language, which differs from all other Italian prose — being really the Tusca[n] of the day that he writes and not a bad imitation of the [ ] trecentisti — the passion and even sublimity of parts rendered it to me a most delightful book.[35]

The quotation shows Mary's confidence as a critic, especially as regards language issues, and knowledge of the contemporary Italian debate on the 'questione della lingua', a discussion on which Italian regional form should be preferred as a national language.[36] Mary was so confident of her language skills, that in 1828 she offered to translate Manzoni's novel and in a letter dated 19 February 1828 she reassured the publisher, John Murray, who had questioned whether she understood standard and non-standard Italian, thus: 'I lived nearly six years in Italy and its language is perfectly familiar to me — and I should not hesitate to undertake a work that required an intimate acquaintance with it.'[37] Yet, to Mary's disappointment,[38] the translation was not assigned, probably because the Italian novel had already been translated in English and published in 1828.[39] Mary Shelley's choice of Manzoni's novel is revealing, for a number of reasons. As de Palacio underlines, it shows her perceptiveness in understanding the evolving canon of Italian literature.[40] Moreover, interest in the story (which had earned a good reputation in the English literary world),[41] may have been aroused by its Gothic traits: the story of a kidnapped young girl, the cruelties of villains, and the plague spreading in the city of Milan.[42]

Mary Shelley claimed the right to translate Manzoni's novel because Italian was familiar to her, and she unquestionably had an advanced knowledge of the language. Her particular fascination of the Italian spoken language enabled her not only to understand the standard but also to detect its regional features. Particularly pleased with the variation of the Italian spoken in Tuscany, in a letter dated 27 June 1825 to Leigh Hunt, who was about to leave Italy and return to England, she wrote: 'We'll talk Tuscan, Hunt, and I shall get more sick than ever for Valle che de' miei lamenti son pieni.'[43] Among the other regional variations of the Italian language, Mary Shelley privileged the Venetian, which she regretted not understanding well, and the Romanesque. Mary Shelley wrote that she was sorry she knew nothing of the Venetian dialect, and was aware that 'Dante himself hesitated whether to write his "Divina Commedia" in Latin or Venetian, till fortunately he became aware that the talk of the common people of Tuscany possessed all the elements of expression'.[44]

Mary Shelley's bicultural identity and conscious manipulation of Anglo-Italianness is perhaps best illustrated by an episode mentioned in a letter to John Howard Payne written on 11 June 1826. Years after she had returned to England, one night at the Opera House[45] with her friend Jane Williams she pretended she was Italian and made fun of a group of English operagoers struggling with the language:

> We spoke Italian all the time. [...] One old lady beside me with her glass tried to follow the English of the Italian in her book. I put her right as far as I could in dumb show. But when she obstinately turned over the pages of the 2^(nd) act of the 'Crociato' in search of the words of Nina I saw no hope of setting her right except by speaking and that was not in the bond — I could understand a little English but not speak a word. The personage before me offered me his book — Apparement, Madame vous être etrangère, voulez-vous vous profitez de mon livre? In my character of Italian I accepted his civility, as an English person I could not.[46]

In this episode, being Anglo-Italian gave Mary an advantage and a mission: since she was familiar with the language she was able to instruct the fellow spectators. She played the educational role of Italianizing her 'un-Italianized English countrymen'[47] initiating them into the delights of Italian culture.

Years later, when travelling back to Italy, she mentioned the pleasure of speaking Italian, which put her at ease when 'inquiring' and 'arranging' her daily life. As she described in her *Rambles*, to her travel companions who did not expect her to be able to speak Italian after so many years, Mary Shelley replied:

> I certainly did speak Italian. It had been strange if I did not; not that I could boast of any extraordinary facility of conversation or elegance of diction, but mine was a peculiarly useful Italian; for having lived long in the country, all its household terms were familiar to me; and I remember the time when it was more natural to me to speak to common people in that language than in my own.[48]

Understandably, after twenty years away from the country, Mary Shelley had become less confident of her language skills and admitted she could no longer consider herself a fluent speaker. However, the 'intimate' relationship with the language remained and Mary Shelley was always at ease with Italy. It might be significant that she chose to end the *Rambles* not by describing her return to England but by giving an account of her stay at the hotel in Sorrento, her new house which she called 'home'.[49]

In her study on *Frankenstein*, Maureen McLane discusses the terms 'nativity' and 'natality', and explains that since the Creature has no place he belongs to — no native land — he constantly migrates to places.[50] Similarly, Mary Shelley the 'traveller' questioned the idea of belonging to *one* place and was more comfortable instead in a hyphenated identity, as the self-appointed title 'Anglo-Italian' underlines. As Maria Schoina notes, she 'identified with routes rather than roots'.[51]

Mary Shelley's interest in Italian literature and language was more than an intellectual attitude, starting at a young age and cultivated throughout her whole life. As de Palacio underlines, she had a 'vocation italienne' ['Italian vocation'], a genuine passion which led her to travel to the land and travel in translation, an empowerment which gave the chance to the Englishwoman in Italy to make Italian her second language, its literature the source of inspiration, and the peninsula her country.[52]

Notes to Chapter 6

1. *European Gothic: A Spirited Exchange, 1760–1960*, ed. by Avril Horner (Manchester: Manchester University Press 2002), p. 1.
2. Roberto Dainotto, *Europe (in Theory)* (Durham: Duke University Press, 2007).
3. David Punter, 'The Uncanny', in *The Routledge Companion to Gothic*, ed. by Catherine Spooner and Emma McEvoy (London: Routledge, 2007), pp. 129–36 (p. 134).
4. Jean de Palacio, *Mary Shelley dans son œuvre*, p. 26.
5. Mary Shelley, *Frankenstein*, in *The Novels and Selected Works of Mary Shelley*, I, 95. Quoted as *Frankenstein*.
6. See Jeanne Moskal, 'Appendix 2: *Monsieur Nongtongpaw*: Verses Attributed to Mary Shelley', in *The Novels and Selected Works of Mary Shelley*, VIII; see also Emily W. Sunstein, 'A William Godwin Letter, and Young Mary Godwin's Part in *Mounseer Nongtongpaw*', in *Keats-Shelley Journal*, 45 (1996), 19–22.
7. Shelley, *Frankenstein*, pp. 194, 203.
8. Ibid.
9. This way of learning languages, which privileged translations to grammar, was a Lockean method. See Lia Guerra, 'Medioevo romantico: Mary Shelley e l'Italia', in *Medioevi Moderni: Modernità del Medioevo*, ed. by Marina Buzzoni, Maria Grazia Cammarota, and Marusca Francini (Venice: Edizioni Cà Foscari, 2013), pp. 171–84 (p. 178).
10. See Timothy Webb, 'Mia Bella Italia: Mary Shelley's Italies', *Journal of Anglo-Italian Studies*, 12 (2013), 63–82. See also Cinzia Mastrascusa, 'Italiano e Inglesi del XIX secolo: Gli scritti di Mary Shelley' (unpublished doctoral thesis, University of Rome, 2002).
11. *MWS Letters*, I, 9. Thomas Jefferson Hogg was well read in Greek, German, French, Italian, and Spanish.
12. *MWS Letters*, I, 18.
13. *MWS Letters*, I, 32.
14. Nora Crook, 'General Editor's Introduction', in *Mary Shelley's 'Literary Lives' and Other Writings*, I, xv.

15. *MWS Journals*, p. 207, pp. 210–11.
16. When he met the Shelleys, Sgricci had been an improviser for four years and had appeared in many major Italian cities. His ability to improvise poems, tragic scenes, and whole tragedies excited both Shelleys. See Elisabetta Marino, *Mary Shelley e l'Italia: Il viaggio, il Risorgimento, la questione femminile* (Florence: Le Lettere, 2011), p. 54.
17. *MWS Letters*, I, 163 (the translation is included in the edition).
18. *Peacock's Memoirs of Shelley with Shelley's Letters to Peacock*, ed. by Herbert Francis Brett Brett-Smith (London: Frowde, 1909), p. 209.
19. Mary Shelley wrote more than twenty-four short stories, seven of which have an Italian subject. Six of her seven novels are set in Italy. See *The Other Mary Shelley*, ed. by Fisch and others, p. 6.
20. Clairmont, *The Journals*, ed. by K. and M. Stoking, p. 103.
21. Mary Shelley, 'Monti', in *Lives of the Most Eminent Literary and Scientific Men*, in *Cabinet Cyclopædia of Biography*, ed. by Lardner, II, 337.
22. *MWS Letters*, I, 112.
23. Most of Mary Shelley's letters in Italy were addressed to Teresa Guiccioli, Byron's lover while he was living in Ravenna (Italy).
24. Mary Shelley, *Valperga*, ed. by Tilottama Rajan (Peterborough, Ontario: Broadview, 1998), p. 435.
25. Shelley, *Valperga*, p. 435.
26. Ibid. Of course, there are different ways in which one may interpret Mary Shelley's choice to use foreign language words without translation: it may be a way of showing her knowledge of the Italian language, or even assume that the English reader is able to understand Italian.
27. Shelley, 'The English in Italy', in *The Novels and Selected Works of Mary Shelley*, II, 149.
28. In 1819, Mary Shelley read and translated Dante's *Purgatorio* with Percy. See 'The Shelleys Reading List', in *MWS Journals*, pp. 631–84. See also de Palacio's detailed study on the influence of Dante in Mary Shelley's writings in his *Mary Shelley dans son œuvre*, pp. 36–66.
29. Roderick Cavaliero, *Italia Romantica: English Romantics and Italian Freedom* (London: Tauris, 2007), p. 40; and *The Novels and Selected Works of Mary Shelley*, II, 2. Mary had read Samuel Richardson's *Pamela* and *Clarissa* in English in 1814. She reread *Clarissa* in English one year later. See Mary Shelley's *Journals* as quoted in Betty T. Bennett, 'Mary Shelley's Letters: The Public/Private Self', in *The Cambridge Companion to Mary Shelley*, ed. by Esther Schor (Cambridge: Cambridge University Press, 2003), pp. 211–25 (p. 224).
30. *MWS Journals*, p. 124
31. *Le Vieux de la Montagne* (1799) is an oriental story translated from the Arabic by the French philosopher Delisle De Sales.
32. Mary Wollstonecraft translated from the French and the German. She was also asked to translate from the Italian. See Claire Tomalin, *The Life and Death of Mary Wollstonecraft* (London: Penguin, 1985), p. 105. William Godwin and Mary Shelley's stepmother, Mary Jane Clairmont Godwin, translated from the French. See Sunstein, *Mary Shelley: Romance and Reality*, p. 31; Lyndall Gordon, *Vindication: A Life of Mary Wollstonecraft* (New York: Harper Collins, 2005), pp. 134–35; de Palacio, *Mary Shelley dans son œuvre*, p. 24.
33. *PBS Letters*, II, 39. Alfieri's *Mirra* was translated into English by Charles Lloyd in 1815.
34. Alfieri's tragedy of incestuous love was based on the story of Myrra and Cinyras in Ovid's *Metamorphoses*. Yet in his study, de Palacio maintains that in *Mathilda* the influence of Mary Shelley's reading of Dante is particularly strong (*Mary Shelley dans son œuvre*, p. 39).
35. *MWS Letters*, II, 48.
36. Alessandro Manzoni discussed the issue of '[l]a questione della lingua' later in 1868 in his essay 'Dell'unità della lingua'.
37. *MWS Letters*, II, 27.
38. Mary Shelley to John Murray, 20 August 1828 (*MWS Letters*, II, 56).
39. Manzoni's novel, translated by Charles Swan, was published in 1828 in English by an Italian publishing house in Pisa, which omitted two chapters. See Alice Crosta, *Alessandro Manzoni nei Paesi Anglosassoni* (Bern: Lang, 2014).
40. De Palacio, *Mary Shelley dans son œuvre*, pp. 499–534.

41. In 1835 Edward Bulwer-Lytton dedicated his work *Rienzi: The Last of the Roman Tribunes* to Manzoni, the 'Genius of the place'. Mary added two other reviews of Manzoni's works, one in her 'Modern Italian Romances', which appeared in *The Monthly Chronicle*, 2 (November–December 1838), and another in her *Rambles in Germany and Italy*, II, 195–200 (Letter XVI, Part III). Hereafter *Rambles*.
42. Unquestionably, Manzoni's novel is eligible to be placed within the canon of European Gothic literature. On Mary Shelley's interest in Gothic literature see de Palacio's chapter 'Le courant "gothique"', in *Mary Shelley dans son œuvre*, pp. 91–138.
43. *MWS Letters*, I, 492. The quotation ('vales that are filled with my laments') ends with an embedded quote from a Petrarchan sonnet (*Canzoniere*, CCCI).
44. *MWS Letters*, I, 244. On the other hand, Mary Shelley thought that the jargon of the Genovese was 'disgusting', an opinion which was understandably influenced by her feelings towards the region tragically connected with the death of her husband. On this issue, see Webb, 'Mia Bella Italia'.
45. See de Palacio, *Mary Shelley dans son œuvre*, p. 308, n. 19; Garrett, *The Palgrave Literary Dictionary of Mary Wollstonecraft Shelley*, p. 304.
46. *MWS Letters*, I, 519.
47. Shelley, 'The English in Italy', in *The Novels and Selected Works of Mary Shelley*, II, 149.
48. Shelley, *Rambles*, I, 56.
49. *Rambles* is not only a travelogue but also a type in the literary genre of writings from Italy. In her texts, Mary Shelley undermined the notion of separate spheres by including in her accounts of Italy topics that were deemed 'unfeminine', i.e. the history and politics of the country visited. See Marino, *Mary Shelley e l'Italia*, p. 60.
50. Maureen McLane, *Romanticism and the Human Sciences: Poetry, Population and the Discourse of the Species* (Cambridge: Cambridge University Press, 2000), p. 93.
51. Schoina, *Romantic Anglo-Italians*, p. 72.
52. De Palacio, *Mary Shelley dans son œuvre*, pp. 23, 78.

CHAPTER 7

Mary Shelley's Italian Scenes

Anna Mercer

I went to Italy young, and visited with ardent curiosity and delight
all of great and glorious which that country contains.

MARY SHELLEY, 'Recollections of Italy'[1]

On 30 March 1818, Mary Wollstonecraft Shelley arrived in Italy with her husband Percy Bysshe Shelley on their second expedition to the continent.[2] This country was to become their home — a 'Paradise of exiles' (l. 57) as expressed in Percy Shelley's poem 'Julian and Maddalo'.[3] It was where the couple spent, as described by Michael Rossington, Percy Shelley's 'last four, richly productive years' prior to the poet's death aged just 29 in 1822.[4] Jane Stabler has explained that after these four years, 'Mary Shelley felt that England was no longer home. Political sympathies in Mary's case, rather than duration of absence from the homeland, shaped her self-designation as an exile.'[5] The Shelleys' relationship(s) with Italian landscapes, architecture, art, and history is far-reaching and complex. Mary Shelley's later travel writing — *Rambles in Germany and Italy* (1844) and her notes to Percy's *Poetical Works* (1839) — recorded her journeys and residences in that 'Beloved Country', Italy.[6] It is the focus of this essay to discuss Mary Shelley's use of Italy as a setting for her fiction, and in relation to her profound understanding of her husband's verse.

I will describe how the Shelleys' experiences of the country during the period 1818–22 are reflected in Mary Shelley's creative writings, and consider her role as a collaborator with Percy on his works composed during that period. Alan Weinberg argued in 1991 that 'the fact that [Percy Shelley's] mature poems were all written and, as it were, nurtured in Italy, is not given sufficient emphasis'.[7] Similarly, there is a rich potential for the Italian scenes in her fiction to show Mary Shelley arguably at her most innovative and versatile; they provide the framework for romance, bathos, and sociological comment enacted through the metaphors of her characters' lives. In my work I pay significant attention to the Shelleys' literary relationship, and on the effect the 'Enchantress' Italy had on their creativity.[8]

On arrival at Milan in 1818, Mary Shelley was delighted. Compared to France, she found everything improved; as Miranda Seymour explains, she 'had not sounded so happy since the visit to Geneva' — the famous summer of 1816 which produced the beginnings of her novel *Frankenstein* (1818).[9] No wonder Italy was to provide her with ample inspiration for her writing. In a letter to her friends Leigh and Marianne Hunt, Mary Shelley explains her first experience of the country:

> We have at length arrived in Italy. After winding for several days through vallies [sic] & crossing mountains and passing Cenis we have arrived in this land of blue skies & pleasant fields. [...] the first evening that we arrived in Italy every thing appeared changed. [...] Italy appears a far more civilised place than France [...]. The inns are infinitely better and the bread which is uneatable in France is here the finest and whitest in the world. There is a disconsolate air of discomfort in France that is quite wretched. In Italy we breathe a different air and every thing is pleasant around us.[10]

This uplift in her spirits and her notable change of attitude is also evident in Mary's journals as she crosses the Italian border. France is 'uninteresting', the countryside 'pleasant' but not beguiling.[11] Italy is 'cultivated', and their first day in that land in the town of Susa presents them with a 'pretty Italian woman' who shows them the 'triumphal arch in honour of Augustus'.[12] Mary Shelley muses that it would 'have pleased Hunt', and inserts the word 'Italy' underneath, a definitive way of marking a new part of her life in the journal.[13] The Shelleys read Italian works (Pietro Antonio Serassi's *Vita del Tasso* and an Italian translation of Samuel Richardson's *Pamela*) and visit the opera during their stay at Milan. By the time of their travels to Como, Mary Shelley declares: 'nothing can be more divine than the shores of this lovely lake.'[14] It was while in Italy that, as Jean de Palacio has discussed, Mary Shelley embarked on her independent study of Latin, demonstrating her admirable skill and dedication to the language; the Shelleys' already impressive reading lists grew, and Mary Shelley developed her skills as a translator whilst living on the continent. In Italy, from June 1818 to July 1820, Mary Shelley 'no longer needed [Percy Shelley's] tutorship [...] while working her way through the forty-five books of Livy's *Decades* almost without intermission for twenty-four months on end'.[15] De Palacio's work has astutely shown that Mary Shelley's Latin exercises — in particular her translation of Apuleius in notebook MSS. 13,290 (now held in the Library of Congress, Washington, DC) — warrant particular study as evidence of her creative mind at work.[16]

In Mary Shelley's fictional and poetical writings, Italian scenes are most famously depicted in the historical novel *Valperga* (1823), set in the fourteenth century, and in her elegiac verses composed after 1822, in which she recalls Percy Shelley and his works and mourns his death. The most famous poem by Mary Shelley is 'The Choice', which navigates the tragedies that befell the Shelleys in Italy, including the deaths of their children in Venice and Rome, as discussed by Valentina Varinelli in the present volume. Elsewhere, Mary Shelley's other portrayals of the country show her personal respect for and enjoyment of the landscape. This response can be found, for example, in the characters of the short story 'Recollections of Italy' (1824), which depicts a conversation about the country. Her works also provide evidence of her fervent admiration for the classical age, as established in the novel *The Last Man* (1826), and Italian scenes are even utilized as a backdrop for satire in another short piece, 'The Bride of Modern Italy' (1824). The Shelleys' mutual appreciation of Italian literature reverberated in their writings: they read Dante together, and praise him in the opening pages of *Valperga* and Percy Shelley's *A Defence of Poetry*.[17]

In London, before they arrived in their adopted land, Percy Shelley once translated some lines of Dante replacing the name Beatrice with 'Mary'.[18]

Although she would write: 'I love Italy with all my heart & all my soul & all my might & all my strength',[19] Mary Shelley's relationship to the country was complicated. In her study *Romantic 'Anglo-Italians'* (2009), Maria Schoina addresses the contradictory terms in which Italy is represented by Mary Shelley, and her 'genuine, though conditional, affection' for the place.[20] Fiona Stafford has considered how in one of Mary Shelley's later novels, *Lodore* (1835), the Italian passages are 'clearly indebted to Mary Shelley's personal knowledge of the country', but 'also draw on a long tradition of English literary depictions of Italy and the Italians'.[21] In other words, Mary Shelley presents a combination of personal reflection and literary heritage in her Italian scenes. As Stafford continues, the 'literary sources' of Mary's writings 'are not always easy to separate from biographical influences, given Mary Shelley's extraordinary family and circle of friends'.[22] Such a myriad of inspirations obscured the originality of Mary's productions beyond *Frankenstein*: Harold Bloom, for instance, implies that he does not class Mary Shelley as one of the 'major figures'[23] in English-language literature, asserting that none of her texts other than *Frankenstein* 'sustain rereading'.[24] I believe that Mary Shelley's lived experiences, and her inquisitive nature, are combined with her astute and far-reaching intellect in her writings, reflecting the intense reading and studying she maintained throughout her adult life. Collectively, these influences are traceable in the strength and worth of her creative productions. The reoccurrence of Italy is a fascinating example that demonstrates the complexity of her literary talent.

7.1. Italy in Mary Shelley's Fiction

> I am still enchanted by the spectacle which diversifies what I have heard called the monotonous blue skies of Italy. — 'Recollections of Italy'[25]

Previous critics have argued that in the Italian period, 1818–22, the Shelleys' relationship was marked by alienation, and therefore a lack of collaborative working. My research demonstrates that this was not always the case, and that the Italian years provide indications of Mary Shelley at her most confident as an advisor to Percy Shelley.[26] Mary Shelley's relationship with Italy is entwined with the life and, post-1822, the memory of her husband and his writings. Allusions to 'Percy Shelley's Italy' (or his works written in Italy) in Mary's oeuvre are not simply derivative. Rather, depictions of Italy — including those landscapes also used in compositions by Percy Shelley, such as the Euganean Hills — demonstrate Mary's innovative rendering of the couples' shared experiences converted into fiction. Mary Shelley even rescued from obscurity a poem by Percy Shelley on this precise topic — a work notably written in a 'Petrarchan rhythmic modulation'.[27] She explains in her notes to his *Poetical Works* in 1839 that she found '[l]ines written among the Euganean Hills' (along with *Rosalind and Helen*) 'among his papers by chance; and with some difficulty urged him to complete them'.[28]

Mary Shelley's short story 'Recollections of Italy' was published in *The London Magazine* in 1824. In this tale, the English character Edmund Malville describes the 'gentler beauty' of the Euganean Hills in comparison to the 'alpine scenery' of the north of the country.[29] Charles E. Robinson and Elizabeth Nitchie have explored the connections this work has with Percy Shelley's writing.[30] Mary Shelley's tale is not simply imitative of her husband's interests, but can be usefully read as an example of her complex literary love affair with the country. Malville is a staunch defender of all Italy has to offer ('he loved Italy, its soil, and all that it contained, with a strange enthusiasm'),[31] but the narrator describes his disappointment following his own travels there. As he explains this view — 'Venice, with its uncleaned canals [...] the smell' — Malville challenges his perceptions in a determined but good-natured discussion: '"Stop, blasphemer!" cried Malville, half angry, half laughing, "[...] Venice, the Queen of the sea, the city of gondolas and romance — "'.[32] Italy is praised for its rareness, yet Mary Shelley's narrator manages to hint at the perhaps alienating qualities of the country. Malville criticizes his interlocutor by suggesting they only spent time amongst other English people on their mere six-month visit, and failed to attend to the natural surroundings.[33] It is intriguing that Malville praises Venice so, as Mary Shelley criticized the city during her residence in Italy — the narrator's distaste at the smell is an echo from her own letters.[34] Overall, the story recalls Mary Shelley's early travel writing in *History of a Six Weeks' Tour* (1817; this was a collaborative effort with Percy Shelley) as she traverses the different landscapes.

Mary Shelley was in part inspired to write travelogues because of her mother Mary Wollstonecraft's *Letters Written During a Short Residence in Sweden, Norway, and Denmark* (1796) which we know she was reading on the Shelleys' first travels through Europe (before their Italian experiences) in 1814.[35] Mary Shelley was just as talented as her mother in her ability to attend to a specific literary form. When Mary's short stories were first published as a collection in 1891, the author of the introduction to that volume, Richard Garnett, described them as 'little tales' by a 'lonely, thwarted, misunderstood woman, who could seldom do herself justice'.[36] Rather, I think that it is Mary Shelley's ability to write within the limits of a short story successfully that so strongly identifies her talent. Robinson argues that in writing in this genre, Mary Shelley can 'discipline her art to restrictions of length and, in the process, anticipate the later development of the short story'.[37] In the collections at Chawton House Library, an apparently contemporary reader of a first edition of *Falkner* (1837) complained in their handwritten notes on the text itself that much of the novel 'was book-making [...] describing verdant lawns [...] autumnal suns & & &'.[38] These insights jotted down on the page were something that struck me as surprising, considering the significance of landscape in *Falkner*, a text that has continued to be neglected and underappreciated. Garnett too laments what he calls Mary Shelley's 'languor' in her novels composed and published after *Frankenstein*, implying they lack the energy of Percy Shelley's influence, and her short stories are 'good' but fail to capture the imagination.[39] Lengthy three-volume novels are marred by descriptive passages apparently inserted arbitrarily into the narrative, and by an unevenness of pace, yet her short stories are meek and 'little': such views have certainly affected Mary Shelley's reputation as a writer to this day, although the staunch work of various scholars (Robinson included) has successfully begun a re-evaluation. Further close study might do well to challenge the image of Mary Shelley as unaware of her audience. Her ability to write for the medium of the literary magazine in a short narrative, and then elsewhere write full-length novels (not forgetting what we also know of her skills in editing and her experimentations in verse), shows her acute awareness of her content and her audience.

In 'Recollections of Italy', for Mary Shelley's Malville, an Italophile, 'Naples is the real enchantress of Italy'; 'Rome is still the queen of the world'; but it is Tuscany where one should take up residence.[40] The narrative ends with a rain-drenched summer boat trip on the Thames — a delightful reminder of the failings of English country life, in comparison to the Tuscan landscape, where 'in spring, nature arises in beauty from her prison, and rains sunbeams and life upon the land'.[41] The memory of Italy in Mary Shelley's narrative serves to present the country as almost a mystical setting, and as such the conflicting views of Malville and the narrator reflect her fluctuating and layered attitude to its charms.

Transmuting travel into fiction was a hallmark of Mary Shelley's writing. In the final pages of *The Last Man*, Italy is a potential home for the last surviving humans on earth. The character Adrian initially suggests that Rome is the ideal place to settle in their despair, since they 'might lose [their] selfish grief in the sublime aspect of its desolation'.[42] Eventually only Lionel remains, and he reaches Rome alone and miserable, finding no way of surpassing his grief, and the very vacancy and desolation of the city is in fact more painful than he can bear: 'I was alone in the Forum; alone in Rome; alone in the world.'[43] Italy is a backdrop for the culmination of this message in Mary Shelley's *The Last Man*. Her use of the country here reinstates the significance of the conflicting effects its scenes have on her protagonists. In Mary Shelley's later novel *Lodore*, Italy represents hope; when the lovers Ethel and Villiers travel to the eternal city, they traverse the 'weed-grown baths of Caracalla' (where Percy Shelley wrote *Prometheus Unbound*) and share an emotional visit to the Coliseum.[44] I have written in my recent monograph about the way in which these two characters represent versions of Percy and Mary Shelley in their youthful love affair, and about the significance of their movements among the sites of Rome. Villers imagines his future life: 'an elegant home, here [England] or in Italy, adorned by Ethel [...], presented itself to his mind with strange distinctness and pertinacity. At no time had Villers loved so passionately as now.'[45] Although Mary Shelley writes that for Villers, 'that was his home where [Ethel] was',[46] it is poignant that Italy becomes for these characters a potential paradise, reflecting a trope in Mary Shelley's fiction, as in *The Last Man* also, where protagonists travel to or through Italian scenes in search of peace.

7.2. Italy and Mary Shelley's Involvement in Percy Shelley's Writings

> 'Do you not hear the Aziola cry?
> Methinks she must be nigh — '
> Said Mary as we sate
> In dusk, ere stars were lit or candles brought —
> And I who thought
> This Aziola was some tedious woman
> Asked, 'Who is Aziola?' How elate
> I felt to know that it was nothing human,
> No mockery of myself to fear or hate! —
> And Mary saw my soul,
> And laughed and said — 'Disquiet yourself not,
> 'Tis nothing but a little downy owl.' (ll. 1–12)[47]

So opens Percy Shelley's charming and tender poem entitled 'The Aziola', written sometime between 8 May and 4 August 1821.[48] The name refers to the scops owl heard in the poem, and in the second and final stanza Percy Shelley goes on to meditate on what he perceives to be its 'sad cry' (l. 21): a contemplation of which makes him love the creature and its call, 'sweeter' than any other 'voice [...] lute [...] wind [...] bird' (ll. 17–19). However, the poem is not so much about the owl's cry as about capturing an intimate moment between Percy and Mary Shelley. In the poem's narrative, the Shelleys hear the bird, and light humour ensues when Percy Shelley assumes that by 'Aziola' Mary actually means a 'tedious woman'; Mary is then able to see his 'soul' and explains the owl's presence. 'Soul' here is used in a profound and intimate way, applied to a short and perhaps unremarkable conversation. I have mentioned in my work elsewhere the relevance of this poem as displaying tenderness and affection between two writers, crucially expressed in verse, but here I wish to consider further what else the poem might suggest about Mary Shelley and Italy.

The word 'Aziola/Aziolo' is the Shelleys' shared nickname for the owl; the Italian name is *l'assiolo*, and a literal English translation as used by the Shelleys is not documented elsewhere.[49] This nickname appears in Mary Shelley's novels *Valperga*, *The Last Man*, and the short story 'The Sisters of Albano' where its 'cry heralds fine weather'.[50] The bird also appears in *Falkner* during a night-time scene when the eponymous hero of the novel begins a confessional narrative: 'It is night; the cooing aziolo, the hooting owl, the flashing fire-fly.'[51] The Aziola's cry embodies a poignant sorrow, similar to Percy Shelley's poem. The bird is the essence of melancholy and contemplation, yet with an undercurrent of purity in its clear 'sad cry'. In Mary Shelley's novel, this presence signifies the redemptive moment when Falkner confesses his sins: 'Can a man speak false in the silence of night, when God and his own heart alone keep watch.'[52]

The use of the noun in *Falkner*, Mary Shelley's final novel, indicates its endurance in her memory and also reminds us of her rereading of 'The Aziola' in her editorial work for Percy Shelley's *Poetical Works* (1839), where it appears under 'Poems Written in 1821'. However, the most significant use of the word in terms of the Shelleys' collaboration is in *Valperga*: the work of Nora Crook and Bruce Barker-Benfield has shown that the physical characteristics of the paper on which Percy Shelley's draft of 'The Aziola' is written are similar to those of the paper used for Mary Shelley's rough transcript of the novel from circa June to July 1821.[53] The image may have been used by the Shelleys at around the same time — both, perhaps, inspired by this conversation documented in Percy Shelley's verse, and I return to my assertion that Italian scenes provided a rich source of idiosyncratic memories for Mary Shelley.

Donald H. Reiman edited one manuscript of the poem (a transcription in Mary Shelley's hand), now held in the Morgan Library, New York. The phrase 'domestic harmony' in the following editorial comment is key to understanding the significance of this poem, as is the comparison to William and Dorothy Wordsworth. We must continue to reassess our view of the Shelleys as creative companions, as their words remind us of the consistency by which they worked so closely together:

> PBS shows here (what we also know from MWS's Journals) that he enjoyed many days of domestic harmony with Mary, his closest friend and confidante, who understood him far better than the world did. In this poem he portrays her treating his foibles kindly, with love and affectionate amusement [...] MWS, like Dorothy Wordsworth, is seen enlightening her poet-companion about one of the slighter forms of nature that he learned to appreciate because of her awareness of both the bird's qualities and his own.[54]

The manuscript itself is intriguing: this particular holograph (there are three transcriptions by Mary Shelley and one untitled draft by Percy) was the basis for the poem's publication in *The Keepsake* in 1829, where many of Mary's short stories also appeared.[55] The final word of the poem in the Morgan manuscript has changed from 'note' to 'cry', an alteration possibly made by Mary: as G. M. Matthews remarks, 'the poem was evidently unfinished, and Mary may have changed the last word so as to make a rhyme.'[56] It is possible she replaced this word after Percy Shelley's death, but the poem was probably discussed by the Shelleys since it appears to depict an experience they had together, and there are three transcriptions of the poem in Mary's hand, reminding us again that her work as copyist helped to preserve the writings of her husband.[57] Betty T. Bennett explains how 'the *assiolo* serves as an example of the couple's mutual influence'; the different ways in which the Shelleys utilize the image of the cooing owl 'more importantly suggest the profound differences in their philosophic perspectives':

> Where Percy Bysshe Shelley translates the owl's voice into something 'sweeter' than 'voice...lute...wind...bird' but inexorably sad, Mary Shelley embraces the owl's existence together with its voice as illuminations of the wonder and potential of the world.[58]

Bennett's argument emphasizes the differences between the Shelleys; however, we can infer a respect for each other's ideas here, and the shared image originates from intimacy and appears to be based on a real conversation.

'The Aziola' is an example of how domestic harmony between the Shelleys post-*Frankenstein* supported and instigated Percy Shelley's poetical writings, yet the image of the Aziola itself is used differently by both authors, in ways that both contradict and allude to the work of the other. The narrative of this poem is evidence for Percy Shelley's creativity intimately involving Mary and drawing on her presence and their dialogue for inspiration. Poems composed in the Italian period, such as 'Julian and Maddalo' and *Epipsychidion*, may offer potentially dark depictions of Mary Shelley conducive to a single narrative, but these interpretations are the construction of critics. Neither poem has an explicit address to Mary Shelley. If the *Vita Nuova* of Dante was the inspiration for the latter work, it is worth remarking that the Shelleys were reading that text together in 1821.[59]

I argue there can be no doubt that in 'The Aziola' Percy Shelley is depicting a scene in which the Shelleys both listen to the noise of the owl in Italy. Mary then transcribed the work and even potentially altered a word prior to its publication in *The Keepsake*, thus building up a sense of the Shelleys' engagement with that poem. 'The Aziola' was published alongside writings by Mary Shelley, Percy Shelley's 'On Love', and two more of his poetic fragments.[60] Mary also used the Shelleys' nickname for the bird in her own writings, including *Valperga*, a text she was working on at the same time as Percy wrote his poem.[61] The adoption of an Italian word, modified in writing for personal use, is a crucial signal of the Shelleys' intertwined creative ideas, and how those ideas were influenced significantly by their time in Italy.

Evidence in holographs from the Italian years indicates Mary Shelley's involvement in the construction of Percy Shelley's poems, including the 'Letter to Maria Gisborne' and other works.[62] She was also an important amanuensis (possibly introducing changes to the original draft) for Percy's poems composed in 1818–22, including *The Mask of Anarchy*[63] — the poem beginning 'As I lay asleep in Italy | There came a voice from over the sea' (ll. 1–2).[64] In finding evidence of Mary Shelley's contributions to her husband's works, we can discern the reciprocal nature of their creative exchange. Percy Shelley's involvement in the composition of *Frankenstein* has been well-documented, and Robinson's assessment that we can never know what Mary 'thought' of Percy's changes to her work is important; his additions and edits were 'for the purpose of improving an already excellent narrative', and we might agree that Mary Shelley 'accepted the suggestions and alterations that she agreed with'.[65] It is by introducing Mary Shelley's ability to influence Percy Shelley's writing that we can successfully challenge the misconception of her subordination to his (assumed) masculine dominance. Byron also used Mary's talents as an amanuensis who 'introduced small changes' when she briefly resided in Italy after Percy's death.[66]

Mary Shelley's significant role in her husband's writing is also measured by her involvement in another Italian project: the retelling of the story of Beatrice Cenci, the noblewoman put to death in the late sixteenth century for the murder of her abusive and corrupt father. Percy Shelley composed and published *The Cenci* in 1819; the work was based on a source translated by Mary Shelley, and both Shelleys were inspired by their visits to the Cenci relics in Rome. Mary Shelley discloses in her notes to *Poetical Works* in 1839: 'we talked over the arrangements of the scenes together', also revealing that Percy Shelley initially insisted she write a tragedy on that subject.[67]

Mary Shelley's own writings would return to this bleak drama: Mary's *Matilda*, for instance, responds to Percy Shelley's play with its incest narrative. 'Recollections of Italy' includes an allusion to *The Cenci* (the 'painted scene of this new world').[68] Mary Shelley cites Beatrice from Percy's play in her journal in 1822, and in her letters post-1822: 'The Time that was, is, & will be presses upon you & standing [in] the centre of a moving circle you " — slide giddily as the world reels."';[69] 'I thought to die myself — wd that I had & "that the flowers of this departed spring were fading on my grave!"'[70] Mary indulges in her love for *The Cenci* to feel a closeness to Percy Shelley after his death. Her choice of the tragic drama might also indicate a nostalgic longing to feel closer to a time in Italy where creativity was fuelled not just by the Shelleys' relationship and the landscape, but by the history of the country, too.

Another of Mary Shelley's short stories is the startlingly comic satire — a tone not often associated with her as an author — 'The Bride of Modern Italy', published anonymously in April 1824 in *The London Magazine*. In this text, Mary Shelley parodies the relationship her husband had with Teresa 'Emilia' Viviani, a teenage girl whom the Shelleys met in Italy in 1821. Emilia would become the addressee of what is perhaps known as Percy Shelley's most strikingly autobiographical and erotic work, *Epipsychidion*. In a work that demonstrates again Mary Shelley's talent in the genre of the short story, the heroine Clorinda falls in love with Marcott Alleyn, a 'young English artist' who thinks to himself on a visit to Clorinda's convent: 'Well [...] I am now in for it; and if I do not lose my heart, I shall at least gain some excellent hints for my picture of the Profession of Eloisa.'[71] The bathos in this tale suggests her experiences in Italy provided Mary Shelley with ample opportunity to explore not just tragic, sincere compositions but also biting, witty ones — a side of Mary Shelley often neglected, and one that I hope will attract more attention in future.

Conclusion

It was when she was living in Italy that Mary Shelley most significantly began to explore alternative genres to prose. She wrote verse dramas (*Proserpine* and *Midas*), and her best-known verse was composed there — the aforementioned 'The Choice', written in Genoa, just a few months after Percy Shelley's death.[72] Pamela Clemit suggests the writing of 'The Choice' took place sometime between May and July 1823. In August 1823, Mary Shelley would then travel to England, although the decision to do so was made in April — but with a determination to return to Italy.[73] Her journal during Percy Shelley's lifetime was a factual record of daily occurrences. Now, in her widowhood, the 'character of the journal changed [...] radically. It ceased to be a day-to-day record of facts, and became instead a form of emotional release'.[74] Schoina explains:

> her journal entries manifest her struggling efforts to overcome her despair and insecurity by nourishing her imagination on the intellectual and spiritual communion that had linked her to her husband, a memory which Italy contained and preserved: 'England I charge thee dress thyself in smiles for my sake.'[75]

'The Choice', according to Schoina, 'depicts Italy in contradictory and confusing colours'.[76] This period of mourning coupled affection and nostalgia with hopelessness and regret, as evidenced in Mary Shelley's journal. Again, these personal exhortations would affect her written engagement with the country in her creative works. Moreover, her characters' relationships with Italy are a crucial feature of their personalities. In 'Recollections of Italy', Malville the idealist is Italy's greatest admirer. He allows the country its faults; something the more logical and matter-of-fact narrator does not.

Like 'Recollections of Italy', 'The Choice' also embodies Mary Shelley's preference for the Tuscan countryside:

> 'Tis thus the Past — on which my spirit leans,
> Makes dearest to my soul Italian scenes.
> In Tuscan fields, the winds in odours steeped
> From flowers and cypresses — when skies have wept,
> Shall, like the notes of music once most dear,
> Which brings the unstrung voice upon my ear
> Of one beloved, to memory display
> Past scenes — past joys — past hopes, in long array. (ll. 122–29)[77]

Italian scenes are dear, yet transient, and tinged with loss, just as the opening lines of the poem declare Italy 'a tomb' (l. 6). Distraught, Mary Shelley wrote to Claire Clairmont in September 1822 explaining that her existence alone in Genoa was fraught and painful: 'am I not melancholy? — here in this busy hateful Genoa where nothing speaks to me of him, except the sea, which is his murderer.'[78] Italy does, however, present a personal comfort for the 'Mary' (l. 49) that speaks in 'The Choice': 'Tear me not hence — here let me live and die, | In my adopted land — my country — Italy' (ll. 59–60). Esther Schor writes that '[i]n Italy, in the tight embrace of the Shelley circle, she withdrew after losing two children to the vagaries of an itinerant, expatriate life'.[79] Her return to England (with her one surviving child Percy Florence) would transform Italy into a place to visit only in recollections for many years. As we have seen, the country was ever present in her mind.

Notes to Chapter 7

1. Mary Wollstonecraft Shelley (hereafter MWS), 'Recollections of Italy', in *Mary Shelley: Collected Tales and Stories*, ed. by Robinson, p. 27 (hereafter 'Recollections of Italy'). For a detailed list of the prominence of Italy in the MWS canon, see Lucy Morrison and Stacey L. Stone, 'Italy', in *A Mary Shelley Encyclopedia*, ed. by Lucy Morrison and Stacey L. Stone (London: Greenwood Press, 2003), pp. 219–21.
2. *MWS Journals*, p. 202.
3. Percy Bysshe Shelley (hereafter PBS), 'Julian and Maddalo', ed. by Ralph Pite, in *The Poems of Shelley* (hereafter *The Poems of Shelley*), ed. by Everest and others, II: *1817–1819*, ed. by Kelvin Everest and G. M. Matthews, Longman Annotated English Poets (London: Longman, 2000), pp. 660–94.
4. Michael Rossington, 'Editing Shelley', in *The Oxford Handbook of Percy Bysshe Shelley*, ed. by O'Neill and Howe, pp. 645–56 (p. 646).
5. Jane Stabler, *The Artistry of Exile: Romantic and Victorian Writers in Italy* (Oxford: Oxford University Press, 2013), p. 7.

6. *MWS Journals*, p. 462.
7. Alan Weinberg, *Shelley's Italian Experience* (London: Macmillan, 1991), p. 1.
8. *MWS Journals*, p. 462.
9. Miranda Seymour, *Mary Shelley* (London: Picador, 2001), p. 204.
10. *MWS Letters*, I, 63–64.
11. *MWS Journals*, pp. 197–98.
12. Ibid., p. 202.
13. Ibid., p. 202.
14. Ibid., p. 204.
15. De Palacio, 'Mary Shelley's Latin Studies', p. 564.
16. Ibid., pp. 564–71.
17. PBS, *A Defence of Poetry*, in *Shelley's Poetry and Prose: A Norton Critical Edition*, p. 526; *MWS Journals*, pp. 297–98.
18. PBS, 'What Mary Is', in *The Poems of Shelley*, I: *1804–1817*, ed. by G. M. Matthews and Kelvin Everest, Longman Annotated English Poets (London: Longman, 1989), p. 447.
19. *MWS Letters*, I, 356.
20. Schoina, *Romantic 'Anglo-Italians'*, p. 58; see also pp. 58–62.
21. Fiona Stafford, 'Introductory Note', in *The Novels and Selected Works of Mary Shelley*, VI: *Lodore*, ed. by Fiona Stafford, pp. ix–xiii (p. xi).
22. Ibid., p. xi.
23. Harold Bloom, *The Anxiety of Influence* (Oxford: Oxford University Press, 1975), p. 5.
24. Harold Bloom, 'Introduction', in Amy Watkin, *Bloom's How to Write About Mary Shelley* (New York: Bloom's Literary Criticism, 2012), pp. vii–ix (p. vii).
25. 'Recollections of Italy', p. 29.
26. For further discussion on the Shelleys' collaboration, including those critics who suggest the Shelleys ceased to collaborate post-*Frankenstein*, please consult my recent monograph and my articles in *The Keats-Shelley Review*: Anna Mercer, *The Collaborative Literary Relationship of Percy Bysshe Shelley and Mary Wollstonecraft Shelley* (2019); 'Beyond *Frankenstein*: The Collaborative Literary Relationship of Percy Bysshe and Mary Shelley', *The Keats Shelley Review*, 30.1 (2016), 80–85; 'Rethinking the Shelleys' Collaborations in Manuscript', *The Keats Shelley Review*, 31.1 (2017), 49–65.
27. Alan Weinberg, 'Shelley and the Italian Tradition', in *The Oxford Handbook of Percy Bysshe Shelley*, ed. by O'Neill and Howe, pp. 444–59 (p. 450).
28. MWS, 'Preface', in PBS, *Poetical Works* (1839), cited in *The Novels and Selected Works of Mary Shelley*, II, 256. 'Rosalind and Helen', composed September 1817–July 1818; 'Euganean Hills', composed late 1818.
29. 'Recollections of Italy', p. 28.
30. *Collected Tales and Stories*, ed. by Robinson, pp. 375–76. Elizabeth Nitchie, *Mary Shelley: Author of Frankenstein* (New Brunswick, NJ: Rutgers University Press, 1953; repr. Westport, Conn.: Greenwood Press, 1970), p. 64.
31. 'Recollections of Italy', p. 25.
32. Ibid., p. 26.
33. Ibid., p. 27.
34. *MWS Letters* I, 81, 225.
35. They also read the works of MWS's father, William Godwin. See e.g. *MWS Journals*, pp. 22, 26, 649–50, 684.
36. Richard Garnett, 'Introduction', in Mary Shelley, *Tales and Stories*, ed. by Richard Garnett (London: Paterson, 1891), p. xi.
37. Charles E. Robinson, 'Introduction', in *Collected Tales and Stories*, pp. xi–xix (p. xiv).
38. MWS, *Falkner*, 1st edn (London: Saunders and Otley, Conduit Street, 1837). Specific copy: Chawton, Hampshire, Chawton House Library, Writers' Sequence SHE, C4283, *Falkner*, III, 319.
39. Garnett, pp. v–xii.
40. 'Recollections of Italy', p. 28.

41. Ibid., p. 29.
42. MWS, *The Last Man*, ed. by Morton D. Paley (Oxford: Oxford University Press, 1994), pp. 326–27.
43. Ibid., p. 463.
44. See PBS, 'Preface to *Prometheus Unbound*', in *The Poems of Shelley*, II, 473; MWS, 'Note on the Prometheus Unbound', in *The Novels and Selected Works of Mary Shelley*, II, 276. MWS, *Lodore*, ed. by Lisa Vargo (Hadleigh: Broadview Press, 1997), p. 267.
45. MWS, *Lodore*, p. 341.
46. Ibid.
47. PBS, 'The Aziola', in *The Poems of Shelley*, IV, p. 349. All further references to this poem are from this edition.
48. *The Poems of Shelley*, IV, 348.
49. *The Novels and Selected Works of Mary Shelley*, VII: *Falkner*, ed. by Pamela Clemit, p. 154, n.
50. *The Poems of Shelley*, IV, 348.
51. *The Novels and Selected Works of Mary Shelley*, VII, 154.
52. Ibid., p. 155.
53. *The Poems of Shelley*, IV, 348.
54. *Fair-Copy Manuscripts of Shelley's Poems in European and American Libraries*, ed. by Michael O'Neill and Donald H. Reiman, Manuscripts of the Younger Romantics, VIII (London: Garland, 1997), p. 322.
55. Robinson, 'Introduction', in *Collected Tales and Stories*, p. xvi. See also *The Poems of Shelley*, IV, 347.
56. *The Poems of Shelley*, IV, 347.
57. Ibid., p. 347.
58. Bennett, 'Mary Shelley's Letters', in *The Cambridge Companion to Mary Shelley*, ed. by Schor, p. 222.
59. See *MWS Journals*, 351; Weinberg, 'Shelley and the Italian Tradition', p. 453.
60. *Fair-Copy Manuscripts of Shelley's Poems*, Manuscripts of the Younger Romantics, VIII, 321.
61. *The Poems of Shelley*, IV, 348.
62. See Mercer, 'Rethinking the Shelleys' Collaborations in Manuscript'.
63. See *The Mask of Anarchy*, ed. by Donald H. Reiman, Manuscripts of the Younger Romantics, II (London: Garland, 1985).
64. PBS, *The Mask of Anarchy*, in *The Poems of Shelley*, III: *1819–1820*, ed. by Jack Donovan and others (Harlow: Longman/Pearson, 2011), pp. 27–63.
65. Charles E. Robinson, 'Introduction', in *The Frankenstein Notebooks* (2 parts), ed. by Charles E. Robinson, part 1 (London: Garland, 1996), pp. vii–cx, (p. lxvii).
66. Jerome J. McGann, 'Introduction', in George Gordon Byron, *The Complete Poetical Works*, ed. by Jerome J. McGann, 7 vols (Oxford: Oxford University Press, 1980–93), V: *Don Juan* (Oxford: Oxford University Press, 1986), pp. i–xxiv (pp. xxi–xxii). For a list of other poems MWS copied for Byron, see Peter Cochran, 'Mary Shelley's Copying of *Don Juan*', *Keats-Shelley Review*, 10 (Spring 1996), 222–41.
67. MWS, 'Note on *The Cenci*', in *The Novels and Selected Works of Mary Shelley*, II, 283.
68. Footnote on 'Recollections of Italy', in *Collected Tales and Stories*, p. 26. Cf. PBS, *The Cenci*, in *The Poems of Shelley*, II, 713–863, V. 1. 78.
69. *MWS Journals*, pp. 395–96. Cf. *The Cenci*, III. 1. 12.
70. *MWS Letters*, I, p. 342. Cf. *The Cenci*, I. 3. 138–39.
71. MWS, 'The Bride of Modern Italy', in *Collected Tales and Stories*, p. 36.
72. Schoina, p. 57.
73. Pamela Clemit, 'Introduction', in *Mary Shelley's 'Literary Lives' and Other Writings*, IV, p. xxx (hereafter *MWS Literary Lives*). See also MWS's dream in *MWS Letters*, I, 329.
74. Paula R. Feldman and Dianna Scott-Kilvert, 'Introduction', in *MWS Journals*, pp. xv–xxv (p. xviii).
75. Schoina, pp. 57–58.
76. Ibid., pp. 57–58.

77. MWS, 'The Choice' [Hunt/Forman printed version], in *MWS Literary Lives*, IV, 117–22. All further references to this poem will be from this edition.
78. *MWS Letters*, I, 258.
79. Esther Schor, 'Introduction', in *The Cambridge Companion to Mary Shelley*, pp. 1–8 (p. 1).

PART III

The Reception of Mary Shelley: Interdisciplinary Approaches (Translation, Theatre, and Iconology)

CHAPTER 8

The British Reception of *Frankenstein* (1818) and the Culture of Early Nineteenth-Century Science

Marjean D. Purinton

From the immense twenty-first-century popularity of Mary Shelley's 1818 novel *Frankenstein; or, The Modern Prometheus*, we might think that its reception by British readers was strong and positive from its inception. This was not the case, however, for as Steven Forry, Audrey Fisch, and William St Clair have demonstrated, the novel might well have fallen out of circulation altogether were it not for the successful stage adaptations (at least fifteen between 1823–26) of Shelley's story, beginning with Richard Brinsley Peake's *Presumption; or, the Fate of Frankenstein* in 1823.[1] According to St Clair, the novel's own publication history was inconsequential in the early nineteenth century, with Lackington, Hughes, Harding, Mavor and Jones initially printing a single edition of only five hundred and taking two-thirds of its net profits. He points out that the three-volume novel sold primarily because of Lackington's reputation as a press specializing in magic, pseudoscience, the illegitimate, the supernatural, and horror.[2] Early reviews of the anonymous novel were harshly negative, with numerous critics citing plot improbabilities, political radicalism, and moral disgust as reasons for the story's deficiencies.

Theatrical entrepreneurs responded to a much broader audience than Lackington's readership, however, and they were savvy in eschewing those aspects of the novel that the reviews deemed inadequate or disturbing and instead turned to the printing press associations with pseudoscience and the supernatural. It was those aspects of the novel that inform the illegitimate adaptations for the stage. Since the Licensing Act of 1737, only theatres receiving Royal Patents (Drury Lane, Covent Garden, and The Haymarket) could perform 'legitimate' drama (conventional or spoken drama). All other theatres had to produce so-called 'illegitimate' dramas that included non-spoken elements, songs, music, dances, pantomimes, and spectacles. The illegitimate theatrical adaptations of Shelley's novel severely compromised the complexities of the original story, emphasizing instead a terrifying and aberrant monster created by a scientist unchecked by professional, ethical, or moral standards. The dramas capitalized on the novel's introduction of experiments and discourses of science, of medical discoveries, of teratology (the study of monstrosities) discussions, of mechanical wonders. These were the aspects of the novel with which theatre-going audiences were fascinated. The stage adaptations of the 'Frankenstein' story became, in fact, a kind of extension of popular scientific demonstrations and lectures, displays and shows, with which they competed as entertainment. Despite critical theatrical reviews that cast the 'Frankenstein' plays as spectacular, melodramatic, and immoral, curious theatregoers turned out to the playhouses with expectations of seeing the controversial scientific content of the novel enacted before them. Between 1818, when the novel was first published, and 1831, the year Mary Shelley sold the novel's copyright to Richard Bentley and wrote the famous 'Preface' to that year's reissue of the novel, the dramas sustained public fascination with *Frankenstein*.

This essay will argue that Mary Shelley's story continued to live in the cultural imagination in the particular form imprinted on it by the stage adaptations. The latter, like the original novel, animated public interest in the medical and scientific discourses that characterize Romantic-period culture. During the early nineteenth century, serious, pedestrian, and quack medicine coexisted in the cultural imaginary. Scientific and medical matters were the subjects of conversation in pubs and coffee houses, the focus of the academies and hospitals, and the materials from which entertainment emanated, so that prominent studies from the late eighteenth-century Scottish Enlightenment and European naturalists of the 1810s participated intertextually with cultural productions and discourses. Over this extended period, theatrical adaptations appealing to cross-classed audiences helped to sustain interest in Mary Shelley's novel.

The medical field of the early nineteenth century was irregular and uncontrolled. Physicians were often dubiously educated, and they did not require license to practice. Apothecaries were often mere pseudo-chemists or untrained shopkeepers. Drugs of all kinds were readily available to the public and were pandered by entrepreneurs disguised as itinerant scientists. The daily newspapers featured columns of medical advice, and readers could procure a diagnosis by merely describing symptoms to the journalist or physician assigned the column. Because medicine operated in an unregulated market, those who offered an exotic treatment, a panacea for pain, an elixir of cure, created spectacles and audiences. The first books of hygiene, the earliest self-help books of health were published and reissued. Two of the popular books were William Buchan's *Domestic Medicine; or, A Treatise on the Prevention and Cure of Diseases by Regime and Simple Medicine*, first published in 1769, with the 1783 edition available to most households at the beginning of the nineteenth century, and Thomas Beddoes's treatise *Hygëia; or, Essays Moral and Medical on the Causes Affecting the Personal State of Our Middling and Affluent Classes*, published in 1802–03. Both Buchan and Beddoes were trained, legitimate physicians, Buchan in Edinburgh and Beddoes in Germany. The line between real medicine and stage quackery was a precarious one, however, and the public was both sceptical and attracted to those who claimed to have medical knowledge. Post-Enlightenment sciences generated hope, but they also fostered anxiety, and this ambivalence is exactly what the theatrical adaptations of Shelley's novel hoped to stir among theatergoers.

Playwrights of staged drama were particularly sensitive to the ways in which physiognomy and anatomy facilitated new perceptions of the body, transforming the body into a text that could be read and interpreted by the trained medical gaze. The widely circulating self-help books were teaching the public how to read the body, how to discern deformity and disease. Serious medical accounts, such as *First Lines of Physiology* (1747) by German physician Albrecht von Haller, available to English audiences thanks to its translation by Dr William Cullen in 1786, or French scientist Geoffrey Saint-Hilaire's *Philosophie Anatomique* (1818–22), contributed to specialized and popular interests in comparative anatomy. Theatregoers could practice their skills, simulating the period's omnipresent medical gaze in their reading of a performing body, a body artificial and fictive, disguised and costumed. Additionally, their theatrical experience replicated that realized by medical students, not unlike Victor Frankenstein, intently watching dissections and demonstrations at the increasing number of anatomical theatres in Europe. At the playhouse, theatregoers could participate as quasi-professionals in the culture's scientific interpretations and diagnoses. Like physicians, theatregoers were especially attracted to malformed, hybrid, monstrous, and sick bodies, not unlike that of the Creature, who excited contradictory responses of sympathy and abomination. Such a body in the theatre was one of terror and curiosity, a text to be deciphered, controlled, and contained, corrected, or discarded. Shelley's Creature was the perfect body for playwrights to recast in their own anatomical theatres.

Playwrights adapting Mary Shelley's story marketed the theatricalization of science popular in the early nineteenth century. Anatomical displays, magnetic demonstrations, freak shows, automaton performances, and curiosity cabinets were all a part of the pseudoscientific culture of early nineteenth-century Britain. These public performances or 'theatrum', as described by Barbara Maria Stafford, invited spectators to peep into spaces that generated feelings of fright and awe similar to those they experienced when they attended the theatre.[3] Spectators paid to see the extraordinary, the bizarre, and the grotesque whether billed as entertainment or as science. Showmen such as the infamous sexologist Dr James Graham lured the paying public to his Temple of Health and Hymen in 1780 at the Adelphi, where he performed electrical treatments, magnetic shock therapy, and applied aethereal balsams. His multimedia spectacles dazzled visitors with theatrical props.[4] Carnivalesque shows featuring giants, midgets, bearded ladies, hermaphrodites, and mad women made their specimens seem scientific in their use of commentary about anatomical studies and teratological taxonomies. Scientists were asked to authenticate monsters. Serious medical men, such as anatomists John and William Hunter, maintained anatomical collections with skulls, feral children, dissected appendages, and aberrant specimens that they made accessible to the public.[5] Among the popularly available scientific lectures were William Hunter's *Two Introductory Lectures* to his course on anatomy, circulated in 1784. Adaptors of Shelley's novel for the stage, therefore, not only recognized the public interest in scientific and medical matters, but their very livelihoods as entertainers were seriously challenged by the new sciences that had taken on theatrical forms.

Theatrical performances were ironically more regulated than the medical and scientific shows that competed for public attention. Since the Licensing Act of 1737, staged drama came under the licensure of the Lord Chamberlain. The stage adaptations of Shelley's novel would have been identified as 'illegitimate', and the non-patent theatres where illegitimate dramas were performed could seat huge audiences. The English Opera House, also known as the Lyceum, had a seating capacity of 1500. Peake's *Presumption; or, The Fate of Frankenstein* ran thirty-seven nights there in 1823. On the basis of this play alone, up to 55,000 persons could come to know Shelley's story by attending the theatre.[6] Also in 1823, Peake's parody *Another Piece of Presumption* was performed at both the Adelphi Theatre and the Surry Theatre, a playhouse that was formerly associated with circus shows.[7]

Frank-in-Steam; or, The Modern Promise to Pay was performed at the Adelphi in 1823 and then again at the Olympic Pavilion Theatre in 1824. The Adelphi marketed itself as a theatre of low life and vulgarity. Little wonder then that its shows were so popular that seats were taken weeks in advance.[8] The Coburg Theatre, with is seating capacity of 3800, is where Henry M. Milner's adaptations were performed: *Frankenstein; or, The Demon of Switzerland* in 1823 and *The Man and the Monster; or, The Fate of Frankenstein* in 1826.[9] *Frankenstein* simply seemed stage ready, malleable material for the various illegitimate theatres of London intent on competing with the science shows already drawing curious audiences.

At the very moment these theatres were presenting variations of Frankenstein's monster for public curiosity and consumption, the medical community was promoting public access to operating and dissecting theatres. For William Hunter, the operating theatre should be particularly 'well constructed, both for seeing and hearing'.[10] The table upon which the body to be dissected is placed 'is not in the centre of the circular room, but about half way between the centre and the circumference'.[11] The circular design of the theatre and the placement of the table creates for spectators a sense of being directly before the object and speaker, which 'both hearing and seeing, makes some compensation for the greater distance' between audience and performers.[12] The teacher/physician, explains Hunter, is positioned not merely to describe human anatomy 'but to shew or demonstrate every part'.[13] Hunter emphasizes how important it is for medical students to 'see' all the principal parts of dissected dead bodies 'over and over again' because when they see 'a number of bodies dissected in succession', they better understand the operations of surgery.[14] Spectators going to the adaptations of Mary Shelley's novel might have expected to see the kind of show promised by Hunter at the operating theatres. They wanted to see the monster over and over again so that they, too, could better understand the operations of human anatomy and death-denying reanimation.

In contrast to efforts to make the work of the medical and scientific fields transparent, the dramaturgy of all the stage adaptations relies on Shelley's hiding of the creation scene from both our theatrical and medical gaze. Readers of the novel are denied details of the monster's creation and must imaginatively conjure the medical procedure. Theatre audiences are likewise denied the opportunity to see the operating theatre where unspeakable anatomical activities occur; but their medical gaze is diverted by stage trickery. The stage frames the scientist's laboratory as though it were a huge curiosity cabinet, but spectators cannot see the specimen inside. The audience is titillated with visual and auditory special effects while characters describe what might be occurring behind closed doors.

At the beginning of Peake's *Presumption; or, The Fate of Frankenstein*, lab assistant Fritz shares his nervousness with the audience over his master's 'fumi-fumi-fumigating all night at his chemistry'.[15] The play's pyrotechnics and music during the creation scene allude to the novel's Promethean fire and build audience expectations of seeing the experiment. According to the stage directions: '*A blue flame appears at the small lattice window [...] from the laboratory. [...] A sudden combustion is heard within. The blue flame changes to one of a reddish hue*' (I. 3). In *Frank-in-Steam; or, The Modern Promise to Pay*, lab assistant Fritz tells the audience that his master has been locked up with his anatomy and supernatural texts in a space where 'the rushlight burns all manner of colours'.[16] He points to Frankinstitch's study and, like the audience, fears to look upon what he will encounter:

> Yonder is the closet where the subject of my enterprise lied stretched in all the horrors of grisly death. How shall I convey it to its proper destination? I have it — I'll box it to prevent discovery. [...] Should I be found out I shall be pummeled by the Populace and receive a body blow that may do one bodily harm. (II. 1, p. 182)

What could be shown in the theatre was even more rigidly controlled than what might be presented in scientific demonstrations. The closeting of science and medicine was a practice challenged by treatises like Hunter's lectures and Buchan's *Domestic Medicine*, which seek to expose the medical science that Frankenstein-like characters hide in closeted laboratories. Secret medicine, argues Buchan, fosters the chicanery of pretenders of science who actually peddle superstition and quackery.[17] For Buchan, quacks depend on secrecy: 'Disguising Medicine not only retards its improvement as a science, but exposes the profession to ridicule, and is injurious to the true interests of society [...] and lays the foundations of quackery.'[18] Buchan promotes the demystification of medicine so that it is not seen as mere trick, as merely theatrical, disguised as entertainment. The *Frankenstein* stage adaptations demonstrate what Buchan feared, the ridiculing and satirizing of serious science as quack shows.

Both Beddoes and Hunter similarly promote transparency in the medical demonstrations orchestrated by physicians and scientists. Hunter recommends that medical students collect anatomical preparations, skeletons, skulls, and organs to serve as props for their own demonstrations and consultations.[19] In *Hygëia*, Beddoes promotes a theatricality of dissecting demonstrations and anatomical lectures in full view of spectators. Like Hunter, he encourages scientists to present 'an assortment of preparations, models, and drawings on a large scale'.[20] Like the illegitimate drama performed at the Lyceum, such as Peake's adaptation of *Frankenstein*, or James Robinson's Planché's *Vampyre*, anatomical demonstrations should be entertaining as well as instructive. Unlike the *Frankenstein* dramatists, however, scientists should not shock spectators by actions such as showing, for example, 'a limb in the dust and leave it to the fancy to make out the entire monster.'[21] Teasing spectators, Beddoes argues, creates images associated with the spectacles of quackery rather than science, and superficial observers cannot discern the difference. Beddoes asserts that if people look to the Lyceum for comfortable and confirming illumination about science, then the anatomical theatres must be enlisted to instruct the public.

The stage adaptations seem intent on obfuscating the science the public desires to see. The Frankenstein of Henry Milner's *Frankenstein; or, The Man and the Monster* conducts his experiments in a private pavilion. The mysterious creation scene is accompanied by smoke and fire, with the top of the pavilion blowing off to reveal its interior. Stage directions indicate: '*On a long Table is discovered an indistinct Form, covered with a black cloth. A small side Table, with Bottles and Chemical Apparatus — a brazier with fire.*'[22] Lab assistant Pietro in John Atkinson Kerr's *The Monster and Magician; or, The Fate of Frankenstein*, reports how his master is isolated in his laboratory 'in the midst of his crucibles, alembecks, and devil's kitchen utensils', evidenced by the blue flame issuing from the laboratory window.[23] Like other lab assistants in the stage adaptations, Pietro directs the audience's gaze when he says: 'I really cant [sic] tell you exactly what I saw — all that I can say is that I thought I beheld in master's laboratory something very unaccountable t'was a figure — a corpse' (II. 1, p. 217). Theatregoers have to see the freak show through Pietro's and other lab assistants' eyes because they cannot perform the scientific gazing first-hand.

Not only are the operations of the laboratory concealed from theatre spectators, but the long-anticipated appearance of the monster is delayed. The layers of spectatorship engendered by performance (Frankenstein beholding the Creature, the audience beholding the Creature, the audience beholding Frankenstein beholding the Creature) invite psychological affinity as well as medical curiosity. While the diseased and deformed among them provided spectacles of horror they avoided, theatergoers attended the Frankenstein plays to gaze at the disfigurations their healthy bodies had been spared. They also sought solutions to the devastating diseases afflicting so many of them. In Peake's *Presumption; or, The Fate of Frankenstein*, the scientist is heard to proclaim offstage:

> It lives! I saw the dull yellow eye of the creature open, it breathed hard, and a convulsive motion agitated its limbs. What a wretch have I formed, I had selected his features as beautiful — beautiful! Ah, horror, his cadaverous skin scarcely covers the work of muscles and arteries beneath, his hair lustrous, black and flowing — his teeth of pearly whiteness — but these luxuriances only form more horrible contrasts with the deformities of the Demon. (I. 3)

Frankenstein identifies with an audience intent on gazing at affliction that medicine seemingly could not alleviate: 'I have seen how the fine form of man has been wasted and degraded — have beheld the corruption of death succeed to the blooming cheek of life!' (I. 1).

Like an itinerant quack selling his miraculous cures, Frankenstein promises the audience that he has found a way for human life to overcome 'the corruption of death' (I. 1). all too ubiquitous in early nineteenth-century Britain, with European pandemics in consumption, cholera, and smallpox making alluring any cure. Buchan points out that in 1783, consumption was responsible for more than one-tenth of the mortality in London, and that it was a disease seldom cured: 'Consumption is a wasting or decay of the whole body from an ulcer, tubercles, or connections of the lungs, an empyema, a nervous atrophy, or a cachexy.'[24] Smallpox, explains Buchan, 'is a most contagious malady; and has, for many years, proved the scourge of Europe.'[25]

Beddoes describes to readers the consequences of diseases on the human body and how, then, that body is rendered a spectacle of disfigurement, disability, and monstrosity. He points to the terror associated with scrofula, which is exceedingly common in Great Britain: 'Nothing can be imagined more disgusting to behold, or more miserable to endure, than the effects it sometimes produces.'[26] Beddoes asks readers to consider how they react to the spectacle of the disfigured, the disabled, the monstrous. He recalls the experiences of a colleague who at nine suffered smallpox, leaving him disfigured. He was harassed at school, and his family withheld from him gestures of kindness and affection. Only his grandfather showed him love, 'for he was stock-blind and could not judge' appearances.[27] Beddoes might well be describing audience reactions to seeing the stage monsters of the Frankensteins' making, their fascination and then aversion at the sight of hideousness. The theatre gives them license to express disgust for disfigurement that polite society requires them to suppress when they encounter it in the appearances of those unfortunate people who have suffered smallpox, scrofula, or other diseases.

Beddoes tries to explain the complex responses generated by the sight of disfiguring and debilitating diseases, a response not afforded to spectators shielded by the artificiality of the theatre:

> What impression [...] does a sallow, unwholesome complexion, seams from the small-pox, scrophulous scars, the blight of beauty, and those marks which debauchery is apt to stamp upon the face, make upon the spectator? Is he not in general disposed to turn away in disgust from these appearances? [...] And in what manner does the mind of those who perceive themselves to be objects of aversion react?[28]

Similarly, Saint-Hilaire points to the mixture of pity and aversion combined in the cathartic response of seeing monsters on exhibit, whether for medical or entertainment purposes:

> Ajoutez à ceci qu'il n'y a ni plus ni moins de monstres chez les animaux que dans l'espèce humaine, et vous en conclurez surabondamment que notre raison et nos affections morales ne sont pour rien dans les déformations qui constituent les faits de la monstruosité.[29]
>
> [If you add the fact that there are no more monsters among animals than among the human species, you will conclude certainly that our reason and our moral affections are not responsible for the deformations that make up monstrosity.][30]

Playwrights exploited human enjoyment at suffering by delaying the appearance of the mysterious creature paradoxically formed from death and promising to curtail disease.

The mysterious and monstrous body withheld from the audience's gaze by its delayed appearance was a strategy of creating dramatic tension and visual anticipation. Like the scientific commentators accompanying freak shows and anatomical demonstrations, the Frankenstein of Peake's *Presumption* explains his arduous experimentation process to theatergoers, as he hints at what they are about to witness: 'I have become the master of the secret of bestowing animation upon lifeless matter. [...] A huge automaton in human form.' According to Fritz, his master's automaton is 'a hob-hob-goblin, 20 feet high! Wrapp'd in a mantle —' (I. 3). Frankenstein concedes that his plastic surgery has resulted in a deformed creature he finds disgusting. He next instructs the audience to listen to sounds and silences emanating from his laboratory and says: 'All is still! The dreadful spectre of a human form — no mortal could withstand the horror of that countenance — a mummy endued with animation could be so hideous as the wretch I have endowed with life!' (I. 3). In the second act, Frankenstein contemplates aborting his creature as he describes its aberrant features to the audience: 'a creature powerful in form, of supernatural and gigantic strength, but with the mind of an infant' (II. 1). According to Stephen Behrendt, Fritz was played by Robert Keeley in Peake's 1823 production of *Presumption*, a part Peake wrote for Keeley, who was just over five feet tall. By contrast, the Creature, played by Thomas Potter Cooke, would appear even taller in statue and larger in frame. James William Wallack played Victor Frankenstein, and at five feet and eight inches, the physically attractive scientist was a visual foil to Fritz as well as to his Creature.[31]

In the Frankenstein adaptations, however, this standard theatrical strategy guided spectators in how to read a body diseased or malformed. *Hygëia* is instructive in reading this process. According to Beddoes, we are conditioned to see normality and difference through artificially determined standards. Then, he elaborates, we attach moral registers to those standards so that we can justify our belief that anyone deviating from them is evil. He illustrates this point with the very standard of height that Peake's *Presumption* emphasizes: 'Malignity is not, I hope, supposed to have any particular affinity with dwarfishness. Yet superiority of stature must be felt as an enviable distinction.'[32] For those of short statue, like Fritz, Beddoes maintains, we tend to treat as children, despite their age and mental capabilities. Because the Frankenstein monsters of the stage are portrayed as exceptionally tall, their distinction could be perceived as threatening. *Hygëia* implores readers to resist the temptation, 'culturally conditioned', to attach moral judgments to physical appearances that deviate from the standards of normality: 'We shall derive from [medical education] sagacity to discern, and firmness to resist, pretentions founded on mere shape and air.'[33] Because the creature does not appear 'normal', Frankenstein pronounces his experiment as a failure, his creature paradoxically a 'spectre of a human form' and a 'mummy endued with animation' (I. 1), a giant with a dwarfed brain, strong but supernatural, a being not categorically distinguished by anatomical taxonomies, a creature outside the accepted scientific discourses of physiology and anatomy, a specimen that had only recently become so named by teratology as monstrous, like those featured in the second volume of Saint-Hilaire's

Philosophie anatomique: Des Monstruosités humaines. While the earlier medical manuals of Beddoes and Buchan examined deformation as a medical phenomenon, in Saint-Hilaire's work monstrous births were mentioned as a means of moving towards the theorizing of embryology and species differentiation. What is important for Mary Shelley's novel is that the scientific discussions over this period of time as well as conceptual change sustained ideas about monstrosity in the popular imagination.

The audience is not treated to even a glimpse of this monster so variously described and secreted until the very end of Peake's first act. Like the creation process itself, the creature eludes the spectators' gaze, both theatrical and medical. In the confusion of explosion and fire, the creature escapes the containment of Frankenstein's laboratory. Frankenstein directs the spectators to avert their gaze when he says: 'Its unearthly ugliness renders it too horrible for human eyes' (I. 3). But of course, all eyes are on Thomas Potter Cooke's embodiment of the creature, as this is the spectacle that has brought most audience members to the theatre. They are also there for a taste of violence, and so on cue, a scuffle ensues, and stage directions indicate: *'The Demon then seizes Frankenstein — loud thunder heard — throws him violently on the floor, ascends the staircase, opens the large windows, and disappears through the casement. Frankenstein remains motionless on the ground'* (I. 3). While the creature does not disappear into the darkness and the distance to commit suicide as he does at the end of Shelley's novel, he does slip containment at the end of the first act of Peake's play, suggesting that even the audience could be at risk from such an abnormal and violent being. Spectators finally get to use their medical gaze and see the infamous creature. They have seen what the new sciences have given birth to.

In Peake's parody *Another Piece of Presumption*, the tailor Frankenstitch makes his new man with the parts of nine journeymen, recently murdered, and he animates his creature with parlour bellows. This Hobgoblin, as he is called, speaks English, and in the second act, he expresses his discomfort with his ill-fitting anatomy, his grafted organs and appendages not quite coordinated and certainly unappealing:

> Is there any thing so infernally ugly in me? I suppose I'm a queer one — my joints don't fit comfortably together — my left hip keeps creating and grating against my back bone like a Coffee Mill — my nose is loose, and my elbows dangle like flails.[34]

Even this humorous creature recognizes his abnormality, his freakish physiology — about which Saint-Hilaire writes. Hobgoblin claims to be merely a *'play thing'* (II. 2, p. 173), suggesting that he might be innocent and innocuous, such as a doll or a puppet, but also indicating that he is merely a prop in this play, a thing for the play, a specimen for show, both medical and theatrical. Frankenstitch worries that his neighbours have 'been disturbed by the freaks of my Infant' (II. 2, p. 174), with a double entendre on 'freaks': first a synonym for antics, mischievous activities, and, more seriously, a reference to abnormal or deformed humans.

Finally, the stage adaptations of Shelley's novel are resurrection enactments, offering victory over the mysteries of death. The anonymous adaptation *Frank-in-Steam; or, The Modern Promise to Pay* features a young medical student heavily in debt. Bailiffs are seeking him for arrest. Frankinsteam's lab assistant Fritz has robbed the grave of Snatch the Bailiff to procure what the scientist needs for his enterprising work. Although the audience is spared the sight of the grave-robbing scene, the phenomenon would have been familiar to theatergoers. When Fritz sees a body emanating from Frankinsteam's study, he surmises that he has snatched a body from its grave that was in fact not dead, but perhaps buried in a trance. The audience's gaze is therefore instructed to see the walking dead, a vampiric figure. To cover his incompetency, Fritz denounces body snatching, noting ironically: 'Plague on all Body Snatching say I — It militates against the liberty of the subject' (II. 1, p. 182). The subject of medical corpses was germane both to Shelley's novel and the theatrical adaptations. William Hunter asserts that for a complete course of anatomy, a physician needs 'a plentiful supply of dead bodies' and 'a complete stock of *preparations*'.[35] In procuring dead bodies, Hunter advises physicians:

> the dead body cannot be too fresh for dissection; every hour that it is kept, it is losing something of its fitness for anatomical demonstrations; the blood is transuding, and bringing all the parts nearer to one colour, which takes off the natural and distinct appearance; and putrefaction is advancing, which makes all the fleshy parts tender and indistinct.[36]

According to Hunter, a dead body is usually 'of little use for demonstration after eight or ten days'.[37] Resurrection men, the period's term for grave robbers, and physicians needed to be wary about the health of the corpse, as Hunter explains, 'diseases frequently alter the state of the parts, so as to render them unfit for a demonstration of their natural condition.'[38]

Frank-in-Steam integrated another reference to Shelley's novel that connects reanimation aspirations to scientific experiments. Frankinsteam refers to Snatch as a 'blue devil' whose 'mixture of Indigo and Whiting' make his touch abhorrent, worse than that of a 'Torpedo' (II. 1, p. 183). The description reminds spectators of electrical experiments conducted by scientists such as Giovanni Galvani and Erasmus Darwin on torpedo fish in efforts to revive them after they had expired. In *First Lines of Physiology*, Albrecht von Haller points to experiments in electrical stimulation and reanimation to which the play alludes. According to von Haller, the power and presence of fibres of the mind can continue 'a considerable time in a dead body, and may be recalled again into action by mechanical causes, as heat, inflation, &c. [...], although the mind may have been a long time separated from the body by a destruction of the brain'.[39] As von Haller explains, recently recovered corpses destined for demonstration at dissecting theatres and anatomy lectures were unlikely to function with healthy brains, even if they were revived. There must be 'consent' between the body and mind (II, 45), a connection that animation might find difficulty to accomplish but which a theatre-going audience might want to see attempted. The indigo and whiting also might hint at bluestockings, an intellectual group with which Mary Shelley herself could be identified, one that clearly resonates with her mother Mary Wollstonecraft.

Milner's adaptation *Frankenstein; or, The Man and the Monster* again emphasizes preoccupations with the scientist's victory over the grave. The audience sees Frankenstein intently engaged in calculations in his pavilion laboratory; he then turns to the audience and exclaims: 'Now that the final operation is accomplished, my panting heart dares scarcely gaze upon the object of its labours' (I. 3, p. 194). He feels the bosom of the figure lying on a table and covered with a black cloth. Frankenstein reports that the figure is breathing, and then the stage directions indicate that he

> rolls back the black covering, which discovers a colossal human figure, of a cadaverous livid complexion; it slowly begins to rise, gradually attaining an erect posture [...]. When it has attained a perpendicular position and glares its eyes upon him, he starts back with horror. (I. 3, p. 194)

Like Frankenstein, the theatergoers no doubt recoil in horror. Frankenstein further instructs the audience's gaze when he describes the creature all are now inspecting: 'a form of horror which I scarcely dare look upon: — instead of the fresh colour of humanity, he wears the livid hue of the damp grave' (I. 3, p. 194). Like Frankinsteam's description of Snatch in *Frank-in-Steam*, Frankenstein's description of his creature in Milner's play reminds spectators of the grave-robbing source of anatomists' work, the contamination and disease associated with such materials.

As with Frankenstein of Peake's *Presumption*, Milner's Frankenstein considers killing his creature, his disgust with his work being so strong. He muses: 'Is this the boasted wonder of my science ... a hideous monster, a loathsome mass of animated putrefaction, whom but to gaze on chills with horror even me, his maker? How, how shall I secrete him, how destroy?' (I. 4, p. 194). Frankenstein reinforces theatregoers' repulsion at what they see when he expresses his concern that mere contact with the wretch would spread a pestilence through his veins, suggesting that monstrosity is contagious. The monster's murder of Prince del Piombino's son does indeed taint Frankenstein with contagion. Lab assistant Strutt comments on the science which has reduced Frankenstein to the status of an outlaw, not for debt, as we saw in *Frank-in-Steam,* but for murder: 'Well, my master has done a nice job himself, it should seem, with all his machinery and magic; the making of a man has rendered him a made man for life' (II. 1, p. 198). Ironically, both *Frank-in-Steam* and Milner's adaptations remind spectators that it was frequently the bodies of hanged criminals that were resurrected by body snatchers as materials for anatomists and medical students. Frankinsteam and Frankenstein have become the very criminals whose corpses might well be the featured subject in a dissecting theatre.

The Monster and Magician; or, The Fate of Frankenstein, Kerr's adaptation, relies similarly on audience recognition of body snatching activities and directs the spectators' gaze through the vision of lab assistant Pietro. Pietro tells the audience he has seen a corpse. Offstage, Frankenstein confirms Pietro's account when he screams: 'Horror! horror! back daemon, fiend, back to the cold and lifeless corpse you were before my folly gave you animation — what fearful monster has hell resigned, oh — I feel his cold and clammy hand upon me still' (I. 3, p. 215). The audience's visual examination of the creature is enriched with tactile directions about the creature's hand that might cause them to recall experiential knowledge of cold and clammy hands of the sick and dying they know from their own circles of family and friends or the cold bodies presented on the tables of anatomical theatres.

Saint-Hilaire admonishes the careless and commercialized science theatricalized as entertainment. Concerned with the structures of organisms, Saint-Hilaire suggests that anatomical specimens based on Mary Shelley's originally conceived monster and represented on stage could dangerously contribute to the very whimsical understanding of human nature that his work sought to suppress:

> Quand à mon début je fus frappé du spectacle de monstruosités si nombreuses et bizarres jusqu'au degré de l'extravagance, il me sembla que je contemplais l'Organisation dans ses jours de saturnales, fatiguée à ce moment d'avoir trop longtemps industrieusement produit et cherchant des délassemens en s'abandonnant à des caprices.[40]

> [When I was first struck by the spectacle of so many bizarre and extravagant monstrosities, it seemed to me that I was contemplating human Organization in the days of unrestrained licentiousness, fatigued at this moment at having too long industriously produced, and looking for leisure by indulging in whims.]

Despite concerns from the scientific community, the theatrical adaptations of Mary Shelley's 1818 novel *Frankenstein* preserved the Frankenstein story for a public fascinated with both science and the supernatural, with both medical and Gothic accounts, with bodies both normal and monstrous. The dramatic productions were instrumental in the reception of Mary Shelley's work in Europe generally and in Great Britain specifically. When we think of *Frankenstein*, we connect the novel to movie adaptations, but we often neglect the extremely influential role played by the stage adaptations in making the novel-movie relationship possible and in maintaining the novel's continued popularity.

Notes to Chapter 8

1. Forry, *Hideous Progenies*, pp. 3–36; Audrey A. Fisch, '*Frankenstein*': *Icon of Modern Culture* (East Sussex: Helm Information, 2009), pp. 85–197; William St Clair, 'The Impact of *Frankenstein*', in *Mary Shelley in her Times*, ed. by Bennett and Curran, pp. 38–63 (pp. 52–54).
2. St Clair, 'The Impact of *Frankenstein*', p. 42.
3. Barbara Maria Stafford, *Artful Science: Enlightenment Entertainment and the Eclipse of Visual Education* (Cambridge, MA: MIT Press, 1999), p. 238.
4. Roy Porter, *Health for Sale: Quackery in England, 1660–1850* (Manchester: Manchester University Press, 1989), pp. 159–60; Marjean D. Purinton, 'George Colman's *The Iron Chest* and *Blue-Beard* and the Pseudoscience of Curiosity Cabinets', *Victorian Studies*, 49.2 (2007), 250–57 (p. 251).
5. Robert Bogdan, 'The Social Construction of Freaks', in *Freakery: Cultural Spectacles of the Extraordinary Body*, ed. by Rosemarie Garland-Thomson (New York: New York University Press, 1996), pp. 23–37 (p. 29).
6. Stephen C. Behrendt, 'Introduction', in Richard Brinsley Peake, *Presumption; or, The Fate of Frankenstein*, ed. by Stephen C. Behrendt (2001), in *Romantic Circles* <http://www.rc.umd.edu/print/editions/peake/apparatus/introduction.html> [accessed 28 November 2019].
7. Jane Moody, *Illegitimate Theatre in London, 1770–1840* (Cambridge: Cambridge University Press, 2000), p. 35.
8. Moody, *Illegitimate Theatre*, pp. 39, 198.
9. St Clair, 'The Impact of *Frankenstein*', p. 52.
10. William Hunter, *Two Introductory Lectures, Delivered by Dr. William Hunter, to his Last Course of Anatomical Lectures, at his Theatre in Windmill-Street [...]* (London: Johnson, 1784), p. 111.
11. Ibid, p. 111.

12. Ibid.
13. Ibid., p. 87.
14. Ibid., p. 109.
15. Peake, *Presumption; or, The Fate of Frankenstein*, ed. by Behrendt, I. 1.
16. *Frank-in-Steam; or, The Modern Promise to Pay*, in Forry, pp. 177–86 (II. 1, p. 182).
17. William Buchan, *Domestic Medicine; or, A Treatise on the Prevention and Cure of Diseases by Regimen and Simple Medicines [...]* (Dublin: printed for Chamberlaine, Williams, Moncrieffe, Burton, and Sleater, 1784), p. xxi.
18. Ibid., pp. xxii, xxv.
19. Hunter, *Two Introductory Lectures*, p. 110.
20. Thomas Beddoes, *Hygëia; or, Essays Moral and Medical on the Causes Affecting the Personal State of our Middling and Affluent Classes*, 3 vols (Briston: Mills, 1802–03), I, Essay 1, 38.
21. Ibid., I, 1, 58.
22. Henry M. Milner, *Frankenstein; or, The Man and the Monster*, in Forry, pp. 187–204 (I. 3, p. 194).
23. John Atkinson Kerr, *The Monster and Magician; or, The Fate of Frankenstein* (1826), in Forry, pp. 205–26 (I. 1, p. 215).
24. Buchan, *Domestic Medicine*, pp. 140–01.
25. Ibid., p. 172.
26. Beddoes, *Hygëia*, II, 6, 6–7.
27. Ibid., I, 1, 32.
28. Ibid., I, 1, p. 30.
29. Geoffroy Saint-Hilaire, *Philosophie anatomique: Des Monstruosités humaines*, 2 vols (Paris: Méquignon-Marvis, 1818; 1822), II, 507–08.
30. Unless otherwise stated, all translations are the author's.
31. Stephen C. Behrendt, 'The Cast and Characters', in *Presumption*, ed. by Behrendt <http://www.rc.umd.edu/print/editions/peake/apparatus/cast-characters.html> [accessed 25 February 2017].
32. Beddoes, *Hygëia*, I, 1, 33.
33. Ibid., I, 1, 34.
34. Richard Brinsley Peake, *Another Piece of Presumption*, in Forry, pp. 161–76 (II. 2, p. 172).
35. Hunter, *Two Introductory Lectures*, pp. 88–89.
36. Ibid., p. 87.
37. Ibid., p. 88.
38. Ibid.
39. Albrecht von Haller, *First Lines of Physiology [...]*, 2 vols (Edinburgh: printed for Charles Elliot, 1786), II, 49.
40. Saint-Hilaire, *Philosophie anatomique*, II, 539.

CHAPTER 9

Jules Saladin's 1821 Translation of *Frankenstein*

Anne Rouhette

Lawrence Venuti provides a significant understanding of translation as a creative exercise:

> Translation is not an untroubled communication of a foreign text, but an interpretation that is always limited by its address to specific audiences and by the cultural or institutional situations where the translated text is intended to circulate and function.[1]

A translation may act as a mask or a screen between the original work and the target audience, as Jacques Béreaud remarks,[2] but the cultural context in which that translation was produced may also work as a screen and may condition some of the choices made by the translator. This essay aims at examining Jules Saladin's 1821 translation of Mary Shelley's *Frankenstein* from this double perspective, reflecting on how this translation may have been influenced by the literary climate in which it came out and how it influenced the latter in its turn.

The translations of *Frankenstein* published in French, either in France or in French-speaking countries, have been well documented and include at least twelve different versions, although Saladin's, which was the first in any language and the only one produced in the nineteenth century, remains to this day the sole French translation of the 1818 text.[3] It was not reissued, however, until 1975, after which it was revised several times by different authors. An exhaustive record of the various translations of *Frankenstein* in French up to 2019, including a few adaptations in other formats (graphic novels, animation films, television series), can be found online on <nooSFere.org>, a non-academic website devoted to science fiction, completing the list compiled in *Romantic Circles* until 2009.[4] That *Frankenstein* should be thus closely linked to fantasy literature might have been expected, but it is worth noting that this association impacts the entire reception of Mary Shelley in France, as we will see below.

The following chart lists, in chronological order of their publication, Shelley's writings (other than *Frankenstein*) as they appeared in French translation:

Title	French Translation	Source	Date
The Last Man (1826) extracts	*Le Dernier homme* (extract), translator unknown	*Bibliothèque universelle des sciences, belles-lettres, et arts [...]* Rédigée à Genève, 34: Littérature[5]	1827
'The Brother and Sister' (1832)	'Le Frère et la sœur', translator unknown	*Le Salmigondis*, 3	1832
Matilda (1819–20, 1st pub. 1959)	*Mathilda*, trans. by Marie-Françoise Desmeuzes	Paris: Éditions des Femmes	1984
The Last Man (1826)	*Le Dernier homme*, trans. by Paul Couturiau	Paris: Éditions du Rocher	1988, repub. 1998
'The Mourner', 'The Mortal Immortal', 'The Dream', 'Transformation'	*L'Endeuillée et autres récits*, trans. by Liliane Abensour ('L'Endeuillée', 'Le Mortel immortel', 'Le Rêve', 'Transformation')	Paris: Corti	1993
'Valerius, the Reanimated Roman' (1st pub. 1976), 'The Invisible Girl' (1832)	'Valérius le ressuscité', trans. by Norbert Gaulard 'La Demoiselle invisible', trans. by Anne-Sylvie Homassel	*Le Visage vert*, 1	1995
'The Invisible Girl', 'A Tale of the Passions', 'Ferdinando Eboli', 'Euphrasia'	*La Jeune fille invisible*, trans. by Nicole Berry ('La Jeune fille invisible', 'Une Histoire de passions; ou, La Mort de Despina', 'Ferdinando Eboli', 'Euphrasia')	Toulouse: Éditions Ombres	1996, repub. 2002[6]
Valperga (1823)	*Valperga*, trans. by Nicole Berry	Lausanne: L'Âge d'homme	1997
'Maurice; or, The Fisher's Cot' (1820, 1st pub. 2000)	*Maurice; ou, Le Cabanon du pêcheur*, trans. by Anna Bellucci	Paris: Gallimard	2001
History of a Six Weeks' Tour (1817) and *Frankenstein* (1818)	*Frankenstein sur la Mer de Glace*, trans. by Christophe Jacquet (contains excerpts from *Frankenstein* and from *History of a Six Weeks' Tour*)	Chamonix: Guérin	2007
The Fortunes of Perkin Warbeck (1830)	*Les Aventures de Perkin Warbeck*, trans. by Anne Rouhette	Paris: Classiques Garnier	2014, repub. 2016
History of a Six Weeks' Tour (1817)	*Histoire d'un voyage de six semaines*, trans. by Anne Rouhette	Aix-en-Provence: Presses Universitaires de Provence	2015
Journal (extracts)	*Que les étoiles contemplent mes larmes: Journal d'affliction*, trans. by Constance Lacroix	Paris: Finitude	2017

TABLE 9.1. French translations of Mary Shelley's writings other than *Frankenstein*

With the exception of an extract from *The Last Man*, published in Geneva in 1827, none of Shelley's other novels were translated until the end of the twentieth century, although *The Last Man* and *Lodore* were both advertised in the French press when they were published in London and could probably be found in Paris. A rise of interest in Mary Shelley and in women's writing in general, corresponding to the rediscovery and publication of her works in English-speaking countries, explains the growing availability of her work in France from the 1980s onwards, but usually without the critical apparatus found in many British or American editions. Thus, the first publishing company to register interest in Shelley's other novels was Éditions des Femmes, founded by an avowed feminist, Antoinette Fouque, who wished to foreground works written by women and brought out a translation of *Mathilda* [sic] in 1984. *The Last Man* followed in 1988, by the publisher Éditions Ombres, *Valperga* in 1997 by L'Âge d'homme, and *Perkin Warbeck* in 2014 by Classiques Garnier. Shelley's travel writing has drawn attention in the twenty-first century, which is partly due to an increasing interest in the genre and to topical considerations: the publishing company which issued *Frankenstein sur la Mer de Glace; ou, Le Voyage des Genève à Chamonix* is situated in Chamonix and specializes in mountain literature, dealing particularly with Alpine sceneries. In this work, the translator Christophe Jacquet interestingly combines excerpts from *Frankenstein* and from *History of a Six Weeks's Tour* to highlight the parallels between the two works.

Apart from Saladin's *Frankenstein* and from the extract from *The Last Man* already mentioned, only one of Shelley's tales was translated into French in the nineteenth century, 'The Brother and Sister', published in December 1832 in an elegant magazine, *Le Salmigondis*, a few weeks after its original publication in *The Keepsake*. Mary Shelley's name was used in *Le Figaro* of 12 February 1832 to advertise *Le Salmigondis*, along with Alexandre Dumas's and Lord Normanby's, suggesting that her reputation was then high enough in France to be considered a commercial asset — on what grounds, that is a question which the end of this essay will address. Other translations of her stories were published in the last decade of the twentieth century, including two versions of 'The Invisible Girl', first published in 1995 together with 'Valerius', in the first issue of *Le Visage vert*.[7]

Since *Le Visage vert* is devoted to fantasy and horror stories, the choice of this magazine is both problematic and illuminating regarding the reception of Mary Shelley in France today. It may have made some sense to include 'Valerius' in such a publication, at least for the basic idea on which the unfinished story rests (that of an inhabitant of Ancient Rome reanimated in nineteenth century Italy), but despite its title, 'The Invisible Girl' bears no trace whatsoever of the fantastic. Those stories were chosen precisely because of their titles and published because they were 'By the Author of *Frankenstein*', as the title page of her other novels indicated, an authorship on which the magazine capitalized. Together with the relative dearth of scientific editions of Mary Shelley's work in French, this points to the partial misunderstanding under which the reception of her writing has been labouring for the general public in France (and elsewhere), a misunderstanding which may be traced to the first translation of *Frankenstein* in French.

At the time of its publication in France,[8] the reception of Saladin's translation was not particularly enthusiastic. As far as I know, it was reviewed only in the *Revue encyclopédique* in July 1821, in which the novel is presented as the 'bizarre production d'une imagination malade' ['bizarre product of a diseased imagination'].[9] Although the reviewer recognizes that the work is not devoid of talent, the judgement is overwhelmingly negative, calling the novel disgusting and absurd, in part, clearly, because it had been written by a woman.[10] Its popular and commercial success is difficult to assess. The three slim volumes of *Frankenstein* were sold for the relatively cheap price of 7.5 francs, probably because the novel was short by contemporary standards — if one volume could reach 10 francs, a complete set of three usually approximated 15 francs at the time.[11] It was not reprinted, but was immediately turned into a play in August 1821, which may reveal a certain degree of popularity. *Frankenstein; ou, Le Prométhée moderne* was announced in *Le Miroir des spectacles* as a melodrama — the Creature was to have been an automaton — although there is no record of a possible performance.[12]

Before dealing with Saladin's translation at greater length, it is necessary to describe briefly the general cultural context in which English novels were translated in France in the 1820s and the literary climate in which the French *Frankenstein* appeared, because they may account for some features of Saladin's version. In 1821, out of 246 novels published in France, 72 were translated from another language, which represents 29.3 per cent.[13] The overwhelming majority of these novels were originally written in English, but the very short delays and low pay explained the poor quality of many translations at the time.[14] However, the liberty taken with the source texts was also the result of a long tradition of literary translation in France which endured through the beginning of the nineteenth century, according to which texts were rewritten according to the neo-classical standards of the eighteenth century in order to better appeal to the French tastes.[15] This was notably the case in the late 1810s and the early 1820s with the translations of Gothic novels, for which French readers were greedier than ever — for instance, there were re-editions both of Ann Radcliffe's *Udolpho* and Matthew Gregory Lewis's *The Monk* in 1819.[16] This fascination for the macabre corresponded to the literary atmosphere in France at a time which saw the early days of what came to be known as 'le Romantisme frénétique'. One of the leading authors of this period was Charles Nodier, who adapted John Polidori's *Vampyre* for the stage in 1820 and, with Justin Taylor, translated Charles Maturin's *Bertram* in 1821. In the same year, which also saw the publication of Saladin's *Frankenstein*, two translations of Maturin's *Melmoth* came out. Neither of them would be considered satisfactory in modern terms, since the two translators cut out about one fourth of the text and freely rewrote numerous passages, altering the style considerably in the attempt to make it more palatable to the French public, as one of them, Mme Bégin, explains:

> J'ai retranché près d'un volume de longueurs qui me semblaient ralentir l'action et l'intérêt [...], j'ai tâché d'affaiblir, autant que me l'a permis le sujet, la couleur romantique de l'auteur anglais, dont je suis souvent parvenue à rendre le style simple et naturel.[17]

> [I have pared down nearly one volume of lengthy descriptions which I thought slowed down the action and diminished interest [...], I have tried to tone down as far as the topic would let me the Romantic quality of the English author, whose style I have often managed to make simple and natural.]

Many of Walter Scott's novels, which became very popular in France in the early 1820s, suffered the same treatment at the hands of his most famous French translator, Jean-Baptiste Defauconpret, who largely rewrote *Old Mortality* (1817), in particular, and headed a whole team of translators more concerned with the tastes of their target audience than with the subtleties of Scott's religious and political plots.[18]

This approach to translation contrasts sharply with Mary Shelley's, both from a practical and a theoretical point of view. In *Mary Shelley dans son œuvre*, Jean de Palacio alludes to her work as a translator for the *Lives* she wrote for Dionysius Lardner's *Cabinet Cyclopædia* between 1835 and 1839 and to the conception of translation which is occasionally evoked in her writing or apparent in her own translations.[19] He emphasizes her concern for the 'literal' character of a translation, in the sense that it should aim at being close to the original in both content and form, and quotes for instance her regret that 'Lord Strangford's translation [of Luís de Camoens' Sonnet XXIV] is not literal'.[20]

Shelley's *Frankenstein* could, however, have fallen into worse hands than those of her French publisher, Alexandre Corréard. One of the few survivors of the Medusa shipwreck, Corréard was himself a translated author: he had written a narrative of his adventures whose English version was published in 1818 to great success. Corréard's interest lay more particularly in political works, including pamphlets which would have been called 'radical' in Britain; he went to jail several times and his company, seen as seditious, was finally closed down in 1822. The dedication to William Godwin, which appears on the French title page of *Frankenstein*, possibly explained Corréard's decision to publish Shelley's first novel, but there were already a few translated novels in his catalogue: for instance, in 1821, he published a version of Scott's *Kenilworth* by Jacques-Theodore Parisot, a much more respectful and careful translator than Defauconpret, which suggests that Corréard may well have paid careful attention to the literary quality of the translations he published, instead of looking exclusively at the money to be made.

At first sight, Jules Saladin would seem to share Mary Shelley's preference for literal translation, stressing his respect for 'literalness' ('la littéralité') in the preface he wrote for his 1822 translation of Thomas Otway's *Don Carlos*. Yet as the following excerpt shows, the term 'literal' holds a different meaning for Shelley and for her translator:[21]

> Il y a bien dans la tragédie de *Don Carlos* quelques images vives, et des expressions peu ménagées, que j'ai cherché à adoucir sans manquer à la littéralité dont je me suis fait une loi; mais elle n'a point le cachet qu'on a pu reconnaître dans quelques ouvrages du même auteur.[22]

> [The tragedy of *Don Carlos* does contain a few forceful images, and some ill-chosen phrases, which I have tried to soften without going against the literalness which I have made my law; but it does not share the same character as that found in some other works by the same author.]

Of course, toning down the style of the source text is not exactly a sign of 'literalness'. Further on, Saladin points out that Otway's style lacks somewhat in 'elegance' ('il s'écarte un peu de ce qu'exige l'élégance', p. 278), a reflexion which would not have come amiss in the heyday of the eighteenth-century *belles infidèles*[23] and hints that as a translator, he might have practised a certain form of cleansing to 'improve' the original and achieve that much sought-after elegance.

However, if one keeps in mind its translator's biases and the translational practices at the time, it seems that the 1821 French *Frankenstein* escapes relatively unscathed and that it may be considered a 'faithful' translation, in the sense that nothing was omitted, added or rewritten and hardly anything was altered. Mary Shelley's style, in particular, is on the whole respected, as Saladin's version does not display the traits which characterize the only other French translation of Shelley's work to appear in the nineteenth century, namely that of 'The Brother and Sister' published in *Le Salmigondis* in 1832. A brief analysis of this translation reveals a clear slant towards sensationalism, characterized in particular by the addition of adverbs, adjectives, and tropes which aim at making the text more dramatic: for example, '[h]e had been wounded' becomes 'il avait été *grièvement* blessé' (emphasis added), while 'hatred to his foes, and love for his native town' is rendered by 'une haine *violente* pour ses ennemis, un *ardent* amour pour sa ville' (emphasis added).[24]

Saladin's translation does, however, present a few notable problems, of which I will give a quick overview before focusing on what represents an actual distortion of Shelley's meaning. The linguistic mistakes are usually trivial and clearly involuntary, sometimes even amusing: for instance, instead of 'la Suisse', Switzerland becomes 'le Switzerland', as though the novel took place in an imaginary country; the notes referring to Samuel Taylor Coleridge or William Wordsworth are reproduced *verbatim*, with the English genitive; for some mysterious reason, Mary Shelley has become Godwin's niece on the title page — the phonetic rendering of her name as 'Mme Shelly', however, was common at the time. From the perspective of today's critics and readers, other changes, however, appear more regrettable. Certain allusions, slight perhaps but suggestive in nature, are eliminated from Shelley's text: thus, when she is first described, Elizabeth Lavenza is no longer presented as a 'summer insect' but as *un papillon* ['a butterfly'], and she is not a 'creature' but a *femme*.[25] The textual web which connects the Creature, also called an 'insect' (p. 67), and the feminine characters in the novel thereby partly disappears.

More profoundly, Saladin's *Frankenstein* arguably suffered from the sensationalist context into which it was published because it consistently displays a series of lexical mistakes that are otherwise inexplicable, all having the effect of stressing the supernatural element in Shelley's novel. Saladin thus almost systematically translated 'chemistry' by *alchimie* and 'chemist' by *alchimiste*, especially in the early parts of the novel.[26] To take just one example: 'I should certainly have thrown Agrippa aside, and, with my imagination warmed as it was, should probably have applied myself to the more rational theory of chemistry which has resulted from modern discoveries' (p. 22) is rendered as 'j'aurais certainement jeté Agrippa de côté, et, avec une imagination échauffée comme la mienne, je me serais probablement appliqué à la théorie d'alchimie, la plus raisonnable qui soit résultée des découvertes modernes' (p. 77–78). *L'alchimie*, not *la chimie*, thus becomes the rational science of the day. In the same line of thought, M. Waldman teaches not only *l'alchimie* but more specifically *l'alchimie moderne* (I, 104), an oxymoron at the time when the novel is supposed to take place, which, together with all the other occurrences of the term, enhances the medieval atmosphere of the novel, as alchemy appears as the modern science, and conveys an aura of magic. Where Shelley manages a complex questioning of science and reaches a delicate balance between ancient and modern conceptions of science, the translation tilts the scales unequivocally in one direction and privileges the magical element — at the cost of a certain incoherence since the chronological indications remain those of the original and locate the novel at the end of the eighteenth century.

Similarly unfortunate effects are produced in other passages. When Saladin renders '[n]ot that, like a magic scene, it all opened upon me at once' (p. 32) by '[t]out se présentait à moi comme une scène magique' (I, 108), he overlooks the 'not' with which the sentence begins and expresses a meaning exactly contrary to that of Shelley's sentence, even though the rest of the passage, in which the difficulty of Victor's work is related, is correctly translated. Not only does this grammatical mistake produce, once again, a certain incoherence, but it likens the creation of the Monster to a magical process precisely where Shelley negates this. Such 'magification' is also perceptible in other translational choices. For example, whereas Shelley carefully distinguishes between natural, unnatural, and supernatural elements in her story, the word 'unnatural' is systematically translated by Saladin as *surnaturel*, a word also used, correctly this time, for 'supernatural', so that the difference between the two disappears. When Victor is animated with an 'unnatural stimulus' (p. 34), he is acted upon, in Saladin's translation, by an *aiguillon surnaturel* (I, 125), suggesting a form of possession. Lastly, the nature of the Creature is no longer ambiguous as in the original version of the novel, but instead presented as entirely supernatural. Where Shelley describes him as 'a figure' (p. 50), he becomes *un fantôme*, a ghost (I, 198), which is indeed a recurring choice on the translator's part; while he is presented by Walton at the very end of Shelley's novel as 'a form' ('over him hung a form', p. 158), the translation transforms him into a spectre ('sur lui était penché un spectre', III, 143). Saladin thus deliberately stressed the supernatural, which may result from a conscious decision to rewrite the text in order to give it a more sensational aspect or from the influence of his literary environment, or both.

Little is known about Shelley's first translator, who signed 'J. S★★★' on the title page of *Frankenstein*, apart from the fact that he translated Francis Lathom's 1820 *Italian Mysteries* (*Les Mystères italiens, ou, Le Château della Torrida*, Paris: Garnot, 1823), which he signed as 'by one of the translators of Walter Scott's historical novels'. This signature suggests that he belonged to Defauconpret's hirelings, although to my knowledge no record exists of such a collaboration. The previous year, he had translated Otway's play *Don Carlos* for the second volume of a series dedicated to the masterpieces of English drama (*Chefs-d'œuvre du théâtre anglais*), a series to whose first volume, also published in 1822, Charles Nodier had contributed. I have not been able so far to establish firmly that Saladin and Nodier knew each other, but this is a reasonable assumption to make given that they both belonged to the circle of Amédée Pichot, one of the most famous French translators of the nineteenth century. A member of Defauconpret's team,[27] Pichot took part in the translations of the *Chefs-d'œuvre du théâtre anglais*, produced French versions of Lord Byron's and Scott's poetry, and would later retranslate *Caleb Williams* (1868).[28] In his translation of Byron's works, prefaced by Nodier, Pichot mentions Saladin as the man who introduced him to Thomas Medwin in Paris and describes him in a note as a man 'qui à toute l'instruction de l'homme de lettres joint l'amabilité de l'homme du monde' ['who, to the knowledge of a man of letters, adds the pleasantness of a man of the world'].[29] Pichot was clearly a link between Nodier and Saladin, who were both interested in the English Romantic circle (witness Nodier's stage adaptation of Polidori's *Vampyre* in 1820 and his preface to the French version of Byron's poems), although the friendship between Pichot and Nodier really only blossomed in 1822 and 1823, so shortly after Saladin's translation of *Frankenstein*.[30] Rather than to the direct influence of one particular man therefore, I would argue that the transformations Saladin brought to *Frankenstein* are attributable to the literary context in which he worked.

Did Saladin's *Frankenstein* influence Nodier and others in its turn? What follows is again speculative. Even if only a manuscript remains of the French play directly based on Shelley's novel and mentioned above, traces of *Frankenstein* are perceptible in *Le Monstre et le magicien*, a very successful *Mélodrame Féerique* that was performed at the Théâtre de la Porte Saint-Martin in June 1826. Charles Nodier contributed to this play by Jean-Toussaint Merle and Antony Béraud, from which the names 'Frankenstein' and 'Mary Shelley' disappeared. The filiation with Shelley's novel was nevertheless obvious: both the press and Mary Shelley herself acknowledged that this play was an adaptation of *Frankenstein*, although apparently it owed more to Richard Brinsley Peake's dramatization of *Frankenstein, Presumption; or, The Fate of Frankenstein* than to the original.[31] The role of Monster was performed by an English artist, Thomas Cooke, who had already played the part of Peake's Creature on the London stage in 1823. As the title indicates, the hero is no longer a scientist but a magician, a sixteenth-century alchemist called Zametti, giving birth to his monster in a puff of smoke. Perhaps inspired by Saladin's view of Shelley's novel, this play offers the audience a purely sensational experience, giving pride of place to the supernatural to the detriment of all the other elements and firmly associating *Frankenstein* with the magical and the satanic. That this association was made by the French audience at least throughout the nineteenth century, and possibly beyond, appears clearly in several summaries purporting to be of Shelley's novel and published in nineteenth-century French literary histories or dictionaries in which the monster becomes an actual demon taking Frankenstein's soul to hell: 'Le malheureux étudiant se laisse mourir: dernier triomphe du monstre qui, ne déguisant plus son origine satanique, vient prendre l'âme du chimiste et la jette aux damnés' ['The unfortunate student languishes and dies — this is the ultimate triumph of the monster who, no longer concealing his satanic origin, steals the chemist's soul and throws it to the damned.'].[32] It seems likely that Mary Shelley's reputation in France suffered from such fantastic misreadings of her first novel, to which her first translator contributed.

Notes to Chapter 9

1. Lawrence Venuti, *The Translator's Invisibility: A History of Translation*, 2nd edn (Abingdon: Routledge, 2008 [1995]), p. 14.
2. Jacques Béreaud, 'La Traduction en France à l'époque romantique', *Comparative Literature Studies*, 8. 3 (1971), 224–44 (p. 225).
3. As a comparison, the first German and Italian versions of *Frankenstein* date respectively from 1912 and 1944. Taking a position which does not appear to reflect recent Shelley scholarship, Alain Morvan chose to translate the 1831 version for the highly prestigious and supposedly authoritative 'Pléiade' collection in 2014; he argued that since, in his view, there are hardly any differences between the two texts, a translator may as well choose the latter, perfected version of the work. See Alain Morvan, 'Note sur le texte', in Mary Shelley, *Frankenstein et autres romans gothiques*, trans. by Alain Morvan and Marc Porée, ed. by Alain Morvan, Bibliothèque de la Pléiade (Paris: Gallimard, 2014), p. 1351.
4. See 'Frankenstein; ou, Le Prométhé moderne', *nooSFere* <https://www.noosfere.org/livres/editionslivre.asp?numitem=1642> [accessed 12 December 2019].
5. I wish to thank Philippe Kassarian for drawing my attention to this nineteenth-century Swiss translation.
6. The 2002 edition, published in Villegly by Encre bleue in their series 'Basse vision', aimed at the visually impaired, contained 'La Jeune fille invisible' and 'Une Histoire de passions'.
7. 'Valérius le ressuscité', trans. by Norbert Gaulard; 'La Demoiselle invisible', trans. by Anne-Sylvie Homassel, Le Visage vert, 1 (October 1995; last revised 14 May 2012). <http://www.levisagevert.com/Revues/visagevert/visagevert/vv01.html> [accessed 19 March 2020].
8. Its publication was announced in the 21 July 1821 issue of *Bibliographie de la France*, p. 33, <https://gallica.bnf.fr/ark:/12148/bpt6k6391319v/f7.item.r=frankenstein> [accessed 20 March 2020].
9. M. A. J. [Marc-Antoine Jullien], review of Mary Shelley, *Frankenstein; ou, Le Prométhée Moderne*, in *La Revue encyclopédique*, 9 (1821), 191–92 (p. 191). Unless otherwise stated, all translations are by the author.
10. 'On voudrait surtout que l'ouvrage d'une femme offrît des peintures aimables et gracieuses au lieu d'objets et de récits toujours révoltans [*sic*] et hideux' ['One wishes especially that a work written by a woman would offer lovely and graceful descriptions instead of always revolting and hideous topics.'], M. A. J., review, p. 192.
11. The average print run was about 2500 copies at the time. See *Histoire des traductions en langue française, XIXe siècle, 1815–1914*, ed. by Chevrel, D'Hulst, and Lombez, p. 276 (hereafter *Histoire des traductions*).
12. Steven Forry, 'Dramatizations of *Frankenstein*, 1821–1986: A Comprehensive List', *English Language Notes*, 25.2 (1987), 63–79 (p. 74); 'Variétés', *Le Miroir des spectacles, des lettres, des mœurs et des arts*, 139 (2 July 1821), 4.
13. *Histoire des traductions*, p. 268.
14. Ibid., p. 270.
15. On the terms on and conditions in which translators worked, see *Histoire des traductions*, pp. 169–85. On the conceptions of translation in France in the first third of the nineteenth century, see *Histoire des traductions*, pp. 51–74; Béreaud, 'La Traduction en France à l'époque romantique', p. 228.
16. *Histoire des traductions*, p. 544. Joëlle Prungnaud notes that the Gothic genre remained very popular in France until at least 1830; see her 'La Traduction du roman gothique anglais en France au tournant du XVIIIe siècle', *TTR: traduction, terminologie, rédaction*, 7.1 (1994), 11–46 (p. 12).
17. Cited in *Histoire des traductions*, p. 545.

18. *Histoire des traductions*, pp. 273–76. On Defauconpret, see for instance Patrick Hersant, 'Defauconpret ou le demi-siècle d'Auguste', *Romantisme*, 29.106 (1999) 83–88; Béreaud, 'La Traduction en France à l'époque romantique'.
19. De Palacio, *Mary Shelley dans son œuvre*, pp. 523–29. Although Palacio focuses more particularly on poetical translation, he notes that Mary Shelley's translations of prose are both accurate and pleasant to read (p. 528).
20. Cited in de Palacio, *Mary Shelley dans son œuvre*, p. 527, n. 227.
21. Béreaud, 'La Traduction en France à l'époque romantique' (pp. 228–30), studies the strange approach to literal translation ('traduction littérale') in France in the late 1820s, which did not preclude, and in fact even encouraged, a form of cleansing ('épuration').
22. Jules Saladin, 'Notice sur *Don Carlos*', in *Chefs-d'œuvre du théâtre anglais*, 5 vols (Paris: Ladvocat, 1822–23), II: *Rowe, Otway, Dodsley* (1822), pp. 267–79 (p. 271).
23. In the seventeenth and eighteenth centuries, the *belles infidèles* (literally: 'beautiful unfaithful ones') were 'translations characterized by strong literary values and highly adaptative or "localizing" translation strategies aimed at making the original author "speak French" according to the standards of taste of the day', as Julie Candler Hayes explains in *Translation, Subjectivity and Culture in France and England, 1600–1800* (Stanford: Stanford University Press, 2009), p. 3.
24. Mary Shelley, 'The Brother and Sister', in *Collected Tales and Stories*, ed. by Robinson, pp. 166–89 (p. 167 for the two quotations); 'Le Frère et la sœur', trans. anon., *Le Salmigondis*, 3 (1832), 159–219 (pp. 161, 163).
25. Mary Shelley, *Frankenstein* [1818], ed. by Hunter, p. 20 for the two quotations; *Frankenstein*, trans. by Jules Saladin, 3 vols (Paris: Corréard, 1821), I, 68 and 69. Further references to these two editions are given in the main text.
26. This is always the case in the first volume but is corrected in the last, where the 'chemical instrument[s]' (pp. 31, 43, 110, 114, 122), earlier rendered as 'instrumens [sic] d'alchimie' (I, 113, 169), become 'instrumens [sic] de chimie' (III, 19, 37, 74).
27. *Histoire des traductions*, p. 595.
28. Laurence Adolphus Bisson, *Amédée Pichot: A Romantic Prometheus* (Oxford: Blackwell, 1942), p. 221. Nodier and Saladin are both among the recipients of the letters published by Pichot in the third volume of his *Voyage historique et littéraire en Angleterre et en Écosse* (1825).
29. Amédée Pichot, 'Avant-Propos', *Œuvres de Lord Byron*, 4th edn, 8 vols (Paris: Ladvocat, 1822–25), VIII (1825), 187–89 (p. 188).
30. See Michel Salomon, *Charles Nodier et le groupe romantique* (Paris: Perrin, 1908), p. 180.
31. 'How goes Frankenstein of Porte St. Martin?', asked Shelley in a letter to John Howard Payne of 11 June 1826 (*MWS Letters*, I, 521).
32. André Delrieu, 'Shelley', *Revue de Paris*, 23 (1843), 183–230 (p. 226). Delrieu attributes to Percy Shelley the authorship of the best parts of *Frankenstein*. His presentation of the novel was reprinted almost *verbatim* in Pierre Larousse's *Le Grand dictionnaire universel du XIXe siècle: Français, historique, géographique, mythologique, bibliographique [...]*, 15 vols (Paris: [n. pub.], 1866–76), VIII: *F–G* (1872), p. 782.

CHAPTER 10

Becoming Human: *Frankenstein* at the National Theatre

Catherine Pugh

Frankenstein is a story that is at home on the stage. Its Gothic atmosphere, highly theatrical narrative, and iconic images make it compelling for a dramatic audience. The extraordinary popularity of the first dramatization, Richard Brinsley Peake's *Presumption; or, The Fate of Frankenstein* (1823),[1] arguably contributed to the publication of the novel's second edition. Within three years of its premiere, *Presumption* inspired fourteen English and French dramatizations, including Jean-Toussaint Merle and Antony Béraud's *Le Monstre et le magicien* (1826) and Henry Milner's *The Man and the Monster* (1826). Together, these three key melodramas established many enduring conventions for both theatrical and cinematic adaptations of the novel, as well as contributing to the public's conception of *Frankenstein* (such as the common assumption that Frankenstein is the Creature and the introduction of a laboratory assistant). Steven Earl Forry summarizes the remoulding of the myth, noting that playwrights charged the tale with alchemy, developed solely the Gothic (or romance) aspects of the story, abandoned the doppelgänger theme in favour of a straightforward Byronic hero-villain (Frankenstein) tormented by a dumb show villain-hero (the Creature), and simplified the plot by removing Walton's narrative, confining the action to twenty-four hours, and reducing the major characters to four types: the hero, the villain, the persecuted heroine, and the comical rustic.[2]

For the most part, dramatic interpretations of *Frankenstein* adhered to these parameters, both on stage and — with the introduction of James Whale's 1931 cinematic adaptation — on screen, turning it into what Forry calls a 'simplistic moral allegory'.[3] Since *Presumption*, Mary Shelley's myth has gradually eroded through countless (re)interpretations, reshaped by massive changes in technology as well as the changing focus of social concern. As her 'hideous progeny'[4] continues to evolve, Shelley's voice is inevitably drowned out. On 5 February 2011, the National Theatre in London premiered a production of *Frankenstein*, adapted by Nick Dear and directed by Danny Boyle. Additionally, the production was screened across cinemas worldwide in March 2011 as part of National Theatre Live broadcasts. It proved to be one of the National's most popular screenings, prompting several national and international encores since 2012. Not only did Dear's script return the Creature's voice and eloquence — features that are strikingly absent in the majority of dramatizations — but the production itself was notable for the two principal actors (Benedict Cumberbatch and Jonny Lee Miller) alternating the roles of Victor Frankenstein and the Creature for every performance.

Constant adaptations and reproductions have fundamentally altered audiences' perceptions of the novel. Pedro Javier Pardo Garcia argues that as 'most films do not take Mary Shelley's text as a point of departure, but previous film versions' the novel instead becomes 'one more version of [the Frankenstein] myth — the founding, but not necessarily the most influential one'.[5] In Dear's adaptation, both writer and director consciously aim to reject traditional dramatic conventions of the Frankenstein myth, endeavouring to put the author Mary Shelley back onto the stage by engaging directly with the novel rather than the myth.[6] Despite the many distinguishing tropes of *Frankenstein*, Dear notes Shelley's lack of a distinctive authorial voice, compounded by the format of the novel. The use of multiple narrators, letters, and Walton's Arctic adventures as a framing device all collude to fragment the narrative, destabilizing any overriding authorial identity. Therefore, in any *Frankenstein* adaptation or reinterpretation, the 'voices' of Victor and (in particular) the Creature become a vital part of establishing the identity of the text. Aspects such as the setting, time period, characters, genre, and even plot can be altered, but Victor and the Creature must remain, to speak for the story and for themselves.

10.1. 'I Will Fight to Live': Early *Frankenstein* Adaptations[7]

Early cinematic adaptations of *Frankenstein* tended to concentrate on the Gothic horror of the text, as special effects meant that cinema was 'the perfect medium of interpreting the Sensation dramas of the 1880s and 1890s' and 'the perfect medium for terror'.[8] Other adaptations explore different techniques and subgenres, such as Whale's German Expressionism-inspired critique on technology and industrialization, Kenneth Branagh's romanticized portrayal (*Mary Shelley's Frankenstein*, 1994), the action-led plot of Stuart Beattie's *I, Frankenstein* (2014), the trauma-centric television series *Penny Dreadful* (2014–16), created by John Logan, and the bio-fiction crime drama *The Frankenstein Chronicles* (2015–17), created by Benjamin Ross and Barry Langford. Dear and Boyle intentionally attempt to avoid popular cinematic conventions, most notably during the Creature's 'birth' from an upright, circular pseudo-womb at the very start of the play. Dear explains that this design was established during pre-production in order to differentiate the play from the outset:

> from the very first image you see in the theatre, it is not going to be the thing on the slab — and we always say 'on the slab' — it is going to be upright. And that informs almost every other decision we make.[9]

Although it features both horror and Romantic elements, Dear's adaptation focuses on exploring what it is to be human, therefore both writer and director moved away from commonly utilized tropes and images. By removing as many stereotypes, inorganic, and extraneous material as possible,[10] Dear's script has been pared down to focus on Victor, the Creature, and the central conflict between them. This conflict is arguably twofold: firstly, exploring in a more general way what it is to be the creator and the created (namely, what it is to be human) and secondly, the specific conflict of the Creature confronting his creator and Victor's responsibility not only for the Creature's life but also his behaviour. Therefore, the return of the Creature's voice is as essential as it is in Shelley's text. In the novel, the Creature not only speaks, but does so with eloquence, reason, and cultural knowledge. Peake's play took away the Creature's voice, simultaneously removing a key part of what makes him a sympathetic, subjective character. Jeanette Laredo clarifies that, 'by rendering him mute Peake accomplished two things: he furthered the moral of the play since an articulate creature would undercut Frankenstein's "impious" act of creation, and made the creature more frightening by stripping him of his humanity.'[11] The Creature devolves from being a coherent, expressive, and rational being to something more akin to a beast or automaton.[12] Dear suggests that the central argument between Victor and the Creature suits theatre better than cinema, partly because the stage offers room for the relationship to play out. Whereas on stage there is 'enough dynamism in the central conflict' to entertain while keeping the action static, cinema 'just wouldn't accept that you could stand there and have an argument for that length of time. [...] It no longer accords with the grammar of editing in the conventional lot of films'.[13]

Forry ponders why dramatizations of the Frankenstein myth were so popular in early nineteenth-century Britain and France. While noting the 'star power' of actor T. P. Cooke playing the Creature in both *Presumption* and *Le Monstre et le magicien*,[14] Forry writes that Peake's dramatization premiering, 'at the height of the popularity of Gothic melodrama accounts for its selection as a subject but fails to explain completely the play's immediate success and the continual outpouring of other dramatizations.'[15] Forry goes on to suggest that the popularity of these dramatizations was, in part, due to the fact that Frankenstein and the Creature are so open to interpretation, primed for adoption by different ideologies. In the nineteenth century, with the onset of huge social upheaval and a wariness brewing over the industrial revolution, the Frankenstein myth inevitably became intertwined with social unrest and the fear of technology:

> Clearly, Frankenstein and his Creature touched a raw nerve in France, a nation in which the anti-tyrannical or 'Bastille' drama evolved in response to the post-Revolutionary maelstrom. Reviewers of *Le Monstre et le magicien* immediately equated the Creature with mob violence [...]. The point would not be lost in England, where conservatives ever since the reign of the Sanscoulottes [sic] had linked social reform and mob rule. The times themselves proved ripe for such a symbol, especially since between 1815 and the mid-century the country stood on the verge of its own revolution. Therefore, on the English stage — to say nothing of the novel's reputation in print — Frankenstein immediately became associated with unbridled revolution, atheism, and blind progress in science and technology.[16]

Forry goes on to argue that gradually Frankenstein's 'scientific quest gave way to alchemical rituals and his Romantic ardour to Victorian censure. So, too, his creation was transformed [...]. Cruel, arrogant, despotic — he usurped and conquered man's rightful prerogatives and punished man's foolish quests'.[17] The Creature symbolized threats as disparate as the Church, Reform Bills, Feminism, homosexuality, and the age of steam. This flexibility is part of society's endless fascination with the myth: the Creature can be whatever the reader or spectator needs him to be. No longer required to stand in for Victorian morality and industry, this more contemporary Creature navigates, amongst other things, questions of reproductive technology, including IVF and cloning, disability, and the romanticized image of the perfect human. Ultimately, however, *Frankenstein* is about being human; how is 'human' defined and created, where is the essence of it formed and housed?

10.2. 'You Are a Poor, Lost Thing': Telling the Creature's Story

Unusually for a dramatization of *Frankenstein*, Dear's play does not include a creation scene as such, immediately distancing it from Whale's adaptation. The play begins with the Creature's 'birth', but Victor — and his clinical gaze — is conspicuously absent. The play begins in darkness, punctuated by the sound of a loud heartbeat. On the revolving stage, the silhouette of a man can be seen moving around inside an artificial womb made of two overlapping translucent, skin-like membranes stretched across an upright circular frame. Hundreds of light bulbs on the ceiling flash a brilliant white as the naked, bald, and horrifically scarred Creature violently emerges from the pseudo-womb. A scientific *mise en scène* is replaced by a more organic, unprocessed outlook; machines become flesh, reanimation becomes birth.[18] The relative (though not complete) silence of the scene underlines its uncanniness. Whereas cinematic creation scenes are usually accompanied by swelling music, loud machinery, shouted orders, and, more often than not, the screams of lightening, Boyle's production is eerily quiet by comparison. The lack of noise — especially for a birth — establishes the divergence of the play from cinematic expectations, while underlying that something is amiss with the 'infant'. Initially, the Creature can only lie on the ground. Gradually, he experiments with moving; at first only able to shake uselessly, he soon drags himself around on his fists without using his legs at all, before eventually standing upright and walking. He can make only the basest of noises and appears bewildered. Watching the Creature develop these basic skills can be painful to witness; unlike seeing a child learn to walk, it is a sequence of violence, humiliation, and frustration as the Creature throws his naked, vulnerable, and highly traumatized body around a cold and barren stage. The Creature frequently trips, falls, and shakes, although he also — eventually — experiences joy and fascination as he learns to run unaided. It is only at the very end of the scene that Victor finally appears only to cruelly reject his creation.

The actors approach the sequence from different perspectives. Cumberbatch researched 'stroke victims and recovery addict people who'd had severe injuries both in war or car crashes trying to re-educate their limbs and their bodies'.[19] Miller, however, focused more on the way a child learns, noting that the Creature is, 'a blank canvas as a body but the brain works extremely fast. It's a fully-grown brain so it's absorbing super-quick.'[20] The difference can be seen in their performances. Miller's Creature initially appears more wide-eyed and clumsier, toddler-like, akin to watching unformed dough begin to take shape. When Cumberbatch performs the same sequence, charm is replaced by pain; the brutality of growth displayed in agonizing detail. Presenting the Creature as childlike and/or as the victim of massive physical trauma helps to foster compassion for a character that the Frankenstein myth presents as a dehumanized monster, in contrast to his eloquent, empathetic narration in the novel. The Creature here is not a horror-villain Other, he is human, exhibiting humankind's capacity for affection, wonder, and intelligence as well as envy, anger, and vengeance. Notably, it is the Creature's human side that ultimately leads to his downfall, not his 'monstrosity'. His very human desires for companionship, revenge, and to understand his origins repeatedly drive him back to Frankenstein and to suffering.

Early adaptations of *Frankenstein* reinforce the Creature's inhumanity. T. P. Cooke's Creature was painted 'a ghastly green-blue to resemble a walking corpse',[21] while Boris Karloff's automaton-inspired design also manifests itself in his robotic physicalization. However, although the practicalities of live theatre restrict how the Creature can be represented on stage, both Dear and Boyle embrace these limitations in order to create a Creature 'clearly human [in] scale and much more resembling someone who's been through surgery'.[22] The bruised, sutured and fully nude body of the Creature is exposed under bright theatre lights for the audiences' scrutiny.[23] Revealing the fragility of the body in this way underscores the Creature's (albeit fragmented) identity as human as well as his inherent vulnerability, while avoiding the legacy of Karloff's infamous image. Visualizing the Creature as essentially human introduces him as a sympathetic character, as well as further establishing him as the alter ego of Victor and underlining the blurring of binaries that is so prevalent in both the narrative and the Gothic in general. The Creature's naked, vulnerable, and traumatized body offers and even encourages the damaging type of stare that Rosemarie Garland-Thomson describes in her work on disability studies.[24] The invasive, critical, and dehumanizing stare magnifies the differences in the disabled body, rendering the Creature object and alien — in other words, monstrous.[25]

The effect of the opening scene, as Dear notes, is that the story is told from the Creature's point of view; the story begins the moment the Creature is born because it is his story.[26] Rather than focusing on Victor's intent or deconstructing his method, the audience is plunged into the middle of the action, immediately aligned with the Creature. The audience watches as an infant is born, gains some control of his body, learns to walk. They watch as he falls and experiences pain, sees his very first struggles and triumphs. It is difficult not to champion this vulnerable creature, exacerbated by Victor's brutal rejection when he strolls on stage at the end of the scene only to immediately run away.

Aligning the audience with the Creature's perspective early on is particularly significant for this production in order to maintain that the Creature is not a monster. As Boyle notes,

[t]here are certain things that [the Creature] does that in other narrative forms like movies would lose you all sympathy for him [...], he kills a child, he burns a house with an old blind man down in it, but because you've kind of inhabited his point of view and you understand in some way why these things are happening, regrettable though they are, you kind of retain sympathy for him.[27]

Fostering empathy between the Creature and the audience therefore becomes particularly important — as indeed it does in the novel with the use of the Creature's narration. If the Creature becomes the Monster then his whole identity is lost, reduced to an Other that can be feared, rejected, and destroyed. Prioritizing the Creature within the theatrical narrative allows his story to be told, not only establishing his subjectivity, but potentially reframing certain events as the products of trauma rather than of horror. In the novel, Victor finding the Creature in his bedroom is a moment of ghastly terror, while in his narration the Creature explains it as a painful and confusing experience. Similarly, in Dear's Creature-orientated script, Victor's abandonment is instant and brutal. It is only later that Victor confesses to the Creature: 'I was terrified — what had I done?'.[28]

For both Shelley and Dear, the hybridity and narrative alignment of the Creature allows difficult questions to be asked about human nature and subjectivity. In Dear's adaptation, the Creature rejects torture in favour of reason; while Frankenstein insists '[t]here is no dialogue with killers!', the Creature immediately replies: 'Yet you'd kill me if you could! Why, you have just tried! So why is your killing justified and mine is not?'.[29] Atop the desolate and suitably Gothic Mont Blanc, it is the 'monster' that reasons, while the human falls to murderous passions and transgressive science. Therefore, when the Creature inevitably submits to these same weaknesses by raping and killing Elizabeth, it is not because he is a Gothic monster, but because he is a Gothic human, driven by uncontrollable desires and the obsessive violation of law and nature.

The production repeatedly underlines that the Creature is not a monster but is in fact human, encouraging the spectator to identify with him. De Lacey calls the Creature a 'lost thing'[30] and his struggle to establish an identity and to belong is universally relatable. Forensic psychotherapist Gwen Adshead suggests that 'Shelley is inviting us to not see this Creature as mad, but you could create something of yourself, and there's a part of yourself that would be murderous and vengeful and lustful and longing and terribly, terribly sad'.[31] In the novel, the Creature never recovers from being abandoned by Victor, a horrific trauma that is constantly exacerbated with continual rejection by everyone he comes into contact with. As Adshead explains, the Creature 'places all his hope on there being these rather idealized people who won't be frightened and when they reject him, hope lost can really cause a type of pain that is unspeakable and can drive people mad'.[32] The psychological complexities of the Creature help to save him from becoming a one-dimensional monster that can be comfortably destroyed at the end of a horror narrative. At times, Boyle's production goes further in its quest to show the Creature as human by directly aligning the audience with his point of view. The theatre auditorium is covered in hundreds of light bulbs sweeping towards the stage that light up at various times. This effect is particularly striking during the play's opening sequence where 'sudden flash[es] of brilliant white light'[33] periodically blind the audience as the Creature first emerges from the pseudo-womb, echoing the Creature blinking in this overwhelming, bright new world. Boyle confirms that

> these flashes of light were literally the darkness and the light [...] and it was to try and somehow suggest through a point of view what it was like to have your eyes closed and then to open them and there be light there.[34]

The opening scene, then, is a creation scene, but it uses a medical, biological framework rather than a scientific one, designed not only to suggest the trauma of birth on an infant, but to induce that trauma in the audience. Eliciting discomfort, disorientation, and disgust binds the spectator and the Creature together. It validates the vulnerability of the Creature in a visceral way, reminding the audience that it is not just the characters on stage that are susceptible to bodily transformations. As Jonathan Lake Crane argues, horror 'will not work if we refuse to involve the body in the spectacle; however, when we give ourselves over to the film we put our own flesh at risk'[35] — a statement that is even more true in the corporal world of the theatre, where there is a constant risk of being affected, even touched, by the sensory input of the surroundings, *mise en scène* of the play, and the actors themselves. Furthermore, these intense flashes of light can be linked back to the novel where, as Paul Marchbank notes, Frankenstein describes being temporarily blinded by bright light reflecting off a lake.[36] Marchbank argues that Shelley 'works to dismantle the blind/sighted binary that dictates two mutually exclusive states' in order to criticize 'flawed social vision'.[37] He goes on to suggest that 'new powers of sight belong to those who can see the invisible and the intangible and who blind themselves to the superficial categories'.[38] Blinding the audience during their first glimpses of the creature disrupts the power of the stare. For brief moments, the Creature becomes simply a figure on stage or is erased completely from sight, the overexposure of the lights working to distort the world for both the Creature and the audience.

10.3. 'You and I, We are One': Doubling Victor and the Creature on Stage

The 2011 production of *Frankenstein* is particularly interested in the symbiotic relationship between Victor and the Creature. Although it is framed as the Creature's story — following him from birth and early development through to his brutal, self-proclaimed inauguration as a 'man' — it is inevitably Victor's story as well. Dear states that the introduction of William's ghost in Victor's dream sequence was designed to balance the intertwining points of view, expositing Victor's backstory and his reasons for his experiments, 'the bit of Victor's story that would have been at the beginning if we'd started with the scientist'.[39] Structurally, the perspective of Victor and the Creature essentially swap places; the narrative begins with the Creature's point of view while Victor has a short middle section to explain his actions and the journey that led him there. The doppelgänger theme of the novel was often absent from early theatrical adaptations as it upset the strict moral framework of melodrama. 'The novel's lack of diametrically opposed characters presents obvious difficulties for the Manichean world of melodrama', writes Forry, 'for how could a melodrama portray the triumph of virtue when the supposed hero perishes with the supposed villain?'[40] Unable to establish a moral hero, playwrights instead established a moral code. Therefore, 'Frankenstein becomes a fallen protagonist, a modern hero-villain whose crimes we exonerate because of his exaggerated remorse.'[41] Simultaneously — and perhaps as a consequence of this — the Creature became a dumbshow villain-hero, allowing the plays to utilize moments such as the Creature discovering fire and sunlight, while avoiding the ambiguity of his journey into self-awareness. Dear's adaptation, however, returns to the doppelgänger premise, exploiting the similarities between Victor and the Creature in the language and structure of the narrative as well as the performances of the actors and even the set design. In a play already rife with doubles, alternating the roles of Victor and the Creature underlines the parallels between Frankenstein and his creation. Dear declares that the double role was — appropriately enough — a 'mad idea'[42] that ultimately helped in the storytelling by highlighting the Victor and the Creature as mirror images of each other:

> The doppelgänger effect was something I always had in mind; it was compounded by the decision to rotate the actors in the two parts [...]. In the story, Victor is a narcissist — he tries to create a being 'as beautiful as myself', or words to that effect. He is like a god trying to make man in his own image — but his technology is not yet sufficiently advanced [...]. So I suppose it is true to say that I have always seen parallels in the two characters. Also, the moment you put this story on a stage, you bring back to it a human element which is missing from the movies. We are dealing with human-sized people, not actual monsters. This tends automatically to emphasise parallels between Victor and Creature.[43]

Although the majority of theatres that have since produced Dear's script have not alternated the roles of Victor and the Creature, both cast and crew have commented positively on the technique breathing extra life into each performance. Cumberbatch, for example, notes that, '[y]ou have to begin each night anew [...] you have to make sure it's about the present which is always at the heart of what good playing should be'[44] whereas Miller argues that, '[w]hat the rest of the company has to deal with is not two actors switching parts but four different characters.'[45] Appropriately enough for a play about creating life, Boyle asserts that, '[i]t always stuck with me as being a wonderful way in which you could stop a play being fixed. You can literally keep it alive the whole time.'[46] As Miller notes in *Doubling Frankenstein and the Creature*, continually switching between the two main roles of Victor and the Creature encourages the actors to become more fluid in their performances; with aspects of the characters being 'carried over' into the opposite role. He goes on to say that the process is, 'a fusing for each of us within our two parts [...] not opposite each other as actors'.[47] For example, Miller's Creature has a pronounced stutter, which reappears when Victor is under intense stress, such as Victor finding his brother's body. Cumberbatch's Creature does not stutter, instead using a broken yet rhythmic delivery that Miller's Victor occasionally copies.

Re-establishing the Creature's ability to speak is essential to Dear's production, not only because it gives him a voice (both literally and figuratively), but because it marks him as Victor's equal. While Shelley's text offers both Victor and the Creature as storytellers, this theatre production returns the Creature's role as a narrator, rejecting Victor's objectifying gaze.

10.4. 'I Had a Vision of Perfection': Passion, Paradise, and Progeny

Victor and the Creature are lost things, isolated from society, only able to find an emotional connection — albeit a cruel and unhealthy one — with each other. They value different characteristics as 'human', therefore chase equally unobtainable goals. In Dear's script, both Victor and the Creature misinterpret 'human' (particularly the idea of women) as 'perfection'. Themes of innocence and responsibility come to the fore in Dear's script through the main characters' quest for this perfection. The Creature is initially an innocent, a literal blank slate, his knowledge and emotions painfully learned. He is not born cruel or violent; he learns these behaviours from bitter experience. 'I am good at the art of assimilation', he tells Elizabeth shortly before he rapes and kills her:

> I have watched, and listened, and learnt. At first I knew nothing at all. But I studied the ways of men, and slowly I learnt: how to ruin, how to hate, how to debase, how to humiliate. And at the feet of my master, I learnt the highest of human skills, the skill no other creature owns: I finally learnt how to lie.[48]

The Creature longs to be human, to find love, and to belong but does not have the foundation or skills to equate this to healthy values, declaring '[n]ow I am a man'[49] after raping Elizabeth. 'The Creature thinks he's defined himself as a human by having sexual intercourse', Dear argues, whereas Victor wants an 'unnatural' procreation without intercourse and/or a woman.[50] Why Victor resists having intercourse with Elizabeth despite her strong attraction towards him and desire for children ('Show me how you'll give me children. Touch me.'[51]) is not resolved in the play. There is some indication within the production that Victor is asexual, seeing both Elizabeth and the Creature through a medical gaze even as he compliments them. His statement to Elizabeth that she will 'make a beautiful wife' while 'star[ing] at her intently'[52] echoes his earlier conversation with the Creature that '[a] bride should be beautiful',[53] causing her to chide him for treating her like a 'specimen'.[54] In the recorded productions, Cumberbatch's Victor underlines this point by picking up her arm, as if measuring her to become the model for the Creature's bride. Furthermore, Victor's initial horror at the Creature's request for a bride quickly turns to enthusiasm at the scientific possibilities: 'If I could make something immaculate. Something that I could — exhibit? Not a demon, but a goddess!'[55] Victor and the Creature verbally align Elizabeth with the Female Creature, continually emphasizing their beauty and perfection, particularly as potential wives.[56] They imbue their wives with imagery from the Garden of Eden, putting them on a pedestal of paradise. Unaware that Victor has just killed the Female, the Creature happily declares: 'I will be Adam, she will be Eve! And all the memory of hell will melt like snow!'[57] Shortly before she too is murdered, Victor tells Elizabeth: 'In you I found paradise. But the apple is eaten, we cannot go back.'[58] Paradise is unattainable, however; just as 'natural' procreation is impossible (with Elizabeth's desire for children going unfulfilled and Agatha De Lacey's unborn child dying with her), supposedly normative (heterosexual, wedded, and consummated) relationships are violently ended.

Despite the Creature's idealistic image of women, throughout Dear's play, it becomes increasingly clear that he understands love far better than Victor, constantly seeking out different kinds of love and affection from the De Laceys, the Female Creature, Elizabeth, and Frankenstein himself. Victor taunts the Creature when presenting him with the almost completed Female. It is Victor who is able to touch her body, even kiss her, demanding: 'Look at her cheeks, her lips, her breasts! Who could not desire those breasts?'[59] Yet it is also Victor who does not desire her; there is no affection or even lust in his actions, in direct contrast to the Creature's passionate proclamation that: 'It feels like all the life is bubbling up in me and spilling from my mouth, it feels like my lungs are on fire and my heart is a hammer, it feels like I can do anything in the world! Anything in the world!'[60] By the final scenes, Victor admits that love (and, therefore, in the context of the play, heterosexual reproduction) is out of his reach, telling the Creature that, '[h]atred is what I understand. Only you give me purpose. You I desire.'[61] Christine M. Crockett maps Victor's physical deterioration throughout the novel onto sexological texts of the eighteenth century, suggesting masturbation as a life-draining obsession. Victor's hesitation to marry and procreate puts him 'at risk from moving from the normative healthy male to the non-normative, and effeminate, invalid'.[62] In the world of *Frankenstein*, there is no 'natural' intercourse or procreation, both nature and supposedly 'natural' desires have been inverted. Victor sees intercourse as something distasteful whereas the Creature uses it for revenge.[63] Yet, in Dear's adaptation, the Creature ultimately takes responsibility for his actions, apologizing and attempting to explain his motivations after committing murder. He points out that he knows that what he has done is wrong. Victor, on the other hand, denies responsibility for everything, even blaming Elizabeth for his brother's death. He admits that he did not consider that the Creature would have emotions while berating the Creature for killing Elizabeth, to which the Creature retorts that Victor had previously killed the Creature's wife with no hesitation or remorse. Victor mocks the Creature for assuming that the female he desires, 'will accept a bargain made before she was even created',[64] yet does not extend this same consideration to the Creature himself, insisting that he is a 'slave' with 'no rights'[65]. Victor wants to improve the world, originally experimenting in order to overcome disease, but by seeking perfection, his arrogance and self-imposed isolation from humankind only begets destruction. Similarly, the Creature, who fruitlessly searches for the paradise that he believes will save him, is willing to destroy everything if he is denied, shouting that he will 'run mad'[66] if the Female Creature rejects him.

As the play continues and the Creature becomes more human, Victor regresses, becoming deformed and monstrous. He is frequently covered in blood, his hair messy, clothes hanging loose with shirt sleeves rolled up. In several scenes his costumes include furs and leather, ostensibly for the cold, yet these alter his outline, making him appear more animal-like and wild. Several characters note that Victor appears unwell, and by the final scenes, Victor crumples to the floor, reduced to dragging himself around and grunting in an uneasy echo of the Creature's 'birth' scene.

By contrast, the Creature's unsteady and awkward movements rapidly evolve as he becomes stronger. He delivers increasingly articulate speeches, demonstrates agility and grace, shows appreciation for music, dancing, and poetry, is able to quote John Milton from memory and, along with his bride, performs a dance 'unlike anything you might have seen before'.[67] On stage, the Creature is drawn to music, both to provide a soothing influence to his savagery[68] and to invoke sympathy by demonstrating the humanity that he cannot vocalize. In both the Peake and Dear productions, the Creature is attracted to the sound of the blind man playing a musical instrument (Felix playing a flute and De Lacey a harp/guitar, respectively). In the Peake adaptation, the Creature '*stands amazed and pleased [...] snatches at the empty air, and with clenched hands puts them to each ear*'.[69] Dear's (at this point nonverbal) Creature also attempts to possess the music that so delights him — clumsily trying to strum the guitar without success — but when listening to De Lacey play he becomes instantly 'captivated' and 'transported' by this 'gift from God'.[70] Writing about the Peake production, Laredo says that: 'Music is an invisible, ethereal force that stirs human emotions and the creature's appreciation for it indicates that he is more than a savage, unfeeling brute.'[71] In Boyle's staging, music is associated with emotion and play, not only in the scenes with De Lacey, but also in the Creature's childlike interactions with the world around him (where he chases birds and tries to catch both sunlight and rain, backed by joyful music), in the celebratory singing at Victor's wedding, and even the powerful chorus of the industrial workers that quickly descends into raunchy merriment. The Creature's willingness to embrace music and play imbues him with life, in direct contrast to Victor, who consistently admonishes both Elizabeth and William for indulging in entertainment.[72] The audience is shown the dreams of both Victor and the Creature. But while the Creature's dream is filled with music, dancing, and affection as he encounters his mate, Victor instead experiences a nightmare where he talks to William's ghost, who questions him relentlessly about the process of bringing the dead to life. Victor's rejection of nature, desire, and emotions is dangerous; he disintegrates into a repressed, unethical void, leaving him vulnerable to the formidable, uncontainable forces of Gothic passions rife within the story.[73] While the Creature learns creative expression and connects with emotional embodiment (though he cannot control it), Victor descends into chaos, cruelty, and powerlessness.[74]

Towards the end of Dear's play, the Creature notes that '[t]he son becomes the father, the master the slave'.[75] In this adaptation, it is the Creature who not only becomes human, but declares himself to be a 'man' only after committing deceitful, violent, and heinous acts. Just as Victor is capable of great cruelty while operating under the façade of a cultured man, the Creature later taunts Victor about Elizabeth while adopting civilized manners such as wearing a frock coat and providing plates, cutlery and 'good wine'[76] in the Arctic. The actors frequently mirror each other on stage, something particularly notable in two of the key 'confrontation' scenes. In the first, where Victor encounters his Creation for the first time since bringing him to life, the two of them stand opposite each other, one angled towards the audience and the other angled away. Additionally, the Creature tends to copy Victor's movements, still in the stages of assimilation. During the final scene in the Arctic, the Creature and Victor sit on the ground together in a mirror image, reaching out to each other in the final moments of the play. Even as Victor continues to deny his Creature, his body admits the connection; in both their monstrosity and their purity, they do belong together. However, after this brief moment of comprehension and conciliation, Victor rejects the Creature yet again, insisting on his destruction, to which the Creature gleefully agrees to lead him on. The stage revolves one way, the Creature walks in the other, and the movement of the stage brings them back together again for the final image of the Creature leading Victor into the light.

Dear notes the difficulty of transferring a dramatic ending to the stage, noting the importance of the 'weird ballet'[77] between Victor and the Creature to suggest the eternal continuation of the story — whether the Frankenstein myth itself, or the thematic complexities it posits, such as questions of creation, individuality, trauma, science versus nature, savagery and culture, and society and the disenfranchised, to name just a few.

'We Have a Compact We Must Keep': Conclusion

The story does continue, bringing to life Victor's fear of (and Shelley's desire for) a propagation of Creatures through 'versions of his monster haunting thousands of cinemas and in the imaginations of millions of spectators'.[78] Since Peake's original production, there have been over ninety theatrical and cinematic adaptations and parodies of the Frankenstein myth, including animation, ballet, opera, television series, and various 'cameo' appearances in other franchises.

The Frankenstein myth endures in many incarnations, nurtured by society's fascination with monstrous creations, whether they are made by a God, evolution, or science. Creations terrible and beautiful, corrupted or pure. As Boyle explains: 'we are made and we want to know who made us. It goes to the essence of what we are.'[79] Victor and the Creature quickly become instruments to navigate difficult questions of existence, including exploring relationships such as father and son, creation and creator, master and slave, 'human' and 'monster'. As Victor and the Creature endure, so do the philosophical questions they embody.

Frankenstein may be better known on the screen, but the animated immediacy of theatre adds muscle to an already powerful narrative, offering a visceral encounter to a story that changes the more it is told. In keeping with the Gothic nature of the novel, the experience of a theatrical production provides opportunity for spectacular visions and tantalizing immersion. However, the stage simultaneously allows space for the subtleties of the story to play out in an intimate environment. Dear argues,

> [t]heatre can do things that movies cannot, it is like a living organism every night. The thing only happens when there is a real audience and people on the

stage. And that creates a certain thing, a certain frisson, a chemistry every night which is different.[80]

The narrative presumptions of any *Frankenstein* adaptation have permanently bound Victor and the Creature together; if a Frankenstein appears within any text, then the audience naturally expects an appearance by a Creature (and vice versa), in the same way that they would anticipate a Hyde to any Jekyll. Furthermore, the fragmented identities of Victor and the Creature mean that they become symbiotic; in terms of both psychology and narrative conventions, neither can exist without the other. They become each other's shadows despite insisting that they are not; the more they strive for autonomy, the more they become like each other until they are trapped in an abusive but codependent relationship. 'We have a compact we must keep', says the Creature, 'He lives for my destruction, I live to lead him on.'[81] The final scene in Dear's adaptation mimics the circular nature of the novel as well as Shelley's desire for her creation's continuance. Not only does Dear's ending imply the endurance of the *Frankenstein* story, but also that events will live to repeat themselves, with the play ending exactly where it began, with the sound of a heart beating loudly into the dark.

Notes to Chapter 10

1. For detailed descriptions of Peake's adaptation, including reviews and the script, see Forry, *Hideous Progenies*; Douglas William Hoehn, 'The First Season of *Presumption!; or, The Fate of Frankenstein*', *Theatre Studies*, 26–27 (1979–81), 79–88.
2. Forry, p. x.
3. Ibid.
4. 'Mary Shelley's Introduction to the 1831 *Frankenstein*', in *The Novels and Selected Works of Mary Shelley*, I, 180.
5. Pedro Javier Pardo Garcia, 'Beyond Adaptation: Frankenstein's Postmodern Progeny', in *Books in Motion: Adaptation, Intertextuality, Authorship*, ed. by Mireia Aragai (Amsterdam: Rodopi, 2005), pp. 223–42 (p. 224).
6. Nick Dear, Interview, led by Catherine Pugh, audio recording, London, 31 May 2017. Hereafter Dear, Interview, 2017.
7. Quotations in the subheadings of this chapter are taken from Nick Dear, *Frankenstein* (London: Faber and Faber, 2011), scenes 16 (10.2), 29 (10.1, 10.4), and 30 (10.3, conclusion).
8. Forry, p. 80. See also the contribution by Marjean D. Purinton in this volume.
9. Dear, Interview, 2017.
10. Including the removal of characters such as Walton, Justine, and Clerval.
11. Jeanette Laredo, 'Unmade and Remade: Trauma and Modern Adaptations of *Frankenstein*', in *Gothic Afterlives: Reincarnations of Horror in Film and Popular Media*, ed. by Lorna Piatti-Farnell (Maryland: Lexington Books, 2019), pp. 123–37 (p. 126).
12. Whale's production makes particular use of the Creature as automaton, as examined in more detail in Laredo, pp. 127–28 (amongst others).
13. Dear, Interview, 2017.
14. Much like the popularity of Benedict Cumberbatch, Jonny Lee Miller, and Danny Boyle in the National Theatre's production.
15. Forry, p. 34.
16. Ibid., pp. 34–35.
17. Ibid., p. 73.
18. A similar representation of the Creature's animation as a procreation appears in *Mary Shelley's Frankenstein*, dir. by Kenneth Branagh (TriStar Pictures, 1994), as written about in detail by

Pardo Garcia, 'Beyond Adaptation', pp. 228–29. However, Boyle's production is more focused on birth, rather than conception.
19. Benedict Cumberbatch, in National Theatre, *Directing 'Frankenstein'*, online video recording, YouTube, 1 September 2015, <https://www.youtube.com/watch?v=E67Ty4diDgE> [accessed 19 March 2020].
20. Jonny Lee Miller, in *Directing Frankenstein*.
21. Laredo, p. 126.
22. Danny Boyle, in *Directing Frankenstein*.
23. Although it was altered slightly for the National Theatre recording, during the live show, all actors portraying both the Creature and Female Creature are introduced fully nude.
24. Specifically, Rosemarie Garland-Thomson, *Staring: How We Look* (Oxford: Oxford University Press, 2009).
25. See Martin F. Norden, *The Cinema of Isolation: A History of Physical Disability in the Movies* (New Brunswick, N.J.: Rutgers University Press, 1994) for a more detailed analysis of the Creature as a physically disabled character.
26. Dear, Interview, 2017.
27. Danny Boyle, in National Theatre, *The Creature: A Character Study*, online video recording, YouTube, 1 September 2015, <https://www.youtube.com/watch?v=lRxOtaPAx1c> [accessed 19 March 2020].
28. Dear, *Frankenstein*, 24, p. 38.
29. Ibid., p. 41.
30. Ibid., 16, p. 18.
31. Gwen Adshead, in National Theatre, *Cruelty, Violence and the Creature*, online video recording, YouTube, 1 September 2015, <https://www.youtube.com/watch?v=irZav2XfPLs> [accessed 19 March 2020].
32. Ibid.
33. Dear, *Frankenstein*, 1, p. 3.
34. Boyle, in *Directing Frankenstein*.
35. Jonathan Lake Crane, *Terror and Everyday Life: Singular Moments in the History of the Horror Film* (Thousand Oaks: Sage, 1994), p. 37.
36. Paul Marchbank, 'A Space, a Place: Visions of a Disabled Community in Mary Shelley's *Frankenstein* and *The Last Man*', in *Demons of the Body and Mind: Essays on Disability in Gothic Literature*, ed. by Ruth Bienstock Anolik (Jefferson, NC: MacFarland, 2010), pp. 21–35 (p. 27).
37. Ibid., p. 27.
38. Ibid., p. 32.
39. Dear, Interview, 2017.
40. Forry, p. 21.
41. Ibid.
42. Dear, Interview, 2017.
43. Nick Dear, Email to Catherine Pugh, 15 March 2016.
44. Benedict Cumberbatch, in National Theatre, *Doubling Frankenstein and the Creature*, online video recording, YouTube, 1 September 2015, <https://www.youtube.com/watch?v=wanlO8fb1co> [accessed 20 March 2020].
45. Jonny Lee Miller, in *Doubling Frankenstein and the Creature*.
46. Danny Boyle, in *Doubling Frankenstein and the Creature*.
47. Miller, in *Doubling Frankenstein and the Creature*.
48. Dear, *Frankenstein*, 29, p. 71.
49. Ibid., 29, p. 72.
50. Dear, Interview, 2017.
51. Dear, *Frankenstein*, 25, p. 49.
52. Ibid., 25, p. 48.
53. Ibid., 24, p. 43.
54. Ibid., 25, p. 48.
55. Dear, *Frankenstein*, 24, p. 44.

56. The Creature also repeatedly notes the beauty of De Lacey's daughter-in-law, Agatha.
57. Dear, *Frankenstein*, 28, p. 61.
58. Ibid., 29, p. 68.
59. Ibid., 28, p. 59.
60. Ibid., 28, p. 60.
61. Ibid., 30, p. 77.
62. Christine M. Crockett, '"The Monster Vice": Masturbation, Malady, and Monstrosity in *Frankenstein*', in *Demons of the Body and Mind*, ed. by Bienstock Anolik, pp. 129–42, (p. 137).
63. For an analysis of both Victor and Creature as 'unnatural procreators', see Crockett '"The Monster Vice": Masturbation, Malady, and Monstrosity in *Frankenstein*'.
64. Dear, *Frankenstein*, 28, p. 59.
65. Ibid., 24, p. 40.
66. Dear, *Frankenstein*, 28, p. 59.
67. Ibid., 19, p. 24.
68. Forry, p. 22.
69. Peake, *Presumption; or, The Fate of Frankenstein*, in Forry, *Hideous Progenies*, p. 147.
70. Dear, *Frankenstein*, 12, p. 13–14.
71. Laredo, p. 126.
72. However, the Creature's attempts at enjoyment do not end well (he is still constantly rejected and abused; De Lacey stops him playing in the snow in order to continue lessons; William is isolated during a game and killed when the Creature realizes he is Victor's brother whilst trying to befriend him).
73. In Dear's play, the Creature's connection with nature suggests an instinctive astuteness towards the natural world that Victor lacks, such as informing an incredulous Victor that the Earth turns round (Dear, *Frankenstein*, 24, p. 43).
74. Branagh's cinematic adaptation also capitalizes on this motif, with the Creature able to play the flute through a fragmented knowledge inherited from one of his body donors. Victor is shown early in the film dancing joyfully with Elizabeth and playfully demonstrating his experiments. However, by the end, his exuberance has turned to frenzy, while music and dancing become an indication of trauma, particularly during and after Elizabeth's reanimation.
75. Dear, *Frankenstein*, 30, p. 75.
76. Ibid., p. 76.
77. Dear, Email to Pugh, 2016. The prominent use of circles in the set design also underlines the eternal continuation of the story, such as a circular incubator, a revolving stage, and rounded sets.
78. Pardo Garcia, 'Beyond Adaptation', p. 223.
79. Danny Boyle, in *Cruelty, Violence and the Creature*.
80. Dear, *Doubling Frankenstein and the Creature*.
81. Dear, *Frankenstein*, 30, p. 75.

CHAPTER 11

Iconographic Portraits of Mary Shelley: A Postmodern Perspective

Jean-Marie Lecomte

11.1. Foreword

Ours is a visual age. The turn of the twenty-first century let loose a flood of digital images. But it was the late nineteenth and early twentieth centuries which laid the foundation of the visual age with the advent of motion pictures, photographs, advertising posters, comic strip characters, and cartoons in magazines and newspapers. These images were aimed at a mass market and came to compete with the traditional iconography of emblems, paintings, prints, etchings, chapbook drawings, or the popular imagery of an earlier age. Portraits of emblematic figures date back to the dawn of time and, like monuments, they serve as visual traces of the real or imaginary person to remember. The art of portraiture has obviously evolved considerably since the advent of photorealism in the nineteenth century. Before, portraits were mainly sculptures, paintings, or drawings. Lifelike portraits were sometimes achieved with optical aids or with the help of reproducing devices such as the physionotrace[1] for profile portraits or 'physionotypes'.

11.2. Portraits by Mary Shelley's Contemporaries

Visual portraits of Mary Shelley are scarce and only one is sure to have been painted from life. None rely on the photorealistic techniques available during her lifetime. Therefore, they are all works of art, mediated through the creative mind of their author. Literary portraits written by her contemporaries run just a few lines, usually stressing her pale skin, abundant, wavy, fair hair, her flat, high forehead, and large melancholy eyes.[2] These salient features will later be used by caricaturists, but her golden-brown hair has been consistently airbrushed by modern visual artists to paint her as either a darksome creature of the night or a fiery redhead.

When she sat to Richard Rothwell in late 1839, Mary was 42 (Fig. 11.2). Her tired, wistful look betrayed her age and revealed little of the beauty she had been in her youth. It is a well-lit frontal portrait against a dark backdrop which brings out the warm chromatic carnation of her face and naked shoulders. The portrait style is classical with the head held straight and the bust slightly oriented towards the sitter's left. Rothwell highlights the roundness of her sloping shoulders, breast, and

Fig. 11.1. Reginald Easton, *Mary Shelley*, between 1851 and 1893, watercolour, Bodleian Library, University of Oxford, Shelley relics (d).

oval face. It is a sad, serene, motherly, and intellectual face, one that would appeal to and assuage Sir Timothy, whose anger at the wild sensual Mary who eloped with his son had not yet abated. The Rothwell portrait at the National Gallery is the only reliable source that gives an idea of what Mary Shelley looked like. As Miranda Seymour points out, Reginald Easton painted a posthumous portrait (Fig. 11.1) probably after a death mask (*c*. 1857).[3] Two 1819 portraits by Amelia Curran and Signor Delicati and a miniature by George Clint are lost. A portrait by Cleobulina Fielding (*c*. 1833) and one (*c*. 1922) in possession of Dr Marcello Pellegrini are privately owned, not for public view. *Portrait of an Unknown Woman*, an 1831 painting by Samuel John Stump, a British artist, has formerly been thought to be that of Mary, but the woman who sat to it remains unidentified.[4]

ICONOGRAPHIC PORTRAITS OF MARY SHELLEY 145

FIG. 11.2. Richard Rothwell, *Mary Shelley*, exhibited 1840, oil on canvas, 73.7 × 61 cm, National Portrait Gallery, London, NPG 1235, © National Portrait Gallery.

11.3. Postmodern Portraits as Prosopography

This essay examines postmodern[5] portraits of Mary Shelley, both print and digital. They mainly consist of caricatures, web art, watercolours, oil paintings, cartoons, book illustrations, comics, and advertising posters. Print illustrations published in newspapers, magazines, and comics can be dated and properly credited, but the author, date, and sources of web illustrations cannot always be ascertained. Only post-1970s iconographic items, belonging to the so-called postmodern period, have been taken to analysis.

These modern portraits are obviously not meant to 'seize' the real-life Mary, to reconstruct her likeness, or to conjure up her avatars. These images are figures of prosopography, attempts to visually represent invisible or fictional people. These 'prosopographs' are not traces (like photos or portraits after life) but aesthetic representations which express how the artists see Mary. In addition to physical traits, Mary Shelley's figures of prosopography can also suggest moral or psychological characteristics. Through them, we see how she, as a popular cultural icon, came to shape modern ideologies, and how a visual artist can appropriate Mary Shelley's image to reflect her or his subjectivity. It is also possible to use some of these portraits to examine how they can function as interpretations of her literary works (although she is solely remembered in the popular imagination as the author of *Frankenstein*). Most of the portraits imagined by postmodern illustrators are inspired by a common mould or '*ur*-image': they are variations or distortions of the Rothwell painting or, less commonly, of the Reginald Easton miniature. A few will use the *Portrait of an Unknown Woman* by Stump. The latter picture is favoured as a model because the Romantic female writer painted by the British artist looks more youthful and appealing, with her rich curls, full lips, and soft skin tone. Several pictures draw their inspiration from film images, especially from the face of Elsa Lanchester, the actress who impersonated Mary Shelley in James Whale's *The Bride of Frankenstein* (1935).

As will be shown in the examples discussed, two opposite tendencies emerge: portraits which cling to the stereotype of Mary Shelley forever wedded to the monstrous creation of her first novel, and portraits which intend to go beyond *Frankenstein* to show Mary Shelley from another perspective and iconography.

11.4. *Frankenstein*-Themed Portraits: Mary the Woman as a Mutilated Female Body

Mary Shelley's portraits in recent popular culture represent her as an icon of the mutilated female body, a fitting bride to her famed creature. Her physical and facial appearance always betrays some aberration of nature or underscores some underlying suffering. *Frankenstein*-themed images are, nearly always, patterned after nineteenth-century portraits. As a rule, they do not depart from the stereotype of the bride of Frankenstein's monster.

Criteria to classify the stereotypical pictures of Mary as a mutilated or suffering woman could possibly be divided into three categories: comic caricatures, horror pictures, and Gothic images. Caricatures resist idealizing the imaginary Mary Shelley (be it Mary the stereotypical Romantic girl, Shelley's scandalous lover, or Mary the writer of *Frankenstein*). In caricatures, the Mary represented by the visual artist has one or several pictorial 'aberrations', but these are not hideous or horrific; they merely raise a smile. Horror pictures, on the other hand, usually show their subject as a hideous or maimed body. They belong to the macabre or horror genre. Gothic portraits tend to point to a narrowed gap between the historical character and its visual representation. They claim to be closer to the epistemic Mary Shelley who penned *Frankenstein*. Gothic portraits aim at underscoring the creative impulse at work behind the creator and her creation. The Gothic mode in a broad postmodern sense will tend to be influenced by movie imagery and themes. As in Francis Ford Coppola's *Dracula* (1992) or Kenneth Branagh's *Mary Shelley's Frankenstein* (1994), the monster's desire for love and humanity is overly stressed, and that implies a sexual and sensual tension between Mary and her creature.

11.5. Beyond *Frankenstein*: Portraits as Counterstereotypes

A few interesting counterstereotypes go against the standardized image of the misshapen Mary who has been vampirized by her *Frankenstein* monster. Some come from comic strips which tell the story of a 'normal' woman who went through the throes of rebellious adolescence, then had to cope with adultery, childbearing, bereavement, solitude, and neglect as a serious writer. These comic strip cartoons are narrative and discursive portraits, biopics featuring Mary Shelley in her adventurous life. They have a story to tell usually with an ideological bias functioning as counterstereotypes, whether comic or melodramatic, and concentrate on action rather than physical traits. No larger-than-life exaggeration is intended here.

Other representations, which steer clear of '*ur*-paintings' and the *Frankenstein* stereotypes, paint Mary as an oneiric woman, a dark lady of the mind. They are not iconic portraits insofar as they do not look for likeness, but pictorial tropes or figures of displacement. In these portraits, Mary acts as 'a portal to dreams'.[6]

11.6. Comic Caricatures

The first set of caricatures to be analysed here are related to the *Frankenstein* theme. They fuse Mary's face with the stereotypical attributes of the Boris Karloff monster in composite images with skin bruises, stiches on her forehead, and bolts through her neck. They imply that Mary was the monster's bride or a female monster herself. These are typical examples of how far a fictional creature can upstage its author.

Fernando Vicente's is a caricatural redrawing of the Rothwell portrait (Fig. 11.3). The size of the head is exaggerated in relation to the bust; the big eyes are dissymmetric and a slight, knowing, ironical smile plays about her mouth. Vicente has added the Boris Karloff flat-top hair and neck bolt. The two wavy, silver bands on either side of her hair recall the hairstyle of the bride of Frankenstein in the eponymous 1935 Hollywood movie. The portrait is curiously desexualized (perhaps androgynous) and euphemistic. The high forehead, traditionally the seat

Fig. 11.3. Fernando Vicente, *Mary Shelley*, 2009, book illustration/print, © Fernando Vicente.

of the intellect, also suggests superiority and pride. The horrific fabrication of the Hollywood creature and the female attraction of Mary the woman have both been killed off by Vicente. They have been emptied of their visual power. There remains a wan figure that winks at the death of a myth by overexposure. Overexposure is a key concept in the birth of the caricature. It means visual wear and tear and leads to grotesque representation, the only way we can treat a myth once it has been debunked and eviscerated as a result of overexposure.

Fig. 11.4. Salvador Heras Muños, *Mary Shelley as her own Dr Frankenstein's Monster Character*, 2007, analogue/digital mixed media, © Salvador Heras Muños.

The cartoon drawn by Salvador Heras Muños (Fig. 11.4), published in *Nocturna Magazine*, is another desexualized representation of Mary Shelley with an original *Frankenstein* theme. This monochrome, sienna-and-copper cartoon uses a quilt design where the pieces are stitched together like the anatomical parts of Frankenstein's creature. It is a closer, altogether more bizarre view of Mary's face but, although it is a caricature, it avoids falling into the grotesque.[7] The bulging lunar eyes hint at an intense inner light or inner life, whereas the manly, elongated chin points to a muscular, hungry jaw. 'Chin', in popular parlance, often signals lower-class or proletarian breeding (English aristocrats are labelled 'chinless'). Does

Heras Muños allude to the relatively humble birth of Mary in contrast to the upper-class or high-birth origins of her circle, Lord Byron and Percy Bysshe Shelley? Possibly, but here again, the idea of maturity and strength rather than sensuality and womanhood comes to the fore. The shining, mesmeric intensity of the woman's gaze enhances the inner, feverish activity of the mind.

David Levine's famous cartoon was designed for an article written by Ellen Moers published in *The New York Review of Books*, in March 1974, and entitled 'Female Gothic: The Monster's Mother'.[8] Levine frames Mary from the waist up, emphasizing the kinesics of writing. Her face is completely dwarfed by her blown-up, pregnant body. This distortion is intended to illustrate the power and physiological ability[9] of the woman writer (and women writers in general) to engender Gothic fiction. Fiction seems to be the fruit of their womb rather than their mind.

These three caricatures, from one American and two Spanish illustrators, share at least one feature. The mature, motherly nature of Mary is brought out to a fine excess. Their authors wish to take us away from the wanton, sexualized Mary who ran away at the age of 16 with a married poet. They highlight the maturity of the female artist who had to face the torment of tragic early pregnancies and exile. These portraits wear the stitched face of saintly martyrdom, in acquiescence not in rebellion. Suffering — they seem to tell the viewer — is the price to pay for fruitful creativity. Artistic creation, as proxy living, speeds up the maturing process in a young girl. She ages faster. These illustrations could also be read as an interpretation of Mary Shelley's early difficult life. By 1822, when Percy Shelley died, she had written *Frankenstein*, settled in Italy, loved and lost two children and a husband, she had matured far beyond her still youthful age. Quite a lot of caricatures similarly portray Mary pregnant with her monster and, like Levine's image, are apt to associate Mary Shelley's creativity with gestation.

Significantly, none of these cartoons, although they are graphic caricatures, have been designed for comic or satirical purposes. The artists remain benevolent toward the sitter. Mary's features appear exaggerated, but the woman depicted is in no way being ridiculed. The portraits evoke 'genial rather than derisive laughter'.[10] From contemporary cartoonists' depictions of Mary Shelley, we can infer their appreciation for her as a literary figure: she is drawn as a plain, ungainly woman with exceptional capabilities shining through her big eyes. Her face is endowed with a charm that is easier felt than explained. The aberrations in her features are not hideous; they merely tend to tone down her sexuality, to dampen her sensual power. They function as counterstereotypes, denying, in her and through her, the normative aspects of what a Romantic or Gothic beauty should look like.

11.7. Horrific Portraits

The second set of popular images depicts Mary Shelley in terms of hideous iconography or 'monstration',[11] usually inspired by popular American Halloween imagery or horror comics. Short of being straight counterstereotypes, they nonetheless tend to keep away from the Frankenstein myth. These portraits of Mary Shelley as a witch, a creature of the night, or a mythical beast aim at teenage or young adult

Fig. 11.5. Tim Seeley, *Mary Shelley Lovecraft*, 2009, comics/print, © Tim Seeley.

audiences. Horror here derives from basic, primal fears, such as fear of predating beasts, of death, blood, etc. These caricatures of Mary as a horror character often fuse her with literary or historical myths such as Dracula, the Hydra, or Bloody Mary. Horror iconography depicting the mutilated body as a genre can be found in medieval religious paintings dealing with demonology, in the representations of the Greek Gorgon, in Japanese prints, in the Decadent[12] paintings of Aubrey Beardsley, in Universal and Hammer film images, in photography showing torture victims, in Jacques Callot's etchings on the horrors of the Thirty Years' War, to name but a few examples taken from this immensely rich imagery. In this genre, the body may also be hideously deformed. Hence the fear and the fascination.

Tim Seeley's pencil and ink frame from a horror comic book (Fig. 11.5) was published in 2009. It plays upon multiple iconographic figures:[13] the Hydra, a monster with several heads; the Shiva, a goddess with several arms; and the Medusa, a Gorgon with snakes instead of hair. The image depicts Mary Shelley with several tentacles in lieu of a right arm. It breaks the concept of the binary anatomical harmony found in humans (two relatively symmetrical eyes, two hands, legs, etc.) and introduces the horror of the proliferation of anatomical parts, a source of primal fear and horror for human beings.[14] Multiple tentacles are deemed indestructible as they regenerate themselves, an animal power that human beings lack. Mary Shelley as a sea monster evokes fears of being dragged, stifled, and drowned by a mythical water creature (a woman, a snake, and a fish all rolled into one). *Spleen et idéal*, a famous illustration drawn in 1900 by Carlos Schwabe,[15] shows such a hybrid creature: a female sea serpent, clinging to and coiling around a beautiful winged angel. Monsters with tentacles have given rise to an iconographic genre in Japanese prints called 'shokushu', which crudely associates multiple arms with sexual potency. Shiva, the Indian goddess, possesses several arms, and the female power of a stifling embrace is often illustrated by depicting women's long locks of hair coiling like snakes (e.g. the Medusa). The tentacular woman is one of the most enduring of all myths, one which probably originates in ancient oriental iconography. But the message is obvious: it is an allegory of female power, both sexual and lethal. It also alludes to the power of women to attract. Tim Seeley has kept the Frankenstein imagery to a minimum, just recalling the stitched face of the Creature. Instead he has foregrounded the profoundly disturbing dark side of the author of *Frankenstein*, as if macabre auctorial creation must, of necessity, be begotten of a disturbed mind.

Jayne Steiger, a young freelance illustrator and web artist, reworked graphically Rothwell's painting to portray Mary as a female vampire (a 'Carmilla'),[16] thus avoiding the *Frankenstein* theme.[17] The colour scheme is sharply contrastive: the complementary colours red and green form her head and her shoulders dripping with blood. Red and green blended together give rise to the black of her dress. Her hair of a dark brown and the deep violet blue of the background round off an extremely sombre and macabre view of the author of *Frankenstein*. 'Undead' Mary Shelley shows the sharply ambivalent and paradoxical life-essence of a woman who — through her dripping blood — comes to evoke both life (red blood) and death (black, violet, burnt umber). The green face — a symptom of bilious temper — underscores the diseased mind of the female vampire. The dreaded undercurrent of female power comes here from the hypnotic fascination evoked by her eyes, eerily alive while everything else recalls death.

The popular portraiture of this 'horrific' Mary is in keeping with postmodern aesthetics. It is apt to recycle several and heterogeneous traits common to time-honoured horror iconography and merge them with some archetypical features redolent of nineteenth-century Gothic literature.

11.8. The Faces of Mary in the Marketing Age

In media advertising portraits of Mary/the Creature abound. Advertising images, an altogether different iconographic mode, also play on figures of Mary Shelley as topoi of uncanny female power, not used as tropes of horror but as advertising devices. Advertisers — always keen to capitalize on stereotypes — have been quick to harness the power inherent in the popular iconography of *Frankenstein*. They, however, do not frequently use the figure of the author of *Frankenstein* as a selling icon, preferring the more marketable images of the mad scientist or its hulking monster. One notable exception is a US advertising poster for beer, promoting a brand of ale strengthened by caffeine.[18] The figure of Mary Shelley is used here to connote strength or potency; hence the hook-line 'galvanized grog'. In the backdrop and on the label of the bottle, the face of Mary Shelley stands for several meanings, as pictures in advertising are always polysemic. But the main concept behind the marketing pitch remains fairly straightforward: advertisers turn Mary Shelley into a brand image, a science fiction writer metonymically associated with electrical potency. They tap into the filmic myth of Dr Frankenstein shocking his monster into life with electricity. Mary Shelley becomes a magician of electric energy who galvanizes consumer products such as a beverage or hard rock music. This is a typical example of the tendency of advertising semiotics to compress the image of a well-known person (dead or alive) into an adjective (here 'energetic' 'live wire') and attribute it to a commercial product.

11.9. Frankenstein-Themed Gothic Portraits: Mary Shelley and her Doppelgänger

A large set of Creature-themed portraits show Mary with her monster (her double, her lover, her father, her inspiration, etc.). More than portraits, these are commentaries on the subjective literary relationship between the writer and her fictional creature. The monster is both hyperbole and allegory. He stands for suffering, love-begging mankind, and that is mostly a postmodern theme imbued with sentimentality and pathos: the monster represents a rejected minority in need of a loving embrace from their creator. He is not rebellious like John Milton's Satan and Percy Bysshe Shelley, or suicidal like a Byronic hero, but he is silently bearing the curse of having been born. The monster is not horrific but pathetic and invites compassion. In Abigail Larson's pencil and ink drawing (Fig. 11.6), the monster's giant size — a hyperbolic trope for his immense misery — is more comforting than repulsive and reminds us of the good giants of fairy tales. Mary sits close to him (a lover, a friend, or a daughter) looking despondent and sad at the blight Doctor Frankenstein (God?) laid upon his creation. Rather like a female Prometheus, Mary Shelley acts as the spokeswoman for suffering man, both advocate and fellow sufferer. These illustrations are good examples of how an image can act as literary criticism, although no definite meaning may be assigned to them. Images are mute, they do not speak, but they invite speech.

Fig. 11.6. Abigail Larson, *Mary Shelley and her Creation*, 2010, pencil & ink drawing/print, © Abigail Larson.

Fig. 11.7. Sarah Dolby, *Portrait of Mary Shelley*, 2008, painting/print, © Sarah Dolby.

11.10. Mary as Romantic Female Angst

Portraits of young Mary as a figure of female angst may be influenced by other representations of extraordinary humans like those found in Tim Burton's movies: big, hollowed eyes; large heads; pale, sickly, bilious faces; wintry lunar landscapes; bat-haunted belfries.

Sarah Dolby's idiosyncratic painting of Mary Shelley (Fig. 11.7) is like a mirror image of a haunted young woman. Sarah has not patterned her Mary on Rothwell's or any other model. The treatment here is closer to surrealism with its emphasis on dream imagery and symbolism. Black tones dominate and even Mary's carmine lips and flowing cloak are darkened by a black pigment. Unlike in a traditional sitting portrait, she is drawn nearly full-length, standing, and in profile, a posture which gives her the appearance of an apparition. Her enormous eyes, severely ringed by shadows, are cast slightly upwards, like a spirit already on her way to another world.

Like the stem of a flower, her long, graceful neck holds up an oversized head, encased in abundant black hair. Creeping flowers entwine her as if she was their own kin. It is not easy to decipher the heavy flower symbolism surrounding her figure. The vegetal woman is a surrealist figure inherited from the baroque period and runs throughout the works of the surrealist painter Félix Labisse. Dolby's vegetal Mary possesses both the frail lability of a green stem and the patient, enduring strength of creepers that suddenly produce flowers or berries like weeping eyes. As if floating against a dark cloudy background, six objects are arranged symmetrically on either of her youthful, almost girlish, body. They look like keepsakes, mementos, or framed pictures that folks keep in their home for sentimental reasons. Perhaps 'they remind Mary of the dead'.[19] But the symbolism goes further and deeper than mere remembrance of the dead. These items are reminders of everything she loved and lost, her *remembrance of things past*, as it were, and her guilt: her mother, her children, Percy Bysshe Shelley, her exile from her homeland, her father, and Fanny Imlay, her stepsister who had committed suicide in 1816.

There is also a bleak Romantic, Keatsian feel to this painting. Something ails Mary: Death (the 'Belle Dame sans merci')[20] has her in thrall. A Blakean and oneiric subtext may also be at work. Womanhood is eerily dead. Mary's sexuality seems to wilt into melancholy. Dolby's portrait of Mary looks like William Blake's 'Sick Rose' whose 'crimson joy' has been destroyed by 'dark secret love'.[21]

We may compare Dolby's take on Mary with Esao Andrews's portrait (Fig. 11.8), in which an early Gothic imagination in the style of Horace Walpole's *Castle of Otranto* permeates Mary.[22]

Whether Frankenstein-themed or not, these post-1960s simulacra of Mary Shelley seem dominated by a pervasive sense of sadness and depressive mood, as if Mary, the female abstract, represented the goddess of the postmodern night (cf. Alan Vest's violet dark sketch of Mary in Fig. 11.9). The western world since the 1960s has reassessed the role of the creative woman, a prime mover in the new aesthetic landscape. Portrait artists have decidedly concluded that Mary Shelley, the ideal or prototypical female author, was doomed to eternal night.

Some illustrations seem to suggest that authorship, or the symbolic activity of

FIG. 11.8. Esao Andrews, *Young Mary Shelley*, 2010, oil on wood/print, © Esao Andrews.

Fig. 11.9. Alan Vest, *Portrait of Mary Shelley*, 2016, watercolour drawing/print, © Alan Vest.

writing fiction originates, for a woman writer, from a deep-seated death impulse. Hence Mary's deathlike masks that prevail in popular iconography. Paradoxically, the female author becomes a figure of 'decreation',[23] a bringer of death, as exemplified in the numerous caricatures associating her with bloodstains, barren nightscapes, corpses, and especially portraits of sleep-starved, ghostly faces.

Similarly, popular art sees her, a wide-eyed, young woman in love with an old, hideous corpse, and this unnatural love fuels her creativity. These clashing, antithetic images or visual oxymorons lend credit to the usual thesis that Mary Shelley created Frankenstein's creature out of the manifold deaths occurring in her circle of family and friends. But this may be too restrictive a view. If we go by the idea that Mary the artist reflected or synthesized the collective or cultural spirit of her age, rather than her own, intimate fantasies, it is highly likely that her works of fiction convert raw events into fictional experience. Deaths, whether from disease, childbirth, mishaps, or wars were all too prevalent in her age. They were unquestionable facts of life that could not be prevented by scientific or social progress. Only God was answerable, but he was inscrutable. Shelley's contemporaries could only choose between blind acceptance of fate or rebellion against God. The Shelleys chose the latter by challenging religion and put man in charge of his fate in an early existentialist philosophic stance. Shelley veered toward atheism but Mary, took a less radical path. She put the experience of her promethean Frankenstein to the fictional test: he failed to bring light and life to mankind. A miserable, revengeful creature is the dismal result of his hubris.

Postmodern popular art shows Mary bonding to a pacified monster so as to portray her commiserating with her outcast creature rather than championing her Prometheus. She did not follow in her husband's footsteps. Popular art therefore resists portraying her as a feminist or a revolutionary, a distinction that her mother is usually honoured with.

Mary remains dominated by the male figures of Shelley and Frankenstein's hulking creature. She even seems to owe them her genius as inspiring ghosts or ghostwriters. As a consequence, her authorship is challenged or belittled in popular caricatures. It is striking to notice that no positive or constructive female empowerment is implied in depictions of the author of *Frankenstein*. She appears in turn, sad, subservient, depressed, broken in body and spirit, or demure. When her power is unleashed, she turns into an agent of decreation, a mother of all chaos, close to some early mythical female monsters found in popular legends.

11.11. Literary or Idiosyncratic Counterstereotypes

A few representations picture Mary in an interesting aesthetic light — neither Gothic, caricatural, or horrific — like the cryptic painting by Alison Silva (Fig. 11.10).

Alison Silva's prosopography of Mary Shelley acts as a portal to the imaginary neuronal woman. Her Mary Shelley is another mutilated body, exhibiting brain damage instead of bodily harm. Neurons show through the two depicted characters'

Fig. 11.10. Alison Silva, *He Comes to Life*, 2017, painting/print, © Alison Silva.

body and their heads are covered in animals. Animals here may allegorize primitive cognition or strange, surreal, inhibited emotions. Be that as it may — Alison Silva painted this 'window' into her mind after suffering a brain haemorrhage and refusing surgery for a brain tumour. Here Silva's hallucinatory world is allegorized by a series of tropes like leprous marks on the walls and animal signs on heads and bodies.

11.12. Literary Portraits

Portraits that illustrate critical or biographical studies of Mary Shelley's works and want to go beyond *Frankenstein* portray Mary as Percy Bysshe Shelley's doppelgänger. Often Mary is seen as her husband's female double and co-worker. Sometimes, Percy is shown as the true genius behind her works, like a ghostwriter. These pictures tend to belittle Mary's creativity and attribute it to her lover. For example, two recent illustrations[24] contrast with the book cover of a biography by Janet Harris where Mary Shelley is depicted pregnant with a baby monster in her womb — a common allusion to Mary's creativity as failed parturition.[25]

11.13. Mary, the Graphic Novel Girl

An altogether new and interesting take on Mary comes from three Belgian cartoonists who have recently illustrated the love life of Mary Shelley. *La Vie amoureuse de l'auteur de Frankenstein* (2014) demystifies the author and her circle, by showing them as teenagers keen to experiment with novel ways of living, loving, and taking risks.[26] They appear as freewheeling youths, practitioners of free love, and there is a decidedly immature and irresponsible side to them. The three daughters of William Godwin vie for the attention of Percy, who comes out the worst of them all: a vain, callous youth who relies on his good looks, scandalous reputation, and high birth to seduce underage girls and lead them to wreck and ruin. A bright, daring but naïve girl is made use of by self-centred and sex-crazed patrician artists (Shelley, Byron). That is the topic of this graphic novel. The ideological undercurrent of this book moves with our feminist times. It sides with Mary against all the callous men in her circle. In a cartoonish, ironic way, even Percy Shelley, her great love, is portrayed as a cynical, unfaithful lover, cheating on her with her half-sister.

In Derek Marks' graphic novel *The Illustrated Life of Mary Shelley*, Marks — a New-York-based illustrator — captures her tragic love life in blue watercolour from the moment she lost her mother (Figs 11.11, 11.12, 11.13, 11.14).[27] Mary seems fated to live under the shadowy spirit of her illustrious mother. Her first kiss is sealed in the graveyard, near her mother's tomb, a herald portending the untimely death of her first three children and her husband. From 1832, her love life grows on barren land. The cartoon illustrating her brief love affair with Washington Irving shows her as a rejected lover rather than a femme fatale. Her youthful beauty is disappearing fast under the features of a plain woman, struggling with financial difficulties (Fig. 11.14).

FIG. 11.11., 11.12, 11.13, 11.14. Derek Marks and Charles Cuykendall Carter, *An Illustrated Biography of Mary Shelley*, [n.d.], comics/print, © Derek Marks and Charles Cuykendall Carter.

11.14. Conclusion

It is difficult to draw together the threads of so many strands of iconographic tendencies and styles and decide where the main pattern lies. One fact comes out most forcefully: postmodern Mary Shelley, viewed from the vantage point of popular iconography, cannot go beyond *Frankenstein*.[28] She seems forever bound to her iconic monster in two respects: first in a metamorphic relationship (she takes on the attributes of her creature or she fuses with her monstrous creation), and secondly in a binary relationship (she and her creature form a pair). These two strands of the same fabric pull in slightly different directions. In the first, Mary and her Creature merge into one being, and Mary is portrayed as the primordial monstress, a kind of modern-day Pandora — but an unwilling mother of all monsters for, in most portraits, she is shown as sorrowful rather than malevolent. In the second type of portrait (the 'double') Mary divides herself, either by parturition (when she is portrayed as pregnant), or by pairing with her creature. In countless pictures,[29] the pair is depicted sitting side by side like partners or seeking each other like platonic halves wishing to reunite.

Mary Shelley has admittedly become a central myth in our postmodern culture: as a victimized female artist who has created a persecuted monster and needs her solace. Victimization in postmodern Gothic culture has replaced horror as a central theme. As a result, fear and repulsion inspired by the monster (a Gothic tenet) have been taken out or deflated by postmodern illustrators or visual artists. The flawed, the atypical, the defective are no longer objects of dread or scorn but beings worthy of commiseration. This deontic attitude is certainly not new; it has run through art and literature since biblical times. But what is new is the prevalence of this representation in our visual age, its proliferation. Stereotypical images of the bond between Mary and her monster and of the protoforms of Mary's traits abstracted from Rothwell's painting, are, like Andy Warhol's silk-screen repetitive portraits, uneasily poised between artistic achievement and mass-produced consumer items.

Notes to Chapter 11

1. See Guillaume Mazeau, 'Portraits de Peu: Le Physionotrace au début du XIXème siècle', *Revue d'histoire du XIXème siècle*, 45 (2012), 35–52.
2. See Sunstein, *Mary Shelley: Romance and Reality*, and Seymour, *Mary Shelley*. Both biographies analyse Mary Shelley's portraits and their history.
3. Seymour, p. 543, n.
4. Now entitled *Unknown Woman, Formerly Known as Mary Shelley* (1831, oil on canvas, 127 × 101 cm), the portrait is held at the National Portrait Gallery, London (Primary Collection NPG 1719). It was purchased in 1913.
5. Postmodernity is a vexed issue. In this paper, we will refer to it as a period in the visual arts of popular culture (comics, digital arts, cinema, press photos, and cartoons) ranging from the 1970s to the present. Admittedly, the definition of aesthetic periods is open to contention. According to Fred Botting, postmodern Gothic in literature starts in the late 1960s with Angela Carter's fiction, whereas American postmodern Gothic cinema will come to the silver screen in the late 1980s with Alan Parker's *Angel Heart* (1986) or Francis Ford Coppola's *Bram Stoker's Dracula* (1992). See Fred Botting, *Gothic* (London: Routledge, 1996), pp. 168–80; Jean-Marie Lecomte, 'Postmodern Verbal Discourse in Coppola's Bram Stoker's Dracula', in *Post/modern Dracula: From*

Victorian Themes to Postmodern Praxis, ed. by John Bak (Newcastle: Cambridge Scholars, 2007), pp. 107–22.
6. See Alison Silva's portrait below (Fig. 11.10).
7. 'Grotesque', as a stylistic figure, is related to imbalance and disharmony and has satirical or comic undertones. See J. A. Cuddon, *A Dictionary of Literary Terms* (London: Deutsch, 1979), p. 290.
8. Ellen Moers, 'Female Gothic: The Monster's Mother', in *The New York Review of Books*, 21 March 1974, online edition <http://www.nybooks.com/articles/1974/03/21/female-gothic-the-monsters-mother> [accessed 20 June 2017].
9. Ellen Moers in her article refers to Gothic fiction engendering 'physiological fear' (ibid.).
10. J. A Cuddon says that 'quite often, the caricature evokes genial rather than derisive laughter' (*A Dictionary of Literary Terms*, p. 102).
11. Concerning Victorian misogynist imagery, see Bram Dijkstra, *Idols of Perversity: Fantasies of Feminine Evil in Fin-de-Siècle Culture* (Oxford: Oxford University Press, 1986).
12. 'Decadent', 'Symbolist', or '*fin-de-siècle* aesthete' are often taken as more or less synonymous, but there are significant differences. See R. K. R. Thornton, ' "Decadence" in Later Nineteenth-Century England', in *Decadence and the 1890s*, ed. by Ian Fletcher (New York: Holmes & Meier, 1980), pp. 15–29.
13. Postmodern iconography is often rhapsodic in its mixing of several stereotypes.
14. At the most basic cognitive level, a human being sees aesthetic balance or equilibrium in polar terms, as structuralist theory has amply explained. Proliferation introduces fear or negativity for the simple reason that unrestrained multiplication in nature (swarms of locusts, plagues, viral outbreaks, rats, nuclear reactions, etc.) threatens humanity. See Gilbert Durand, *Les Structures anthropologiques de l'imaginaire* (Paris: Dunod, 1960).
15. Carlos Schwabe, *Spleen et idéal*, 1907, oil on canvas, 146 × 97 cm, Musées royaux des Beaux-Arts de Belgique, Brussels.
16. See Joseph Sheridan Le Fanu's 'Carmilla', in *In a Glass Darkly* (London: Bentley & Son, 1872), and *Carmilla: A Critical Edition*, ed. by Kathleen Costello-Sullivan (Syracuse, NY: Syracuse University Press, 2013).
17. Jayne Steiger, *Mary Shelley Undead*, published on 5 December 2009, ©Jayne Steiger (USA) <https://www.deviantart.com/raevynewings/art/Mary-Shelley-Undead-145821895> [accessed 26 March 2020].
18. 'Craft Beer Author Posters', *Sabodesign19*, 27 December 2012, < https://sabodesign19.wordpress.com/2012/12/27/craft-beer-author-posters/> [accessed 25 January 2020].
19. See the commentaries posted online on the *Heresy and Beauty* website. 'Mary Shelley by Sarah Dolby', *Heresy and Beauty* (21 April 2010) <https://heresyandbeauty.wordpress.com/2010/04/21/mary-shelley-by-sarah-dolby> [accessed 20 June 2017].
20. John Keats, 'La Belle Dame sans Merci', in *Norton Anthology of Poetry*, ed. by Margaret Ferguson, Mary Jo Salter, and Jon Stallworthy (New York: Norton, 2005), pp. 1–4.
21. William Blake, 'The Sick Rose', in *Blake's Poetry and Designs*, ed. by Mary Lynn Johnson and John E. Grant, A Norton Critical Edition (New York: Norton, 1979), pp. 47–48.
22. Horace Walpole, *The Castle of Otranto: A Gothic Story* (London: printed for William Bathoe, 1764). See also Andrew L. Cooper, 'Horace Walpole', in *Encyclopedia of the Gothic*, ed. by William Hughes, David Punter, and Andrew Smith (Chichester, West Sussex: Wiley, 2016), pp. 723–25.
23. 'Decreation' is a concept whereby the artist (or God) feels a deep-seated or unconscious impulse to destroy or 'unmake' his or her works of art, conceived as dangerous or badly executed. I have found this theme prominent in Gerard Manley Hopkins's poetry where God is always on the verge of unbinding, untwisting, unmaking his own creation. In postmodern cinema, decreation occurs frequently in American apocalyptic movies. See Jean-Marie Lecomte, 'Création et décréation dans le cinéma de King Vidor', unpublished paper delivered at the seminar of the CICLAHO (research centre for classical cinema studies), University of Paris Nanterre, February 2008; Jean-Marie Lecomte, 'Inscape: Hopkins et le formalisme halluciné', *Scapes, Cahiers Charles V*, special issue on *Scapes: Poésie anglophone. English Language Poetry* (2006), 83–94.

24. See the book cover illustration for Scott D. de Hart's *Shelley Unbound: Uncovering Frankenstein's True Creator* (Port Townsend, WA: Feral House, 2013), cover design by Karl Tozzi, book cover, 2013, ©Feral House <https://feralhouse.com/shelley-unbound/> [accessed 25 March 2020]; and the poster for the production of the play *Mary Shelley* by Helen Edmundson, directed by Peter Leslie Wild, and performed by third-year undergraduates at the University of Birmingham in 2014, © Birmingham University <https://www.birmingham.ac.uk/events/events/mary-shelley.aspx> [accessed 7 November 2019].
25. Janet Harris, *The Woman Who Created Frankenstein* (New York: Harper Collins, 1979).
26. David Vandermeulen and Daniel Casanave, *La Vie amoureuse de l'auteur de Frankenstein* (Brussels: Le Lombard, 2014).
27. Derek Marks and Charles Cuykendall Carter, *An Illustrated Biography of Mary Shelley*, [n.d.] <http://www.derekmarks.net/mary-shelley-an-illustrated-biography> [accessed 22 January 2020].
28. Mary Shelley, the writer, did go beyond *Frankenstein* and wrote several novels after 1818, but popular culture has so far refused to acknowledge that.
29. Most are not analysed or reproduced here for lack of space or due to copyright issues.

BIBLIOGRAPHY

MSS

Chawton, Hampshire, Chawton House Library

MARY SHELLEY, *Falkner*, 1st edn (London: Saunders and Otley, Conduit Street, 1837), Writers' Sequence SHE, C4283, *Falkner*, III, 319

London, Victoria and Albert Museum, National Art Library

MS, MSL/1876/Forster/228

New York, New York Public Library

Carl H. Pforzheimer Collection of Shelley and his Circle, MWS 0203 *Pforz 558L 11

Oxford, Bodleian Library

MS. Abinger c. 45
MS. Shelley adds. c. 5

For the reproduction and transcription of the MSS of Mary and Percy Shelley's works held at the Bodleian, see *The Bodleian Shelley Manuscripts: A Facsimile Edition, with Full Transcriptions and Scholarly Apparatus*, ed. by Donald H. Reiman and others, 23 vols (New York: Garland, 1986–2002). The volumes cited are:

II: *Bodleian MS. Shelley adds. d. 7: A Facsimile Edition with Full Transcription and Textual Notes*, ed. by Irving Massey, The Bodleian Shelley Manuscripts (1987)
IX: *The Prometheus Unbound Notebooks: A Facsimile of Bodleian MSS. Shelley e.1, e.2, e.3*, ed. by Neil Fraistat, The Bodleian Shelley Manuscripts (1991)
XII: *The 'Charles the First' Draft Notebook: A Facsimile of Bodleian MS. Shelley adds. e. 17*, ed. by Nora Crook, The Bodleian Shelley Manuscripts (1991)
XXII/2: *Bodleian MS. Shelley adds. c. 5*, ed. by Alan M. Weinberg, The Bodleian Shelley Manuscripts (1997)

Manuscripts of the Younger Romantics: Percy Bysshe Shelley, ed. by Donald H. Reiman and others, 9 vols (London: Garland, 1985–97). The volumes cited are:

II: *The Mask of Anarchy*, ed. by Donald H. Reiman, Manuscripts of the Younger Romantics (1985)
VIII: *Fair-Copy Manuscripts of Shelley's Poems in European and American Libraries*, ed. by Michael O'Neill and Donald H. Reiman, Manuscripts of the Younger Romantics (1997)
IX: *The Frankenstein Notebooks: A Facsimile Edition of Mary Shelley's Manuscript Novel, 1816–17*, ed. by Charles E. Robinson, Manuscripts of the Younger Romantics, 2 vols (1996)

For Mary Shelley's edition of Percy Shelley's works, see also *Posthumous Poems of Shelley: Mary Shelley's Fair Copy Book, Bodleian MS. Shelley adds. d. 9 collated with the holographs and printed texts*, ed. by Irving Massey (Montreal: McGill-Queen's University Press, 1969)

Databases, Indices, and Online Resources

Curran Index to Victorian Periodicals <http://victorianresearch.org/curranindex.html> [accessed 3 March 2017]

'Frankenstein ou le Prométhé moderne', *nooSFere* <https://www.noosfere.org/livres/editionslivre.asp?numitem=1642> [accessed 12 December 2019]

'List of Works by Mary Shelley', *Wikipedia* <https://en.wikipedia.org/wiki/List_of_works_by_Mary_Shelley> [accessed 3 March 2017]

Lives of the Most Eminent Literary and Scientific Men, *Wikipedia* <https://en.wikipedia.org/wiki/Lives_of_the_Most_Eminent_Literary_and_Scientific_Men> [accessed 27 February 2020]

Marks, Derek, and Charles Cuykendall Carter, *An Illustrated Biography of Mary Shelley*, [n.d.] <http://www.derekmarks.net/mary-shelley-an-illustrated-biography> [accessed 22 January 2020]

'Mary Shelley by Sarah Dolby', *Heresy and Beauty* (21 April 2010) <https://heresyandbeauty.wordpress.com/2010/04/21/mary-shelley-by-sarah-dolby> [accessed 20 June 2017]

Poster for the production of Helen Edmundson, *Mary Shelley* (2014) at the University of Birmingham, © Birmingham University <https://www.birmingham.ac.uk/events/events/mary-shelley.aspx> [accessed 7 November 2019]

'Responses to and Adaptations of Frankenstein in Film and Elsewhere: A Selective Chronological Bibliography', taken from the NASSR-L discussion list, September 1999, compiled by Melissa J. Sites for *Romantic Circles Scholarly Resources* (1999) <https://www.rc.umd.edu/reference/misc/ficrep/frankenstein.html> [accessed 03 November 2019]

Victorian Women Writers Project <http://webapp1.dlib.indiana.edu/vwwp/welcome.do> [accessed 27 March 2020]

Interview, Filmography, Podcast, Videos

Branagh, Kenneth, dir., *Mary Shelley's Frankenstein* (TriStar Pictures, 1994)

Dear, Nick, Interview, led by Catherine Pugh, audio recording, London, 31 May 2017

'Frankenstein: Les 200 ans du premier monstre de la science', *La Méthode scientifique*, Radio France Culture, 2 March 2018, <https://www.franceculture.fr/emissions/la-methode-scientifique/la-methode-scientifique-du-vendredi-02-mars-2018> [accessed 4 November 2019]

National Theatre, *The Creature: A Character Study*, online video recording, YouTube, 1 September 2015, <https://www.youtube.com/watch?v=lRxOtaPAx1c> [accessed 19 March 2020]

National Theatre, *Cruelty, Violence and the Creature*, online video recording, YouTube, 1 September 2015, <https://www.youtube.com/watch?v=irZav2XfPLs> [accessed 19 March 2020]

National Theatre, *Directing Frankenstein*, online video recording, YouTube, 1 September 2015, <https://www.youtube.com/watch?v=E67Ty4diDgE> [accessed 19 March 2020]

National Theatre, *Doubling Frankenstein and the Creature*, online video recording, YouTube, 1 September 2015, <https://www.youtube.com/watch?v=wanlO8fb1co> [accessed 20 March 2020]

Whale, James, dir., *Frankenstein* (Universal Pictures, 1931)

Works of Art

See 'List of Illustrations' for information on works of art included in this publication.

'Craft Beer Author Posters', *Sabodesign19*, 27 December 2012, <https://sabodesign19.wordpress.com/2012/12/27/craft-beer-author-posters/> [accessed 25 January 2020]

DE VILLAIN [AFTER ANON.], *Théâtre de la Porte S.t Martin, Le monstre, acte premier, scène dernière*, 1826, engraving, *Gallica* <https://gallica.bnf.fr/ark:/12148/btv1b531169025/f1.item.r=le%20monstre%20et%20le%20magicien?rk=150215;2> [accessed 12 January 2020]

'Locket Containing Shelley's and Mary's Hair', *Shelley's Ghost: Reshaping the Image of a Literary Family* <http://shelleysghost.bodleian.ox.ac.uk/locket-containing-shelleys-and-marys-hair> [accessed 2 March 2020]

SCHWABE, CARLOS, *Spleen et idéal*, 1907, oil on canvas, 146 × 97 cm, Musées royaux des Beaux-Arts de Belgique, Brussels

STEIGER, JAYNE, *Mary Shelley Undead*, published 5 December 2009, © Jayne Steiger (USA) <https://www.deviantart.com/raevynewings/art/Mary-Shelley-Undead-145821895> [accessed 26 March 2020]

STUMP, SAMUEL JOHN, *Unknown Woman, Formerly Known as Mary Shelley*, 1831, oil on canvas, 127 × 101 cm, National Portrait Gallery, London

Printed Sources

French Translations of Mary Shelley's Works:

SHELLEY, MARY WOLLSTONECRAFT, *Les Aventures de Perkin Warbeck*, trans. and with an introduction by Anne Rouhette, Collection 'Littératures du Monde' (Paris: Classiques Garnier, 2014)

—— *Le Dernier homme*, trans. by Paul Couturiau (Paris: Éditions du Rocher, 1998 [1988])

—— *L'Endeuillée et autres récits*, trans. by Liliane Abensour (Paris: Corti, 1993)

—— *Frankenstein et autres romans gothiques*, trans. by Alain Morvan and Marc Porée, ed. by Alain Morvan, Bibliothèque de la Pléiade (Paris: Gallimard, 2014)

—— *Frankenstein; ou, Le Prométhée Moderne*, trans. and with an introduction by Germain d'Hangest (Paris: La Renaissance du livre, 1922)

—— *Frankenstein; ou, Le Prométhée Moderne*, trans. by Jules Saladin, 3 vols (Paris: Corréard, 1821)

—— *Frankenstein sur la Mer de Glace; ou, Le Voyage des Genève à Chamonix*, trans. by Christophe Jacquet (Chamonix: Guérin, 2007)

—— 'Le Frère et la sœur', trans. anon., in *Le Salmigondis: Contes de toutes les couleurs*, 3 (1832), 159–219

—— *Histoire d'un voyage de six semaines*, trans. by Anne Rouhette (Aix-en-Provence: Presses Universitaires de Provence, 2015)

—— *La Jeune fille invisible* ('La Jeune fille invisible', 'Une histoire de passions; ou, La Mort de Despina', 'Ferdinando Eboli', 'Euphrasia'), trans. by Nicole Berry (Toulouse: Éditions Ombres, 1996)

—— *Mathilda*, trans. by Marie-Françoise Desmeuzes (Paris: Éditions des Femmes, 1984)

—— *Maurice; ou, Le Cabanon du pêcheur*, trans. by Anna Bellucci (Paris: Gallimard, 2001)

—— *Que les étoiles contemplent mes larmes: Journal d'affliction*, trans. by Constance Lacroix (Paris: Finitude, 2017)

—— 'Valérius le ressuscité', trans. by Norbert Gaulard; 'La Demoiselle invisible', trans. by Anne-Sylvie Homassel, *Le Visage vert*, 1 (1995; last revised 14 May 2012) <http://www.levisagevert.com/Revues/visagevert/visagevert/vv01.html> [accessed 19 March 2020]

—— *Valperga*, trans. by Nicole Berry (Lausanne: L'Âge d'homme, 1997)

French Translations of Percy Bysshe Shelley's Works

SHELLEY, PERCY BYSSHE, *Les Cenci: Drame de Shelley*, trans. by Tola Dorian (Paris: Lemerre, 1883)

—— *Œuvres poétiques complètes de Shelley*, trans. by Félix Rabbe, 3 vols (Paris: Savine, 1885–87)

Works Cited

AKTULUM, KUBILAY, 'What is Intersemiotics? A Short Definition and Some Examples', *International Journal of Social Science and Humanity*, 7.1 (January 2017), 33–36

ALLEN, GRAHAM, *Mary Shelley*, Critical Issues (Houndmills, Basingstoke: Palgrave Macmillan, 2008)

'The Annuals for 1844', *The Athenæum*, 838 (1 November 1843), 1026

APULEIUS, *Metamorphoses*, ed. and trans. by J. Arthur Hanson, 2 vols (Cambridge, MA: Harvard University Press, 1989)

'The Attacked Escort: A Spanish Scene', *Forget-Me-Not for 1827* (1826), 333–43

AVELING, EDWARD B., and ELEANOR MARX AVELING, *Shelley's Socialism* (London: Journeyman Press, 1975)

BALDICK, CHRIS, *In Frankenstein's Shadow: Myth, Monstrosity, and Nineteenth-Century Writing*, Clarendon Paperbacks (Oxford: Oxford University Press, 1990 [1987])

BANN, STEPHEN, ed., *Frankenstein: Creation and Monstrosity* (London: Reaktion Books, 1994)

BARKER-BENFIELD, B. C., *Shelley's Guitar* (Oxford: Bodleian Library, 1992)

BARTHES, ROLAND, *S/Z*, trans. by Richard Millen (Oxford: Blackwell, 2002 [1990])

BATILLIAT, MARCEL, *La Beauté* (Paris: Mercure de France, 1900)

BEDDOES, THOMAS, *Hygëia; or, Essays Moral and Medical on the Causes Affecting the Personal State of our Middling and Affluent Classes*, 3 vols (Bristol: Mills, 1802–03)

BEHRENDT, STEPHEN C., 'The Cast and Characters', in *Presumption; or, The Fate of Frankenstein*, ed. by Stephen C. Behrendt (2001) <http://www.rc.umd.edu/print/editions/peake/apparatus/cast-characters.html> [accessed 25 February 2017]

BENNETT, BETTY T., 'Mary Shelley's Letters: The Public/Private Self', in *The Cambridge Companion to Mary Shelley*, ed. by Esther Schor (Cambridge: Cambridge University Press, 2003), pp. 211–25

—— *Mary Wollstonecraft Shelley: An Introduction* (Baltimore: Johns Hopkins University Press, 1998)

—— 'The Political Philosophy of Mary Shelley's Historical Novels: *Valperga* and *Perkin Warbeck*', in *The Evidence of Imagination: Studies of Interactions Between Life and Art in English Romantic Literature*, ed. by D. H. Reiman, M. C. Jaye, and Betty T. Bennett (New York: New York University Press, 1978), pp. 354–71

—— 'Radical Imaginings: Mary Shelley's *The Last Man*', *Wordsworth Circle*, 26.3 (Summer 1995), 147–52

—— AND CURRAN, STUART, eds, *Mary Shelley in her Times* (Baltimore: The Johns Hopkins University Press, 2000)

—— AND ROBINSON, CHARLES E., eds, *The Mary Shelley Reader* (New York: Oxford University Press, 1990)

BÉRAUD, ANTONY, and JEAN-TOUSSAINT MERLE, *Le Monstre et le magicien: Mélodrame Féerique en trois actes* (Paris: Bezou Libraire, 1826)

BÉREAUD, JACQUES, 'La Traduction en France à l'époque romantique', *Comparative Literature Studies*, 8.3 (1971), 224–44

BESLAIS, HENRI, *Le Plectre*, (Paris: Jouve, [1913]), pp. 237–39

BISSON, LAURENCE ADOLPHUS, *Amédée Pichot: A Romantic Prometheus* (Oxford: Blackwell, 1942)

BLAKE, WILLIAM, 'The Sick Rose', in *Blake's Poetry and Designs*, ed. by Mary Lynn Johnson and John E. Grant, A Norton Critical Edition (New York: Norton, 1979), pp. 47–48
BLOOM, HAROLD, *The Anxiety of Influence* (Oxford: Oxford University Press, 1975)
——ED., *Mary Shelley*, Bloom's Classic Critical Views (New York: Infobase Publishing, 2008)
[BLUNDEN, EDMUND], 'An Oxford Poet', *TLS*, 2332, 12 October 1946, p. 493
BOGDAN, ROBERT, 'The Social Construction of Freaks', in *Freakery: Cultural Spectacles of the Extraordinary Body*, ed. by Rosemarie Garland-Thomson (New York: New York University Press, 1996), pp. 23–37
BOIS, JULES, 'Baiser rouge', *Le Courrier français*, 5 October 1890, p. 8
——*Le Mystère et la volupté* (Paris: Ollendorff, 1901)
BOTTING, EILEEN HUNT, *Mary Shelley and the Rights of the Child* (Philadelphia: University of Pennsylvania Press, 2018)
BOTTING, FRED, *Gothic* (London: Routledge, 1996)
——*Making Monstrous: Frankenstein, Criticism, Theory* (Manchester: Manchester University Press, 1991)
BOURDIEU, PIERRE, *Homo Academicus* (Paris: Éditions de Minuit, 1984)
BRAIDA, ANTONELLA, 'La Notion d'intraduisible dans l'Europe du dix-huitième siècle: le débat en Italie', in *Recherches en littérature et civilisation européennes et hispano-américaines: Mélanges Brey*, ed. by Angelo Colombo (Besançon: Presses Universitaires de Franche-Comté, 2009), pp. 329–38
BRETT-SMITH, HERBERT FRANCIS BRETT, ed., *Peacock's Memoirs of Shelley with Shelley's Letters to Peacock* (London: Frowde, 1909)
BRIGGLE, ADAM, 'As Frankenstein Turns 2000, Can We Control our Modern "Monsters"?', *Scientific American* (29 December 2017), online edition <https://www.scientificamerican.com/article/as-frankenstein-turns-200-can-we-control-our-modern-monsters/?wt.mc=SA_Twitter-Share> [accessed 03 November 2019]
BUCHAN, WILLIAM, *Domestic Medicine; or, A Treatise on the Prevention and Cure of Diseases by Regimen and Simple Medicines: With an Appendix, Containing a Dispensatory for the Use of Private Practitioners* (Dublin: printed for Chamberlaine, Williams, Moncrieffe, Burton, and Sleater, 1784)
BULLEN, J. B., 'Browning's "Pictor Ignotus" and Nineteenth-Century "Christian" Art', *Nineteenth-Century Contexts*, 26.3 (September 2004), 273–88
BUTTER, PETER, REVIEW OF JEAN DE PALACIO, *Mary Shelley dans son œuvre*, in *The Yearbook of English Studies*, 2 (1972), 300
BUXTON FORMAN, HARRY, ed., *The Choice: A Poem on Shelley's Death, by Mary Wollstonecraft Shelley* (London: printed for the editor for private distribution, 1876)
BYRON, GEORGE GORDON, *The Complete Poetical Works*, ed. by Jerome J. McGann, 7 vols (Oxford: Oxford University Press, 1980–93)
BYRON, GLENNIS, and SHARON DEANS, 'Teen Gothic', in *The Cambridge Companion to the Modern Gothic*, ed. by Jerrold E. Hogle (Cambridge: Cambridge University Press, 2014), pp. 87–106
CAMERON, KENNETH NEILL, 'The Planet-Tempest Passage in *Epipsychidion*', *PMLA*, 63 (1948), 950–72
——AND DONALD H. REIMAN, eds, *Shelley and his Circle: 1773–1822*, 10 vols (Cambridge: Harvard University Press, 1961–2002)
CAMERON, LAUREN, 'Mary Shelley's Malthusian Objections in *The Last Man*', *Nineteenth-Century Literature*, 67.2 (September 2012), 177–203
CANDLER HAYES, JULIE, *Translation, Subjectivity and Culture in France and England, 1600–1800* (Stanford: Stanford University Press, 2009)

CANTOR, PAUL A., 'The Apocalypse of Empire: Mary Shelley's *The Last Man*,' in *Iconoclastic Departures: Mary Shelley after 'Frankenstein'*, ed. by Syndy M. Conger, Frederick S. Frank, and Gregory O'Dea (Madison, NJ: Associated University Presses, 1997), pp. 193–211

CARLYLE, THOMAS, *Critical and Miscellaneous Essays: Collected and Republished by Thomas Carlyle* (Boston: James Munroe, 1839)

CASANOVA, NONCE, *La Libertine* (Amiens: Bibliothèque du hérisson, 1923)

CAVALIERO, RODERICK, *Italia Romantica: English Romantics and Italian Freedom* (London: Tauris, 2007)

CESAROTTI, MELCHIORRE, L'*Iliade di Omero*, in *Opere dell'Abate Melchior Cesarotti Padovano*, 40 vols (Pisa: Dalla Tipografia della Società Letteraria, 1802), VI

CHAMPSAUR, FÉLICIEN, *Paris. Miss América* (Paris: Ollendorff Éditeur, 1885)

CHARLE, CHRISTOPHE, and RÉGINE FERRÉ, eds, *Le Personnel de l'enseignement supérieur en France aux XIXème et XXème siècles* (Paris: Éditions du CNRS, 1985)

CHATTERJEE, RANITA, ed., *European Romantic Review*, special issue on Mary Shelley's *The Last Man*, 25.1 (February 2014)

CHEEKE, STEPHEN, 'Browning, Renaissance Painting, and the Problem of Raphael', *Victorian Poetry*, 49.4 (Winter 2011), 437–61

CHERVEL, ANDRÉ, *Histoire de l'Agrégation* (Paris: Institut National de Recherche Pédagogique, Éditions Kimé, 1993)

CHEVREL, YVES, 'La Société française de littérature générale et comparée (1956–2006): Évolution et problèmes d'une institution associative', (2007) <http://sflgc.org/sflgc/notre-histoire> [accessed 22 February 2020]

——LIEVEN D'HULST and CHRISTINE LOMBEZ, eds, *Histoire des traductions en langue française, XIXe siècle, 1815–1914* (Paris: Verdier, 2012)

CLAIRMONT, CLAIRE, *The Journals of Claire Clairmont*, ed. by Marion K. Stocking and David M. Stocking (Cambridge, MA: Harvard University Press, 1969)

CLARKE, STEVE, and TRISTANNE CONNOLY, eds, *British Romanticism in European Perspective: Into the Eurozone* (London: Palgrave Macmillan, 2015)

CLEMIT, PAMELA, *The Godwinian Novel: The Rational Fictions of Godwin, Brockden Brown, Mary Shelley* (Oxford: Clarendon Press, 1993)

——AND DAVID WOOLLS, 'Two New Pamphlets by William Godwin: A Case of Computer-Assisted Authorship Attribution', *Studies in Bibliography*, 54 (2001), 265–84

COCHRAN, PETER, 'Mary Shelley's Copying of *Don Juan*', *Keats-Shelley Review*, 10 (Spring 1996), 222–41

COOPER, ANDREW L., 'Horace Walpole', in *Encyclopedia of the Gothic*, ed. by William Hughes, David Punter, and Andrew Smith (Chichester, West Sussex: Wiley, 2016), pp. 723–25

[CORELLI, MARIE], *The Silver Domino* (London: Lamley, 1893)

—— *The Sorrows of Satan* (London: Methuen, 1895)

—— *The Soul of Lilith*, 3 vols (London: Bentley, 1892)

—— *The Young Diana* (London: Hutchinson, 1918)

CRANE, JONATHAN LAKE, *Terror and Everyday Life: Singular Moments in the History of the Horror Film* (Thousand Oaks: Sage, 1994)

CRARY, J., *Techniques of the Observer: On Vision and Modernity in the Nineteenth Century* (Cambridge, MA: Massachusetts Institute of Technology, 1992)

CREED, BARBARA, *The Monstrous-Feminine* (Routledge: London and New York, 1993)

CRISAFULLI, LILLA MARIA, and GIOVANNA SILVANI, eds, *Mary versus Mary: Saggi per il bicentenario di Mary Wollstonecraft e Mary Shelley* (Napoli: Liguori, 2001)

CROCKETT, CHRISTINE M., '"The Monster Vice": Masturbation, Malady, and Monstrosity in *Frankenstein*', in *Demons of the Body and Mind: Essays on Disability in Gothic Literature*, ed. by Ruth Bienstock Anolik (Jefferson, NC: MacFarland, 2010), 129–42

CROLY, GEORGE, *Tales of the Great St Bernard*, 3 vols (London: Colburn, 1828)
CROOK, NORA, 'Counting the Carbonari: A Newly-Attributed Mary Shelley Article', *Keats-Shelley Review*, 23 (2009), 39–50
—— 'Germanizing in Chester Square: Mary Shelley, Cecil, and Ida von Hahn-Hahn', *TLS*, 6 June 2003, p. 14
—— 'Fourteen New Letters by Mary Shelley', *Keats-Shelley Journal*, 62 (2013), 37–61
—— 'Mary Shelley's Concealing "To ——": (Re)addressing Poems', *The Wordsworth Circle*, 43 (2012), 12–20
—— 'Mary Shelley: Geology, Statuary, and "The Attacked Escort"', *The Wordsworth Circle*, 50.3 (Summer 2019), 348–69
—— 'Mary Shelley: A Waxing Moon', *The Cambridge Quarterly*, 19.1 (1 January 1990), 47–52
—— 'Sleuthing towards a Mary Shelley Canon', *Women's Writing*, 6 (1999), 417–24
—— 'That Crabbed German', in *Romantic Dialectics: Culture, Gender, Theater: Essays in Honor of Lilla Maria Crisafulli*, ed. by Serena Baiesi and Stuart Curran (Bern: Lang, 2018), pp. 81–97
CROSTA, ALICE, *Alessandro Manzoni nei Paesi Anglosassoni* (Bern: Lang, 2014)
CUDDON, J. A, *A Dictionary of Literary Terms* (London: Deutsch, 1979)
DAINOTTO, ROBERTO, *Europe (in Theory)* (Durham: Duke University Press, 2007)
DEAR, NICK, *Frankenstein* (London: Faber and Faber, 2011)
DÉDÉYAN, CHARLES, *Dante en Angleterre*, 2 vols (Paris: Didier, 1961)
DE HART, SCOTT D., *Shelley Unbound: Uncovering Frankenstein's True Creator* (Port Townsend, WA: Feral House, 2013)
D'HUMIÈRES, ROBERT, *Du Désir aux destinées* (Paris: Mercure de France, 1902)
DELRIEU, ANDRÉ, 'Shelley', *Revue de Paris*, 23 (1843), 183–201
DELYON, AYMÉ, REVIEW OF PERCY B. SHELLEY, *Les Cenci: Drame de Shelley*, trans. by Tola Dorian, in *Le Zig-Zag* (18 November 1883)
—— REVIEW OF PERCY B. SHELLEY, *Hellas*, trans. by Tola Dorian, in *Le Zig-Zag* (23 November 1884)
DENSON, SHANE, *Postnaturalism: Frankenstein, Film and the Anthropotechnical Interface* (Bielefeld: Transcript, 2014)
DE PALACIO, JEAN, 'Byron traducteur et les influences italiennes', *Rivista di Letterature Moderne e Comparate*, 11.3–4 (December 1958), 209–30
—— *La Décadence: Le Mot et la chose* (Paris: Les Belles Lettres/Essais, 2011)
—— 'Encore du nouveau sur Godwin', *Études anglaises*, 22.1 (January–March 1969), 49–57
—— 'État présent des études godwiniennes', *Études anglaises*, 20.2 (April–June 1967), 149–59
—— *Figures et formes de la décadence [première série]* (Paris: Séguier, 1994)
—— 'La Fortune de Godwin en France: le cas d'Elizabeth Hamilton', *Revue de littérature comparée*, 41.3 (July–September 1963), 321–41
—— 'Godwin et la tentation de l'autobiographie (William Godwin et J.-J. Rousseau)', *Études anglaises*, 27.2 (April–June 1974), 143–57
—— *Mary Shelley dans son œuvre: Contribution aux études shelleyennes* (Paris: Klincksieck, 1969)
—— 'Mary Shelley and *The Last Man*: A Minor Romantic Theme', *Revue de littérature comparée*, 42.1 (January–March 1968), 37–49
—— 'Mary Shelley's Latin Studies: Her Unpublished Translation of Apuleius', *Revue de littérature comparée*, 38.4 (October–December 1964), 564–71
—— 'Music and Musical Themes in Shelley's Poetry', *The Modern Language Review*, 59.3 (July 1964), 345–59
—— 'Shelley and Dante: An Essay in Textual Criticism', *Revue de littérature comparée*, 35.1 (January–March, 1961), 105–12

—— 'Shelley et D'Annunzio: Motifs rapportés ou influence créatrice?', in *Le Romantisme anglo-américain: Mélanges offerts à Louis Bonnerot*, Études anglaises, 39 (Paris: Didier, 1971), pp. 181–200
—— 'Shelley's Library Catalogue: An Unpublished Document', *Revue de littérature comparée*, 36.2 (April–June 1962), 270–76
—— 'The Shelley Studies: New Trends and Texts', *Les Langues modernes*, 9.5 (September–October 1966), 69–73
—— 'Shelley traducteur de Dante: Le Chant XXVIII du *Purgatoire*', *Revue de littérature comparée*, 26.4 (October–December 1962), 571–78
—— 'Shelley traducteur de soi-même', *Revue de sciences humaines*, 40.158 (April–June 1975), 223–44
—— 'La Quête de l'Éden: Mary Wollstonecraft entre Milton et Rousseau', *Revue de littérature comparée*, 49.2 (April–June 1975), 217–34
—— 'William Godwin, Ariosto, and the Grand Tour; or, *Caleb Williams* Reconsidered', *Rivista di Letterature Moderne e Comparate*, 23.2 (June 1970), 111–20
—— *William Godwin et son monde intérieur* (Lille: Presses Universitaires de Lille, 1980)
DIJKSTRA, BRAM, *Idols of Perversity: Fantasies of Feminine Evil in Fin-de-Siècle Culture* (Oxford: Oxford University Press, 1986)
DURAND, GILBERT, *Les Structures anthropologiques de l'imaginaire* (Paris: Dunod, 1960)
EBERLE-SINATRA, MICHAEL, 'Gender, Authorship and Male Domination: Mary Shelley's Limited Freedom in *Frankenstein* and *The Last Man*', in *Mary Shelley's Fictions: From Frankenstein to Falkner*, ed. by Michael Eberle-Sinatra and Nora Crook (New York: Macmillan, 2000)
EILITTÄ, LEENA, and CATHERINE RICCIO-BERRY, eds, *Afterlives of Romantic Intermediality: The Intersection of Visual, Aural and Verbal Frontiers* (Lanham, Maryland: Lexington Books, 2016)
ESPAGNE, MICHEL, *Le Paradigme de l'étranger: Les Chaires de littérature étrangère au XIXe siècle* (Paris: Cerf, 1993)
FEDERICO, ANNETTE R, *Idol of Suburbia: Marie Corelli and Late-Victorian Literary Culture* (Charlottesville: University of Virginia Press, 2004)
FISCH, AUDREY A., *'Frankenstein': Icon of Modern Culture* (East Sussex: Helm Information, 2009)
—— 'Plaguing Politics: AIDS, Deconstruction, and *The Last Man*', in *The Other Mary Shelley: Beyond Frankenstein*, ed. by Audrey A. Fisch, Anne K. Mellor, and Esther H. Schor (New York: Oxford University Press, 1993), pp. 267–86
—— ANNE K. MELLOR, and ESTHER H. SCHOR, eds, *The Other Mary Shelley: Beyond Frankenstein* (New York: Oxford University Press, 1993)
FLORESCU, RADU and MATEI CASACU, *Frankenstein* (Paris: Tallandier, 2013)
FORRY, STEVEN EARL, 'Dramatizations of *Frankenstein*, 1821–1986: A Comprehensive List', *English Language Notes*, 25.2 (1987), 63–79
—— '"The Foulest Toadstool": Reviving *Frankenstein* in the Twentieth Century', in *The Fantastic in World Literature and the Arts*, ed. by Donald E. Morse (New York: Greenwood, 1987), pp. 183–209
—— *Hideous Progenies: Dramatizations of 'Frankenstein' from the Nineteenth Century to the Present* (Philadelphia: University of Pennsylvania Press, 1990)
FUMAROLI, MARC, *Quand l'Europe parlais français* (Paris: Éditions de Fallois, 2001)
GARLAND-THOMSON, ROSEMARIE, *Staring: How We Look* (Oxford: Oxford University Press, 2009)
GARNETT, RICHARD, ed., *Relics of Shelley* (London: Moxon, 1862)
GARRETT, MARTIN, *The Palgrave Literary Dictionary of Mary Wollstonecraft Shelley*, Palgrave Literary Dictionaries (London: Palgrave Macmillan, 2019)

'The Ghost of the Private Theatricals', *The Keepsake for 1844* (1843), 9–34
GIDE, ANDRÉ, PIERRE LOUŸS, and PAUL VALÉRY, *Correspondance à trois voix*, ed. by Peter Fawcett and Pascal Mercier, with a preface by Pascal Mercier (Paris: Gallimard, 2004)
GINZBURG, CARLO, *The Cheese and the Worms: The Cosmos of a Sixteenth-Century Miller* (1976), trans. by John and Ann C. Tedeschi (Baltimore: The Johns Hopkins University Press, 2013 [1980])
[GODWIN, WILLIAM] BALDWIN, EDWARD, *The History of England for the Use of Schools and Young Persons* (London: printed for Baldwin, Cradock and Joy, 1827)
―― *Life of Chaucer, The Early English Poet: Including Memoirs of his Near Friend and Kinsman, John of Gaunt, Duke of Lancaster, With Sketches of the Manners, Opinions, Arts and Literature of English in the Fourteenth Century*, 4 vols (London: printed by Davison, for Phillips, 1804)
―― *Of Population: An Enquiry Concerning the Power of Increase in the Numbers of Mankind. Being an Answer to Mr. Malthus's Essay on that Subject* (London: printed for Longman, Hurst, Rees, Orme and Brown, 1820)
―― *Travels of St Leon* (London: Colburn, 1831)
GOTTLIEB, EVAN, ed., *Global Romanticism: Origins, Orientations, and Engagements, 1760–1820* (Lewisburg: Bucknell University Press, 2015)
GLUT, DONALD, *The Frankenstein Archive: Essays on the Monster, the Myth, the Movies and More* (Jefferson, NC: McFarland, 2002)
―― *The Frankenstein Catalog* (Jefferson, NC: McFarland, 1984)
GORDON, CHARLOTTE, *Romantic Outlaws: The Extraordinary Lives of Mary Wollstonecraft and Mary Shelley* (London: Windmill Books, 2015)
GORDON, LYNDALL, *Vindication: A Life of Mary Wollstonecraft* (New York: Harper Collins, 2005)
GRAITSON, JEAN-MARIE, ed., *Actes du colloque 'Frankenstein': Littérature/cinéma*, with a preface by Gilles Ménégaldo, Les Cahiers de paralittérature (Liège: Éditions du Céfal, 1997)
GREEN FREDMAN, ALICE, REVIEW OF JEAN DE PALACIO, *Mary Shelley dans son œuvre*, in *Keats-Shelley Journal*, 23 (1974), 129–38
GROSS, JONATHAN, 'Byron and *The Liberal*: Periodical as Political Posture', *Philological Quarterly*, 72 (1993), 471–85
GROTE, HARRIET, *Philosophical Radicals of 1832: Comprising the Life of Sir William Molesworth, and Some Incidents Connected with the Reform Movement from 1832 to 1842* (London: Savill and Edwards, 1866)
GRYLLS, ROSALIE GLYNN, *Claire Clairmont, Mother of Byron's Allegra* (London: Murray, 1939)
GUERRA, LIA, 'Mary Shelley's Contributions to Lardner's *Cabinet Cyclopædia*: Lives of the Most Eminent Literary and Scientific Men of Italy', in *British Romanticism and Italian Literature: Translating, Reviewing, Rewriting*, ed. by Laura Bandiera and Diego Saglia (Amsterdam: Rodopi, 2005), pp. 221–35
―― 'Medioevo romantico: Mary Shelley e l'Italia', in *Medioevi Moderni: Modernità del Medioevo*, ed. by Marina Buzzoni, Maria Grazia Cammarota, and Marusca Francini (Venice: Edizioni Cà Foscari, 2013), pp. 171–84
H., R. W., 'Gift of Shelley Manuscripts', *Bodleian Library Record*, 2 (1946), 144–45
HALL, STUART, 'Cultural Identity and Diaspora', in *Identity and Difference*, ed. by K. Woodward (London: SAGE Publications, 1997), pp. 51–59
―― 'New Cultures for Old', in *A Place in the World? Places, Cultures and Globalization*, ed. by Doreen Massey and P. M. Jess (Oxford: Oxford University Press, in association with The Open University, 1995), pp. 175–214
HALLER, ALBRECHT VON, *First Lines of Physiology: By the Celebrated Baron Albertus Haller, Translated from the Correct Latin Edition, Printed under the Inspection of William Cullen, M.D.*, 2 vols (Edinburgh: printed for Charles Elliot, 1786)

HAMBURGER, JOSEPH, *Intellectuals in Politics: John Stuart Mill and the Philosophic Radicals* (New Haven: Yale University Press, 1965)

HAMILTON, PAUL, ed., *The Oxford Handbook of European Romanticism* (Oxford: Oxford University Press, 2016)

HARRIS, JANET, *The Woman Who Created Frankenstein* (New York: Harper Collins, 1979)

HEMANS, FELICIA, *Selected Poems, Prose and Letters*, ed. by Gary Kelly (Peterborough, Ontario: Broadview Press, 2002)

HERSANT, PATRICK, 'Defauconpret ou le demi-siècle d'Auguste', *Romantisme*, 29.106 (1999), 83–88

HINDLE, MAURICE, *Mary Shelley: Frankenstein*, Penguin Critical Studies (Harmondsworth: Penguin, 1994), pp. 173–76

HOEHN, DOUGLAS WILLIAM, 'The First Season of *Presumption!; or, The Fate of Frankenstein*', *Theatre Studies*, 26–27 (1979–81), 79–88

HOLMES, RICHARD, *Shelley on Love* (London: Flamingo, 1996)

HORNER, AVRIL, ed., *European Gothic: A Spirited Exchange, 1760–1960* (Manchester: Manchester University Press 2002)

HUNT, LEIGH, 'Letters from Abroad', *The Liberal*, 2 (1823), 251–64

——— LORD BYRON, and PERCY BYSSHE SHELLEY, *The Liberal: Verse and Prose from the South*, 2 vols (London: Hunt, 1822–23)

——— *The Poetical Works of Leigh Hunt*, ed. by Thornton Hunt (London: Routledge, Warne, & Routledge, 1860)

——— *The Selected Writings of Leigh Hunt*, ed. by Robert Morrison and Michael Eberle-Sinatra, The Pickering Masters, 6 vols (London: Pickering & Chatto, 2003)

HUNTER, WILLIAM, *Two Introductory Lectures, Delivered by Dr. William Hunter, to his Last Course of Anatomical Lectures, at his Theatre in Windmill-Street: As They Were Left Corrected for the Press by himself. To Which are Added, Some Papers Relating to Dr. Hunter's Intended Plan, for Establishing a Museum in London, for the Improvement of Anatomy, Surgery, and Physic* (London: Johnson, 1784)

INGPEN, ROGER, *Shelley in England: New Facts and Letters from the Shelley-Whitton Papers* (London: Paul, Trench, Trubner, 1917)

JAKOBSON, ROMAN, *Essais de linguistique générale* (Paris: Minuit, 1963)

JAMES, KATHRYN, *Death, Gender and Sexuality in Contemporary Adolescent Literature* (New York: Routledge, 2009)

JAUFFRET, LOUIS FRANÇOIS, *Dramas for Children; or, Gentle Reproofs of their Faults, Imitated from the French of L. F. Jauffret by the Editor of Tabart's Popular Stories* [trans. by Mary Jane Godwin and William Godwin] (London: for Godwin, at the Juvenile Library, 1817)

[JEWSBURY, MARIA JANE], 'Lacy de Vere', in *Forget-Me-Not for 1827* (1826), 275–94

JOHNSON, BARBARA, 'The Last Man,' in *The Other Mary Shelley: Beyond Frankenstein*, ed. by Audrey A. Fisch, Anne K. Mellor, and Esther H. Schor (New York: Oxford University Press, 1993), pp. 258–66

JONES, FREDERICK L., 'Unpublished Fragments by Shelley and Mary', *Studies in Philology*, 45 (1948) 472–76

J., M. A. [MARC-ANTOINE JULLIEN], REVIEW OF MARY SHELLEY, *Frankenstein; ou, Le Prométhée Moderne*, in *La Revue encyclopédique*, 11 (1821), 191–92

JUMP, HARRIET DEVINE, '"My Dearest Geraldine": Maria Jane Jewsbury's Letters', *Bulletin of the John Rylands Library*, 81.1 (1999), 63–74

KEATS, JOHN, 'La Belle Dame sans Merci', in *Norton Anthology of Poetry*, ed. by Margaret Ferguson, Mary Jo Salter, and Jon Stallworthy (New York: Norton, 2005), pp. 1–4

KOSZUL, ANDRÉ, *La Jeunesse de Mary Shelley* (Paris: Librairie Bloud, 1910)

——— *Proserpine and Midas: Two Unpublished Mythological Dramas* (London: Milford, 1922)

KRZYWKOWSKI, ISABELLE, and SYLVIE THOREL-CAILLETEAU, eds, *Anamorphoses décadentes:*

l'art de la défiguration (1880–1914), Études offertes à Jean de Palacio (Paris: Presses Universitaires de Paris Sorbonne, 2002)

LARDNER, DIONYSIUS, ed., *Lives of the Most Eminent Literary and Scientific Men of France*, 2 vols (London: Longman, Pees, Orme, 1838–39)

—— *Lives of the Most Eminent Literary and Scientific Men of Spain and Portugal*, 3 vols (London: Longman, Pees, Orme, 1835–37)

LAREDO, JEANETTE, 'Unmade and Remade: Trauma and Modern Adaptations of *Frankenstein*', in *Gothic Afterlives: Reincarnations of Horror in Film and Popular Media*, ed. by Lorna Piatti-Farnell (Maryland: Lexington Books, 2019), pp. 123–37

LAROUSSE, PIERRE, *Le Grand dictionnaire universel du XIXe siècle: Français, historique, géographique, mythologique, bibliographique [...]*, 15 vols (Paris: [n. pub.], 1866–76), VIII: *F–G* (1872)

LAVALLEY, ALBERT, 'The Stage and Film Children of *Frankenstein*', in *The Endurance of Frankenstein*, ed. by George Levine and U. C. Knoepflmacher (Berkeley: University of California Press, 1974), pp. 243–89

LECOMTE, JEAN-MARIE, 'Inscape: Hopkins et le formalisme halluciné', *Cahiers Charles V*, special issue on *Scapes: Poésie anglophone. English Language Poetry* (2006), 83–94

—— 'Postmodern Verbal Discourse in Coppola's Bram Stoker's Dracula', in *Post/modern Dracula: From Victorian Themes to Postmodern Praxis*, ed. by John Bak (Newcastle: Cambridge Scholars, 2007), pp. 107–22

LE FANU, JOSEPH SHERIDAN, 'Carmilla', in *In a Glass Darkly* (London: Bentley & Son, 1872)

—— *Carmilla: A Critical Edition*, ed. by Kathleen Costello-Sullivan (Syracuse, NY: Syracuse University Press, 2013)

LE ROUX, HUGUES, 'La Cenci', *Le Journal*, 18 September 1898

LEVI, GIOVANNI, 'On Microhistory', in Peter Burke, *New Perspectives on Historical Writing* (Cambridge: Polity Press, 1991), pp. 93–94

LEVINE, GEORGE, and U. C. KNOEPFLMACHER, eds, *The Endurance of Frankenstein* (Berkeley: University of California Press, 1974)

LOMAX, WILLIAM, 'Epic Reversal in Mary Shelley's *The Last Man*: Romantic Irony and the Roots of Science Fiction', in *Contours of the Fantastic; Selected Essays from the Eighth International Conference on the Fantastic in the Arts*, ed. by Michele K. Langford (Westport, CT: Greenwood Press, 1990), pp. 7–17

LORRAIN, JEAN, *L'École des vieilles femmes* (Paris: Ollendorff, 1905)

—— *Très Russe* (Paris: Giraud, 1886)

LYLES, W. H., *Mary Shelley: An Annotated Bibliography* (New York: Garland, 1975)

MARCHBANK, PAUL, 'A Space, a Place: Visions of a Disabled Community in Mary Shelley's *Frankenstein* and *The Last Man*', in *Demons of the Body and Mind: Essays on Disability in Gothic Literature*, ed. by Ruth Bienstock Anolik (Jefferson, NC: MacFarland, 2010), pp. 21–35

MARINO, ELISABETTA, *Mary Shelley e l'Italia: Il viaggio, il Risorgimento, la questione femminile* (Florence: Le Lettere, 2011)

MASSON, JEAN-YVES, 'Le Cosmopolitisme littéraire de Charles Dédéyan', *Revue de littérature comparée*, 336, (2010), 485–92

MASTRASCUSA, CINZIA, 'Italiano e Inglesi del XIX secolo: Gli scritti di Mary Shelley' (unpublished doctoral thesis, University of Rome, 2002)

MATTHEWS, G. M., 'Shelley and Jane Williams', *Review of English Studies*, n.s., 12 (1961), 40–48

—— '"The Triumph of Life": A New Text', *Studia Neophilologica*, 32 (1960), 271–309

MAXWELL, CHRISTABEL, *Mrs Gatty and Mrs Ewing* (London: Constable, 1949)

MAZEAU, GUILLAUME, 'Portraits de Peu: Le Physionotrace au début du XIXème siècle', *Revue d'histoire du XIXème siècle*, 45 (2012), 35–52

McLane, Maureen, *Romanticism and the Human Sciences: Poetry, Population and the Discourse of the Species* (Cambridge: Cambridge University Press, 2000)

Mercer, Anna, 'Beyond *Frankenstein*: The Collaborative Literary Relationship of Percy Bysshe and Mary Shelley', *The Keats Shelley Review*, 30.1 (2016), 80–85

—— *The Collaborative Literary Relationship of Percy Bysshe Shelley and Mary Wollstonecraft Shelley* (London: Routledge, 2019)

—— 'Rethinking the Shelleys' Collaborations in Manuscript', *The Keats Shelley Review*, 31.1 (2017), 49–65

Micha, Béatrice, review of Jean de Palacio, *Mary Shelley dans son œuvre*, in *Arcadia*, 8.2 (1973), 228–30

Mill, John Stuart, *Autobiography*, 3rd edn (London: Longmans, 1874)

Mitchell, W. J. T, *Iconology: Image, Text, Ideology* (Chicago: University of Chicago Press, 1986)

Moers, Ellen, 'Female Gothic: The Monster's Mother', in *The New York Review of Books*, 21 March 1974, online edition <http://www.nybooks.com/articles/1974/03/21/female-gothic-the-monsters-mother> [accessed 20 June 2017]

Montesquieu, *Œuvres complètes*, ed. by Roger Caillois, Bibliothèque de Pléiade, 2 vols (Paris: Gallimard, 1951)

Moody, Jane, *Illegitimate Theatre in London, 1770–1840* (Cambridge: Cambridge University Press, 2000)

Morice, Charles, *La Littérature de tout à l'heure* (Paris: Libraire académique Perrin et Co., 1889)

Morrison, Lucy, 'Listen While You Read: The Case of Mary Shelley's *The Last Man*', in *Mary Shelley, Her Circle and her Contemporaries*, ed. by Adam Meckler and Lucy Morrison (Newcastle: Cambridge Scholars Publishing, 2010), pp. 151–68

—— and Staci L. Stone, eds, *A Mary Shelley Encyclopedia* (London: Greenwood Press, 2003)

Nesbitt, G. L., *Benthamite Reviewing* (New York: Columbia University Press, 1934)

Nestrick, William, 'Coming to Life: *Frankenstein* and the Nature of Film Narrative', in *The Endurance of Frankenstein*, ed. by George Levine and U. C. Knoepflmacher (Berkeley: University of California Press, 1974), pp. 290–316

Newell, Adam, ed., *The Ghost of the Private Theatricals: A True Story. By M. S. Now Attributed to Mrs Shelley with [...] an Afterword by Adam Newell* (Penrith: printed for Newell and Newell, 2018)

Nitchie, Elizabeth, *Mary Shelley: Author of Frankenstein* (New Brunswick, NJ: Rutgers University Press, 1953; repr. Westport, Conn.: Greenwood Press, 1970)

Norden, Martin F., *The Cinema of Isolation: A History of Physical Disability in the Movies* (New Brunswick, NJ: Rutgers University Press, 1994)

Norman, Sylva, *Flight of the Skylark: The Development of Shelley's Reputation* (London: Reinhardt, 1954)

O'Dea, Gregory, '"Perhaps a tale you'll make it": Mary Shelley's Tales for *The Keepsake*', in *Iconoclastic Departures: Mary Shelley after Frankenstein*, ed. by Syndy M. Conger and others (Madison, NJ: Fairleigh Dickinson University Press, 1997), pp. 62–78

O'Neill, Michael, '"Trying to make it as good as I can": Mary Shelley's Editing of P. B. Shelley's Poetry and Prose', in *Mary Shelley in her Times*, ed. by Betty T. Bennett and Stuart Curran (Baltimore: Johns Hopkins University Press, 2000), pp. 185–97

Paley, Morton D., '*The Last Man*: Apocalypse without Millennium,' in *The Other Mary Shelley: Beyond Frankenstein*, ed. by Audrey A. Fisch, Anne K. Mellor, and Esther H. Schor (New York: Oxford University Press, 1993)

Pardo Garcia, Pedro Javier 'Beyond Adaptation: Frankenstein's Postmodern Progeny', *Books in Motion: Adaptation, Intertextuality, Authorship*, ed. by Mireia Aragai (Amsterdam: Rodopi, 2005), pp. 223–42

PEAKE, RICHARD BRINSLEY, *Presumption; or, The Fate of Frankenstein*, ed. by Stephen C. Behrendt (2001), in *Romantic Circles* < https://romantic-circles.org/print/editions/peake/> [accessed 12 March 2020]
PÉLADAN, JOSÉPHIN, *A Cœur perdu* (Paris: Edinger, 1888)
PENNACCHIA PUNZI, MADDALENA, ed., *Literary Intermediality: The Transit of Literature through the Media Circuit* (Bern: Lang, 2007)
PERKINS, PAM, 'John Moore, Ann Radcliffe and the Gothic Vision of Italy', *Gothic Studies*, 8.1 (May 2006), 35–51
PICARD, EMANUELLE, 'L'Histoire de l'enseignement supérieur français: Pour une approche globale', *Histoire de l'éducation*, 122 (1 April 2009), 11–33
PICART, CAROLINE JOAN S., *Remaking the Frankenstein Myth on Film: Between Laughter and Horror* (Albany: State University of New York Press, 2003)
PICHOT, AMÉDÉE, 'Avant-Propos', *Œuvres de Lord Byron*, 4th edn, 8 vols (Paris: Ladvocat, 1822–25), VIII (1825), 187–89
PORTER, ROY, *Health for Sale: Quackery in England, 1660–1850* (Manchester: Manchester University Press, 1989)
'Preface', *The Monthly Magazine*, 1 (1796), iii–iv
PROST, ANTOINE, 'Faut-il rétablir la thèse d'état ?', *Vingtième Siècle, Revue d'histoire*, 47.1 (1985), 191–93
PRUNGNAUD, JOËLLE, 'La Traduction du roman gothique anglais en France au tournant du XVIIIe siècle', *TTR: Traduction, terminologie, rédaction*, 7. 1 (1994), 11–46
PUNTER, DAVID, 'The Uncanny', in *The Routledge Companion to Gothic*, ed. by Catherine Spooner and Emma McEvoy (London: Routledge, 2007), pp. 129–36
PURINTON, MARJEAN D., 'George Colman's *The Iron Chest* and *Blue-Beard* and the Pseudoscience of Curiosity Cabinets', *Victorian Studies*, 49.2 (2007), 250–57
R. J. E., 'Mary Shelley and "Orpheus"', *TLS*, 1102, 1 March 1923, p. 143
RAJEWSKY, IRINA, *Intermedialität* (Tübingen: Francke, 2002)
REBELL, HUGUES, *Baisers d'ennemi* (Paris: Sauvaitre, 1892)
REDDING, CYRUS, *Fifty Years Recollections, Literary and Personal*, 3 vols (London: Skeet, 1858)
REGGIO, ALBERT, *La Sonate des heures* (Paris: Perrin, [n.d.; ca. 1905])
REIMAN, DONALD H., *Shelley's 'The Triumph of Life': A Critical Study* (Urbana: University of Illinois Press, 1965)
REVIEW OF JOSIAH CONDER, *Italy*, and James Johnson, *Change of Air; or, Pursuit of Health: An Autumnal Excursion through France, Switzerland, and Italy, in the Year 1829*, in *Westminster Review*, 15 (October 1831), 335–38
REVIEW OF WILLIAM BROCKEDON, *The Passes of the Alps* and *Italy: A New Illustrated Road-Book*, in *Westminster Review*, 15 (July 1831), 177–80
REYNOLDS, MATTHEW, *Translation: A Very Short Introduction* (Oxford: Oxford University Press, 2016)
ROBINSON, CHARLES E., ed., *The Frankenstein Notebooks*, 2 parts (London: Garland, 1996)
—— REVIEW OF *Mary Shelley's 'Literary Lives' and Other Writings*, ed. by Nora Crook and others, 4 vols (London: Pickering & Chatto, 2002), in *Romanticism on the Net*, 43 (August, 2006) <https://www.erudit.org/fr/revues/ron/2006-n43-ron1383/013595ar/> [accessed 19 February 2020]
RODENBACH, GEORGES, *L'Art en exil* (Paris: Librairie moderne, 1889)
ROE, NICHOLAS, ed., *Romanticism: An Oxford Guide* (Oxford: Oxford University Press, 2008 [2005])
ROGERS, NEVILLE, *Shelley at Work: A Critical Inquiry* (Oxford: Clarendon Press, 1956)
—— 'The Shelley-Rolls Gift to the Bodleian: I — Shelley at Work', *TLS*, 2582, 27 July 1951, p. 476

'Rome in the First and Nineteenth Centuries', *New Monthly Magazine*, 10 (March 1824), 217–22

'Rome in the First and Nineteenth Centuries', *Romantic Circles* <http://www.rc.umd.edu/editions/mws/lastman/rome.htm> [accessed 27 February 2020]

ROSSINGTON, MICHAEL, 'Editing Shelley', in *The Oxford Handbook of Percy Bysshe Shelley*, ed. by Michael O'Neill and Anthony Howe, with the assistance of Madeleine Callaghan (Oxford: Oxford University Press, 2013), pp. 645–56

—— 'Mary Shelley's Short Stories Notebook in the Bodleian Library', *La Questione Romantica*, Mary Shelley special issue in memory of Betty T. Bennett, n.s., 1.1 (1 June 2009), 113–18

—— AND SCHMID, SUSANNE, eds, *The Reception of P. B. Shelley in Europe* (London: Continuum, 2008)

ROUVIN, CHARLES, *Poésie de l'art et de des lettres* (Montmorency: Imprimerie Gaubert, 1892)

ST CLAIR, WILLIAM, 'The Impact of *Frankenstein*,' in *Mary Shelley in her Times*, ed. by Betty T. Bennett and Stuart Curran (Baltimore: The Johns Hopkins University Press, 2000), pp. 38–63

—— *The Reading Nation in the Romantic Period* (Cambridge: Cambridge University Press, 2004)

—— *Trelawny: The Incurable Romancer* (London: Murray, 1977)

SAINT-HILAIRE, GEOFFROY, *Philosophie anatomique: Des Monstruosités humaines*, 2 vols (Paris: Méquignon-Marvix, 1818; 1822)

SALADIN, JULES, 'Notice sur *Don Carlos*', in *Chefs-d'œuvre du théâtre anglais*, 5 vols (Paris: Ladvocat, 1822–23), II: *Rowe, Otway, Dodsley* (1822), pp. 267–79

SALISBURY, MARK, *Burton on Burton* (London: Faber and Faber, 1995)

SALMONSON, JESSICA AMANDA, 'Marie Corelli and her Occult Tales', *The Victorian Web* (12 August 2012) <http://www.victorianweb.org/authors/corelli/salmonson1.html> [accessed 15 January 2020]

SALOMON, MICHEL, *Charles Nodier et le groupe romantique* (Paris: Perrin, 1908)

SANDY, MARK, *Romanticism, Memory, and Mourning* (Farnham: Ashgate, 2013)

SARRAZIN, GABRIEL, *Poètes modernes de l'Angleterre* (Paris: Ollendorff, 1885)

SCHEIDHAUER, CHRISTOPHE, 'Les Langues de l'Europe: un régime paradoxalement durable', *Langage et société*, 125.3 (2008), 125–43

SCHOINA, MARIA, *Romantic 'Anglo-Italians': Configurations of Identity in Byron, the Shelleys and the Pisan Circle* (Farnham: Ashgate, 2009; Abingdon: Routledge, 2016)

SCHWARZKOPF, JUTTA, *Women in the Chartist Movement* (New York: St. Martin's Press, 1991)

SEYMOUR, MIRANDA, *Mary Shelley* (London: Picador, 2001)

SHELLEY, LADY JANE, ed., *Shelley and Mary*, 3 vols (London: privately printed, 1882)

SHELLEY, MARY WOLLSTONECRAFT [MWS], 'The Bravo', *Westminster Review*, 16 (January 1832), 180–92

—— '1572 Chronique du temps de Charles IX', *Westminster Review*, 13 (October 1830), 495–502

—— *Collected Tales and Stories*, ed. by Charles E. Robinson (Baltimore, MD: The Johns Hopkins University Press, 1976)

[——], 'The English in Italy', *Westminster Review*, 6 (October 1826), 325–41

—— *Frankenstein; or, The Modern Prometheus*, by the author of *The Last Man, Perkin Warbeck*, &c. &c. revised, corrected, and illustrated with a new introduction, by the author (London: Colburn and Bentley, 1831)

—— *Frankenstein; or, The Modern Prometheus*, ed. by J. Paul Hunter (New York: Norton, 2012 [1996])

—— 'Illyrian Poems — Feudal Scenes', *Westminster Review*, 10 (January 1829), 71–81

—— 'Journal of a Tour in Italy, and also in a Part of France and Switzerland. From October 1828, to September 1829', *Westminster Review*, 14 (January 1831), 174–80
—— *Journals of Mary Shelley: 1814–1844*, ed. by Paula R. Feldman and Diana Scott-Kilvert, 2 vols (Oxford: Clarendon Press, 1987; repr. (with light corrections and in one volume) Baltimore: Johns Hopkins University Press, 1995)
—— *The Last Man*, 3 vols (London: Colburn, 1826)
—— *The Last Man*, ed. by Hugh J. Luke, Jr, with an introduction by Anne K. Mellor (Lincoln: University of Nebraska Press, 1993)
—— *The Last Man*, ed. by Morton D. Paley (Oxford: Oxford University Press, 1994)
—— *The Letters of Mary Wollstonecraft Shelley*, ed. by Betty Bennett, 3 vols (Baltimore: The Johns Hopkins University Press, 1980–88)
—— *Lives of the Most Eminent Literary and Scientific Men of Italy, Spain and Portugal*, in *Cabinet Cyclopædia of Biography*, ed. by Dionysius Lardner, 3 vols (London: Longman, 1837)
—— *Lodore*, ed. by Lisa Vargo (Hadleigh: Broadview Press, 1997)
—— 'Loves of the Poets', *Westminster Review*, 11 (October 1829), 472–77
—— *Mary Shelley's 'Literary Lives' and Other Writings*, ed. by Nora Crook and others, 4 vols (London: Pickering & Chatto, 2002)
—— *Italian Lives*, ed. by Tilar J. Mazzeo, *Mary Shelley's 'Literary Lives' and Other Writings*, I
—— *Spanish and Portuguese Lives*, ed. by Lisa Vargo, *Mary Shelley's 'Literary Lives' and Other Writings*, II
—— *French Lives*, ed. by Clarissa Campbell Orr, *Mary Shelley's 'Literary Lives' and Other Writings*, III
—— *Life of William Godwin, Poems, Uncollected Prose, Translations, Post-Authored and Attributed Writings*, ed. by A. A. Markley and Pamela Clemit, *Mary Shelley's 'Literary Lives' and Other Writings*, IV
[——] 'Modern Italian Romances, I', *Monthly Chronicle*, 2 (November 1838), 415–28
[——] 'Modern Italian Romances, II', *Monthly Chronicle*, 2 (December 1838), 547–57
—— 'Modern Italy', *Westminster Review*, 11 (July 1829), 127–40
—— 'The Mortal Immortal', *The Keepsake for 1834* (1833), 71–87
—— *The Novels and Selected Works of Mary Shelley*, ed. by Nora Crook and others, Pickering Masters, 8 vols (London: Pickering & Chatto, 1996)
—— *Frankenstein*, ed. by Nora Crook with introduction by Betty Bennett, *The Novels and Selected Works of Mary Shelley*, I
—— *Matilda, Dramas, Reviews and Essays*, ed. by Pamela Clemit, *The Novels and Selected Works of Mary Shelley*, II
—— *Valperga; or, The Life and Adventures of Castruccio, Prince of Lucca*, ed. by Nora Crook, *The Novels and Selected Works of Mary Shelley*, III
—— *The Last Man*, ed. by Jane Blumberg with Nora Crook, *The Novels and Selected Works of Mary Shelley*, IV
—— LODORE, ED. BY FIONA STAFFORD, *The Novels and Selected Works of Mary Shelley*, VI
—— *Falkner*, ed. by Pamela Clemit, *The Novels and Selected Writings of Mary Shelley*, VII
—— *Travel Writing*, ed. by Jeanne Moskal, *The Novels and Selected Works of Mary Shelley*, VIII
—— *Proserpine & Midas: Two Unpublished Mythological Dramas by Mary Shelley*, ed. by A. Koszul (London: Milford, 1922)
—— *Rambles in Germany and Italy in 1840, 1842, and 1843*, 2 vols (London: Moxon, 1844)
—— *Tales and Stories*, ed. by Richard Garnett (London: Paterson, 1891)
—— *Valperga*, ed. by Tilottama Rajan (Peterborough, Ontario: Broadview, 1998)
—— 'Velluti', *Examiner*, 12 June 1826, pp. 372–73
SHELLEY, PERCY BYSSHE [PBS], *The Letters of Percy Bysshe Shelley*, ed. by Frederick L. Jones, 2 vols (Oxford: Clarendon Press, 1964)

—— *The Poems of Shelley*, ed. by Kelvin Everest and others, 4 vols (London: Longman, 1989–2014):
—— *1804–1817*, ed. by G. M. Matthews and Kelvin Everest, Longman Annotated English Poets (London: Longman, 1989), *The Poems of Shelley*, I
—— *1817–1819*, ed. by Kelvin Everest and G. M. Matthews, Longman Annotated English Poets (London: Longman, 2000), *The Poems of Shelley*, II
—— *1819–1820*, ed. by Jack Donovan and others (Harlow: Longman/Pearson, 2011), *The Poems of Shelley*, III
—— *1820–1821*, ed. by Michael Rossington, Jack Donovan, and Kelvin Everest with the assistance of Andrew Lacey and Laura Barlow, Longman Annotated English Poets (London: Routledge, 2014), *The Poems of Shelley*, IV
—— *The Poetical Works of Percy Bysshe Shelley*, ed. by Mrs [Mary] Shelley, 4 vols (London: Moxon, 1839)
—— *The Poetical Works of Percy Bysshe Shelley*, with an introduction by A. H. Koszul, 2 vols (London: Dent, 1907)
—— *Posthumous Poems of Percy Bysshe Shelley* (London: Hunt, 1824)
—— *Posthumous Poems of Shelley: Mary Shelley's Fair Copy Book*, ed. by Irving Massey (Montreal: McGill-Queen's University Press, 1969)
—— *Shelley's Poetry and Prose: A Norton Critical Edition*, 2nd edn, ed. by Donald H. Reiman and Neil Fraistat (London: Norton, 2002)
SNYDER, ROBERT LANCE, 'Apocalypse and Indeterminacy in Mary Shelley's *The Last Man*', *Studies in Romanticism*, 17.4 (Autumn 1978), 435–52
STABLER, JANE, *The Artistry of Exile: Romantic and Victorian Writers in Italy* (Oxford: Oxford University Press, 2013)
STAFFORD, BARBARA MARIA, *Artful Science: Enlightenment Entertainment and the Eclipse of Visual Education* (Cambridge, MA: The MIT Press, 1999)
STELZIG, EUGENE, ed., *Romantic Autobiography in England* (Farnham, Surrey: Ashgate, 2009)
STOCK, PAUL, 'The Shelleys and the Idea of "Europe"', *European Romantic Review*, 19.4 (2008), 335–49
SUNSTEIN, EMILY W., *Mary Shelley: Romance and Reality* (Baltimore, MD: Johns Hopkins University Press, 1991 [1989])
—— 'A William Godwin Letter, and Young Mary Godwin's Part in *Mounseer Nongtongpaw*', *Keats-Shelley Journal*, 45 (1996), 19–22
SUZUKI, RIEKO, 'Browning on Romanticism: "Fra Lippo Lippi" and Leigh Hunt', *The Keats-Shelley Review*, 27.1 (2013), 31–38
TAYLOR, BARBARA, *Eve and the New Jerusalem: Socialism and Feminism in the Nineteenth Century* (London: Virago, 1983)
TAYLOR, CHARLES H., JR, *The Early Collected Editions of Shelley's Poems: A Study in the History and Transmission of the Printed Text* (New Haven: Yale University Press, 1958)
TENARG, PAUL, *Cahiers d'un faux Don Juan* (Paris: Antony, 1898)
THORNTON, R. K. R., '"Decadence" in Later Nineteenth-Century England', in *Decadence and the 1890s*, ed. by Ian Fletcher (New York: Holmes & Meier, 1980), pp. 15–29
TOMALIN, CLAIRE, *The Life and Death of Mary Wollstonecraft* (London: Penguin, 1985)
TOOMAN, ZACHARY, 'Her "Whole Soul Was Ear": Novel Sound, Experimental Music, and Artistic Community in Mary Shelley's *The Last Man*', *Style: A Quarterly Journal of Aesthetics, Poetics, Stylistics, and Literary Criticism*, 51.2 (2017), 167–86
TOURY, GIDEON, *Translation Studies and beyond* (Amsterdam: Benjamins, 1995)
TUILIER, ANDRÉ, *Histoire de l'Université de Paris et de la Sorbonne*, 2 vols (Paris: Nouvelle Librairie de France, 1994)
TURNEY, JON, *Frankenstein's Footsteps: Science, Genetics and Popular Culture* (Yale: Yale University Press, 1998)

TWITCHELL, JAMES, *Dreadful Pleasures* (Oxford: Oxford University Press, 1985)
VACQUIN, MONETTE, *Frankenstein aujourd'hui: Égarements de la science moderne* (Paris: Belin, 2016)
VALLETTE, ALFRED, 'Les Cenci au Théâtre d'Art', *Mercure de France*, 1 March 1891, pp. 181–82
VANDERMEULEN, DAVID and DANIEL CASANAVE, *La Vie amoureuse de l'auteur de Frankenstein* (Brussels: Le Lombard, 2014)
VARGO, LISA, 'The Aikins and the Godwins: Notions of Conflict and Stoicism in Anna Barbauld and Mary Shelley', *Romanticism*, 11.1 (2005), 84–98
—— 'Writing for *The Liberal*', in *Mary Shelley: Her Circle and her Contemporaries*, ed. by L. Adam Mekler and Lucy Morrison (Newcastle: Cambridge Scholars, 2010), pp. 131–49
'Variétés', *Le Miroir des spectacles, des lettres, des mœurs et des arts*, 139 (2 July 1821), 4
VENUTI, LAWRENCE, *The Translator's Invisibility: A History of Translation*, 2nd edn (Abingdon: Routledge, 2008 [1995])
VOISINE, JACQUES, REVIEW OF JEAN DE PALACIO, *Mary Shelley dans son œuvre*, in *Revue de littérature comparée*, 45 (1971), 284–87
WAGNER, PETER, ed., *Icons — Texts — Iconotexts: Essays on Ekphrasis and Intermediality* (Berlin: De Gruyter, 1996)
WALPOLE, HORACE, *The Castle of Otranto: A Gothic Story* (London: printed for William Bathoe, 1764)
WATKIN, AMY, *Bloom's How to Write About Mary Shelley* (New York: Bloom's Literary Criticism, 2012)
WEBB, TIMOTHY, 'Mia Bella Italia: Mary Shelley's Italies', *Journal of Anglo-Italian Studies*, 12 (2013), 63–82
WEINBERG, ALAN, 'Shelley and the Italian Tradition', in *The Oxford Handbook of Percy Bysshe Shelley*, ed. by Michael O'Neill and Anthony Howe, with the assistance of Madeleine Callaghan (Oxford: Oxford University Press, 2013), pp. 444–59
—— *Shelley's Italian Experience* (London: Macmillan, 1991)
Wellesley Index of Victorian Periodicals, 1824–1900, ed. by Walter E. Houghton and Esther Rhoades Houghton, 5 vols (Toronto: University of Toronto Press, 1966–89)
'The Westminster Review. No. XIX. January 1929 [...]', *The Edinburgh Literary Review; or Weekly Register of Criticism and Belles Lettres*, 21 January 1829, pp. 205–06
WHITE, NEWMAN IVEY, *Shelley*, 2 vols (New York: Knopf, 1940)
WOLF, WERNER, 'Literature and Music: Theory', in *Handbook of Intermediality: Literature, Image, Sound, Music*, ed. by Gabriele Rippl (Berlin: De Gruyter, 2015), pp. 459–73
—— *The Musicalization of Fiction: A Study in the Theory and History of Intermediality* (Amsterdam: Rodopi, 1999)
—— *Selected Essays on Intermediality by Werner Wolf (1992–2014): Theory and Typology, Literature-Music Relations, Transmedial Narratology, Miscellaneous Transmedial Phenomena*, ed. by Walter Bernhardt (Leiden: Brill, 2018)
WOLLSTONECRAFT, MARY, and MARY SHELLEY, *Mary Wollstonecraft, 'Mary and Maria'; Mary Shelley, 'Mathilda'*, ed. by Janet Todd (London: Penguin, 1991)
WRIGHT, ANGELA, *Mary Shelley*, Gothic Authors: Critical Revisions (Cardiff: University of Wales Press, 2018)

INDEX

Abensour, Liliane 119
Adlington, William 53
Adshead, Gwen 133
Aikin, John 72
Aikin, Lucy 72
Alfieri, Vittorio 84–85, 104 n. 33–34
Alighieri, Dante 5, 7–8, 15 n. 42 & 48, 21, 50, 53–54, 84, 86, 88 n. 28 & 34, 91–92, 97
   Divina Commedia 5, 86
   Vita Nuova 5, 97
   'Voi che 'ntendendo il terzo ciel movete' 21
Andrews, Esao 156–57
Apuleius 52–53, 91
Ariosto, Ludovico 84

Baldick, Chris 10–11
Barker-Benfield, Bruce 95
Batilliat, Marcel 28
Baudelaire, Charles 27, 29
Baxter Booth, Isabel 33
Beardsley, Aubrey 151
Beattie, Stuart 129
Beddoes, Thomas 106, 109–13
Behrendt, Stephen 112
Bellucci, Anna 119
Bennett, Betty T. 5, 7, 9, 25, 33, 35–38, 41, 46 n. 30, 96
Bentham, Jeremy 72, 75, 79 n. 18
Bentley, Richard 29, 106
Bentley Standard novels 11, 22
Béraud, Antony:
   Le Monstre et le magicien 11, 125, 128
Béreaud, Jacques 118
Berry, Nicole 119
Beslais, Henri 28
Bhabha, Homi 2
Bibliothèque Nationale de France, Paris 22
Blunden, Edmund 49
Boccaccio, Giovanni 26
Bode, Cristoph 2–3
Bodleian Library, Oxford 5, 21, 23, 49–51
Bois, Jules 27
Bonnerot, Louis 27
Boswell, Thomas Alexander 22
Botting, Fred 11, 164 n. 5
Bowring, John 74–75, 79 n. 18
Boyle, Danny 128–29, 131–35, 138–39

Braida, Antonella 1–18, 24
Branagh, Kenneth:
   Mary Shelley's Frankenstein 129, 140 n. 18, 142 n. 74, 147
British Museum 22–23, 25
British Romanticism 2–3, 7, 13 n. 8
Brockedon, William 41–42
Browning, Robert 15 n. 50, 22, 30 n. 13
Buchan, William 106, 109, 111, 113
Bullen, J. B. 8
Bury, Charlotte 22
Butter, Peter 24
Byron, George Gordon 2, 7, 12, 27, 29, 37, 52–53, 58, 61, 71–73, 97, 125, 128, 150, 153, 161

Callot, Jacques 151
Cameron, Lauren 9
Cantor, Paul A. 9
Carlyle, Thomas 40
Casanova, Nonce 27
Cellini, Benvenuto 39
Champsaur, Félicien 28
Chatterjee, Ranita 9
Clairmont, Claire 1, 23, 39, 44, 46, n. 34, 82–83, 99
Clarke, Steve 2
Clemit, Pamela 9, 16 n. 55, 45 n. 14, 64, 98
Clint, George 144
Cobbett, James P. 35, 43, 75
Cobbett, William 35
Coleridge, Samuel Taylor 3, 123
Comparative Literature 3, 6–8, 10, 15 n. 15, 36 & 41, 24, 48, 53
Conder, Josiah 43
Connolly, Tristanne 2
Cooke, Thomas Potter 112–13, 125, 130, 132
Cooper, James Fenimore 75
Coppola, Francis Ford 147, 164 n. 5
Corbould, Edward 76
Corelli, Marie 28–30
Corréard, Alexandre 122
cosmopolitanism 3–5, 7, 13, 15 n. 41
Couturiau, Paul 119
Crane, Jonathan Lake 134
Crary, Johnathan 12
Crisafulli, Lilla Maria 2
Crockett, Christine M. 137
Crook, Nora 5, 10, 12, 24, 33–47, 48, 54 n. 2, 59, 83, 95

Cullen, William 107
Cumberbatch, Benedict 12, 129, 131–32, 135–36
Curran, Amelia 144

D'Annunzio, Gabriele 27
d'Hangest, Germain 21
d'Humières, Robert 28
Dainotto, Roberto 81
Darwin, Erasmus 114
De Palacio Jean 1–13, 21–32, 33–36, 48–56, 62, 64, 71, 76, 78, 81, 85, 87, 91, 122
    Mary shelley dans son œuvre 1, 5, 8–10, 12, 21–25, 48–56, 71, 81, 122
De Quincey, Thomas 24
De Staël, Madame 3
Dear, Nick 12, 128–40
Decadence 27–28
Dédéyan, Charles 7, 15 n. 39 & 41
Defauconpret, Jean-Baptiste 122, 124–25
Delicati, Signor 144
Denlinger, Elizabeth 49
Desmeuzes, Marie Françoise 119
Dolby, Sarah 155–56
Dorian, Tola 27
drama 105–17, 128–42
Dumas, Alexandre 120

Easton, Reginald 144, 146
Edinburgh Review 74–75
Europe 1–8, 10–13, 26, 33, 44, 48–49, 53–54, 81–82, 84, 93, 106–07, 110, 111, 116
exile 4, 90, 150, 156

Federico, Annette R. 28
Fielding, Cleobulina 144
fin de siècle 3, 7, 27–28
Finden, William 62
Fisch, Audrey 9, 105
Forget-Me-Not 36–37
Forman, Harry Buxton 57
Forry, Steven Earl 105, 128, 130, 134
Foscolo, Ugo 4, 84
Fraistat, Neil 49
France 1, 4, 11, 21–25, 33, 42–43, 48, 53, 90–91, 118–27, 130
Franklin, Benjamin 26
Fredman, Alice Green 24, 36

Galvani, Giovanni 114
Gardiner, Marguerite, Lady Blessington 40
Garland-Thomson, Rosemarie 132
Garnett, Richard 21, 50–51, 93
Gaulard, Norbert 119
Geneva 7, 34, 37, 82, 90, 120
Ghirlandaio, Domenico 8
Gide, André, 28

Gillet, Louis 28
Gisborne, Maria 63, 65 n. 24, 79 n. 18, 83, 97
Godwin, Catherine Grace 35
Godwin, William 7, 22–23, 25, 26, 38, 43, 58, 74, 82, 38–39, 122–23, 161
    'Juvenile library' 23
    Caleb Williams 22, 26, 125
    Cloudesley 22, 33
    Deloraine 22
    Enquiry Concerning Political Justice 25–26
    Fables Ancient and Modern 23
    Fleetwood 22
    History of England 23
    Life of Geoffrey Chaucer 25
    Mandeville, 22
    Of Population 24–26
    Pantheon 23
    St Leon 43
Goethe, Johann Wolfgang 39
Gore, Catherine 22
Gosse, Edmund 29
Gothic genre 4, 12, 28, 81–82, 86, 116, 121, 128–30, 132, 133, 138–39, 147, 150, 152, 153, 156, 159, 164
Gozzi, Carlo 84
graphic novels 118, 161–63
Graham, James 107
Great Britain 1, 2, 4, 49, 54, 107, 110, 111, 116, 122, 130
Greece 2, 4, 71, 76–78
Grillparzer, Franz 40
Gross, Jonathan 72
Grote, Harriet 74

Haller, Albrecht von 107, 114
Hamilton, Paul 3
Heras Muños, Salvador 149
Hogg, Thomas Jefferson 82
Homassel, Anne-Sylvie 119
Hope, Thomas 22, 38
Horner, Avril 81
Hunt, Leigh 57, 64 n. 3, 65 n. 10, 72, 78, 82–83, 86
Hunter, William 108, 114
Huysmans, Joris-Karl 29

interdisciplinarity 6, 9
intermediality:
    literary intermediality 10
    mediamorphosis 10
Italy 1–2, 5, 10, 41–44, 48, 53–54, 58–59, 63–64, 71, 75, 77, 81–89, 90–102, 150
Italian literature 1–3, 5, 7–8, 21, 26–27, 30, 33–34, 84–86, 91–92, 97
Italian language 5, 33, 85–87, 91
    Bagni di Lucca 43
    Bologna 13
    Genoa 57–58, 98–99

Leghorn 43
Milan 86, 90–91
Naples 42–43, 53, 60, 94
Padua 85
Pisa 35, 63, 83
Rome 5, 13, 38–39, 42, 61–62, 91, 94, 97, 120
Venice 5, 13, 91, 93

Jacquet, Christophe 119–20
Jameson, Anna 73, 75
Jauffret, Louis-François 23
Jewsbury, Maria Jane 37
Johnson, Barbara 9
Johnson, James 43

Karloff, Boris 11, 21, 132, 147
Keats, John 53, 156
Keeley, Robert 112
Keepsake 22, 33–35, 38–41, 43, 51, 62, 75–76, 96–97, 120
Kerr, John Atkinson:
    The Monster and Magician; or The Fate of Frankenstein 110, 115
Koszul, André, 7, 48, 51

Labisse, Félix 156
Lackington 11, 105
Lacroix, Constance 119
Lardner, Dyonisius:
    Cabinet Cyclopædia 1, 3, 25, 34–35, 122
Lathom, Francis 124
Le Roux, Hugues 27
Lecomte, Jean-Marie 12, 143–66
Lesage, Alain-René 38
Levine, David 150
Lewis, Matthew Gregory 40, 121
Liberal 34, 58, 72, 75
liberalism 71–80
Logan, John 129
London Magazine 34, 43, 98
Lorrain, Jean 28
Louÿs, Pierre 28
Lyles, W. H.:
    Annotated Bibliography 10, 34–35
Lytton, Bulwer 75

Macpherson, James 28
Malthus, Thomas 25–26
    Essay on Population 25–26
Manzoni, Alessandro 84–86
Marchbank, Paul 134
Markley, Arnold 34, 36–38
Marks, Derek 161, 163
Martineau, Harriet 22
Marx Aveling, Eleanor 71
Marx, Karl 71

Matthews, Geoffrey Maurice 49, 96
Maturin, Charles 121
Mayoux, Jean-Jacques 6
McLane, Maureen 87
medical science 105–17
Medwin, Thomas 38, 125
Mellor, Anne K. 9
Mercer, Anna 4–5, 90–102
Mérimée, Prosper 33, 74–76
Merle, Jean-Toussaint:
    Le Monstre et le magicien 11, 125, 128
Micha, Béatrice 24
Mill, James 72
Mill, John Stuart 72, 75
Miller, Jonny Lee 12, 131–32, 129, 135
Milner, Henry H.:
    Frankenstein; or The Demon of Switzerland 108
    The Man and the Monster; or The Fate of Frankenstein 108, 110, 114–15, 128
Milton, John 59, 138, 153
Moers, Ellen 150
Montesquieu, Charles de 25
Monthly Chronicle 36
Monthly Review 72
Monti, Vincenzo 84
Moore, Thomas 33
Morice, Charles 28
Morrison, Lucy 9
Motte-Fouqué, Freidrich 39
Moxon, Edward 21
Murray, John 85

Neale, William Johnson 22
New Monthly Magazine 38, 41
Newell, Adam 39–40
Nitchie, Elizabeth 33–34, 93
Nodier, Charles 121, 124–25
Norton, Caroline 22

O'Malley, Glenn 52
O'Neill, Michael 50
Ollier, Charles 39
Otway, Thomas 122–24
Owen, Robert Dale 74

Pacchiani, Francesco 83
Paganini, Niccolò, 43–44
Paley, Morton D. 9
Pardo Garcia, Pedro Javier 129
Parrino, Maria 4, 81–89
Pater, Walter 53
Peacock, Thomas Love 59
Peake, Richard Brinsley:
    Another Piece of Presumption 108
    Presumption; or The Fate of Frankenstein 105, 109-10, 112–13, 115, 125, 128, 130, 138–39

Péladan, Joséphin 27
Pellegrini, Marcello 144
Pennacchia Punzi, Maddalena 10
Perronet Thompson, Thomas 75
Phillips, Richard 72
Pichot, Amédée 125
Planché, James Robinson 109
Plutarch 82
Polidori, John 121, 125
Pomfret, John 58
Prost, Antonie 6
Pugh, Catherine 12, 128–42
Punter, David 81
Purinton, Marjean D. 11, 105–17

Quarterly Review 74

Rabbe, Felix 27
Radcliffe, Ann 121
Rebell, Hugues 27
Reggio, Albert 28
Reiman, Donald H. 49, 96
Revue encyclopédique 121
Reynolds, Frederic Mansel 51
Reynolds, Matthew 11
Richardson, Samuel 84, 91
Robinson, Charles E. 3, 34, 38–39, 41, 93, 97
Robinson, H. 76
Rodenbach, Georges 28
Rogers, Neville 49–50
Rossetti, Dante Gabriel 28
Rossington, Michael 9, 48–56
Rothwell, Richard 143–47, 152, 156, 164
Rouhette, Anne 11, 118–27
Rouvin, Charles 28

Saglia, Diego 2
Said, Edward 2
Saint-Hilaire, Geoffrey 107, 111–13, 116
Saladin, Jules 11, 118–27
Salmigondis, (Le) 119–20, 123
Salmonson, Jessica Amanda 28–29
Sandy, Mark 5
Sarrazin, Gabriel 27
Scarlett, James Richard 8th Baron Abinger 5, 23
Schlegel, August Wilhelm 3
Schoina Maria 2, 4, 24, 87, 92, 98–99
Schwabe, Carlos 152
science 29, 41, 105–17
Scott, Margaret 39
Scott, Walter 122, 124–25
Seeley, Tim 151–52
Seymour, Miranda 90, 144
Sgricci, Tommaso 75, 83, 88 n. 16
Sharp, William 29

Shelley, Jane Gibson, Lady 49
Shelley, Mary:
   attribution of articles and canon 33–47
   and Germany 40
   and Greece 1–2, 4, 71, 76–78
   and Italy 1–3, 5, 7, 8, 10, 41–44, 48, 53–54, 57–67, 71, 75, 77, 81–89, 90–102, 120, 150
   and France 1, 4, 11, 21–28, 33, 42–43, 48, 53, 90–91, 118–27, 130
   and Europe 1–18, 33, 44, 48–56, 81–82, 84, 93, 107, 110–11, 116
   editor 9, 39, 48–56, 57–67
   in de Palacio's work 21–26, 28–32, 48–56
   liberalism 71–80
   portraits 143–66
   translator 3–4, 9, 10, 34–35, 38, 39, 48, 52–53
   'A Dirge' 62
   'A Night Scene' 33, 71, 76–78
   'Euphrasia' 72, 76–78, 119
   'Maurice' 41, 71
   'Recollections of Italy' 90–92, 94, 98–99
   'Roger Dodsworth, the Reanimated Englishman' 41
   'The Bride of Modern Italy' 83, 91, 98
   'The Choice' 5, 57–67, 98
   'The Mortal Immortal' 29
   'The Sisters of Albano' 38, 95
   'The Tide Was at my Feet' 33
   Falkner 22, 93, 95
   Frankenstein 1, 4, 8, 10–13, 21–22, 24, 29, 34–35, 37, 39–40, 73, 81–82, 85, 87, 90, 92–93, 96–97, 105–17, 118–27, 128–42
      film adaptations 11, 21, 128–29, 131
      stage adaptations 105–17, 128–42
      translations 118–27
   History of a Six Weeks' Tour 4, 34, 42, 63, 93, 119–20
   Literary Lives 3, 24, 34–36, 38, 122
   Lodore 22–23, 92, 94
   Mathilda 34, 85, 119–20
   'Modern Italian Romances' 36
   (ed.) *Posthumous Poems of Percy Shelley* 49, 51–52, 57–58, 60–63
   Proserpine and Midas 7, 51, 98
   Rambles in Germany and Italy 1, 4, 8, 22–23, 34, 39–42, 86–87, 90
   Review of *Chronique du règne de Charles IX* 33
   Review of *Cloudesley* 33
   Review of J. P. Cobbett's *Tour of Italy* 35, 43, 75
   'The English in Italy' 75, 84
   The Fortunes of Perkin Warbeck 22–23, 36–37, 119–20
   The Last Man 1, 9, 22–23, 25–26, 37, 60, 94, 119–20
   translations of her works 118–42
   Valperga 1, 22, 33, 84, 91, 95, 97, 119–20
Shelley, Percy 1–2, 4–5, 7, 9, 12, 21–22, 26–29, 34, 48–57, 59–64, 71–72, 74–75, 78, 82–83, 85, 90–99, 150, 153, 156, 161

'Fiordispina' 51
'Julian and Maddalo' 60–61, 90, 97
'Lines Written among the Euganean Hills' 92–93
'Lines Written at the Bay of Lerici' 49
'Orpheus' 51–52
'Summer and Winter' 51
'The Boat on the Serchio' 51
'The Triumph of Life' 49
'To a Sky-Lark' 60
Adonais, 58, 62
Epipsychidion 21, 28, 58–59, 97–98
Hellas 27
'Letter to Maria Gisborne' 63, 97
Prometheus Unbound 94
The Cenci 27, 97–98
translation of Dante 21, 50
Shelley, Percy Florence 59, 62
Shelley-Rolls, John, Sir 49–50
Silva, Alison 159–61
Simond, Louis 75
Smith, Horace 10, 38, 41
St Clair, William 73–74
Stafford, Barbara Maria 107
Steiger, Jayne 152
Stock, Paul 4
Stump, Samuel John 144, 146
sublime 27, 41–43, 62, 94
Sunstein, Emily 33–36, 38–39
Suzuki, Rieko 8
Swinburne, Algernon 27–28

Tasso, Torquato 84, 91

Taylor, Charles H. 49
Tenarg, Paul 28
Tennyson, Alfred 28
Tooman, Zachary 9
Trelawny, Edward John 22, 72–74, 76

Vallette, Alfred 27
Vargo, Lisa 4, 35, 71–80
Varinelli, Valentina 4–5, 57–67
Venuti, Lawrence 118
Vicente, Fernando 147–48
Viglianti, Raffaele 49
Viviani, Teresa Emilia 21, 59, 83, 98
Voisine, Jacques 24

Wadewitz, Adrianna 34
Wallack, James William 112
Warhol, Andy 164
Westminster Review 4, 33–34, 41, 43, 44, 71–72, 74–80, 84
Whale, James:
    Frankenstein 11, 21, 128–29, 131, 146
White, Newman Ivey 21, 59
Williams, Edward 58
Williams, Jane 58, 63, 85–86
Wilson, John 26
Wolf, Werner 10
Wollstonecraft, Mary 54, 72, 93, 114
Wordsworth, Dorothy 96
Wordsworth, William 24, 75, 96, 123
Wright, Frances 72

Zola, Émile 29

www.ingramcontent.com/pod-product-compliance
Lightning Source LLC
Chambersburg PA
CBHW050454110426
42743CB00017B/3351